ESCAPING THE MATRIX

How We the People can change the world

We've lived so long under the spell of hierarchy – from god-kings to feudal lords to party bosses – that only recently have we awakened to see not only that "regular" citizens have the capacity for self-governance, but that without their engagement our huge global crises cannot be addressed. The changes needed for human society simply to survive, let alone thrive, are so profound that the only way we will move toward them is if we ourselves, regular citizens, feel meaningful ownership of solutions through direct engagement. Our problems are too big, interrelated, and pervasive to yield to directives from on high.
—Frances Moore Lappé, *Time for Progressives to Grow Up*

Blessed are the meek; for they shall inherit the earth.
—Matthew 5:5

To the people of Ireland, whose humor and humanity brighten each day, sun or no sun.

ESCAPING THE MATRIX

How We the People can change the world

Richard Moore

a publication of
The Cyberjournal Project
http://cyberjournal.org/
http://escapingthematrix.org/

Escaping the Matrix: How We the People can save the world
by Richard Moore

Published by The Cyberjournal Project
570 El Camino Real #117, Redwood City, CA 94063
and Wexford, Ireland.
http://cyberjournal.org/
http://escapingthematrix.org/

November 2005   First Edition

Portions of this material have previously appeared in *Whole Earth Review*.

ISBN: 0-9770983-0-3

Library of Congress Control Number: 2005932961

Acknowledgements

To all those people who, over the years, have contributed to the author's understanding by sharing their ideas, and by joining in the dialog on the Cyberjournal email lists. A special thanks to those who have generously "redistributed" some of their wealth from time to time, enabling the author to devote full-time to this project.

To Chris Thorman, James Macgregor, and Jackson Davis, whose ongoing support and assistance in the development of the book has been invaluable and much appreciated.

To Karl Amatneek, Benjamin Kelly, and others, who patiently reviewed drafts.

To Tom Atlee, Tree Bressen, Jim Rough, and Rosa Zubizarreta, who graciously shared their experiences with facilitation processes and their visions of the human potential – and who helped me develop the material in Chapter 5.

Contents

Foreword

If fifteen years ago, when the USSR was collapsing, I had noticed a book on the shelves about "changing the world," I imagine I would have passed it by. Such topics, I would have assumed, were for philosophers, mystics, or ideological fanatics. Such a slogan had no real political relevance, either as a desired goal or as a likely possibility. Our Western societies certainly needed reforming, but few people thought in terms of whole new systems, or questioning the wisdom of such basic things as progress and capitalism.

A lot has changed in the last fifteen years. In that time we've seen the rise of globalization, as the dominant economic force in the world, and along with that have come the destabilization of our national economies and a general decline in our quality of life. With holes in the ozone layer, global warming, and disappearing rainforests, topsoil, water tables, and oil reserves, there is a growing recognition that our modern societies are headed for some kind of major collapse, sooner or later. Meanwhile, in the sphere of geopolitics, we've seen a dramatic rise in civil wars and armed interventions, and a growing fear that conflict may develop among nuclear powers. By comparison, the Cold War era is beginning to seem like 'the good old days.'

Without exaggeration, I can say that our modern civilization is facing a major crisis, indeed a crisis of survival. The full scope of the crisis has become increasingly apparent to more and more people over these past fifteen years. There were some, however, who were able to see the signs of this crisis long ago. Fortunately for the rest of us, there have been scientists, economists, journalists, and others, who have devoted their talents to investigating the roots of our current crisis, exploring how humanity might be able to avoid falling over the precipice – and publishing their results as part of a new genre of transformational literature. (See: *Bibliography and online resources.*)

One of the common themes that emerges in this genre is *interconnectedness*. Our economic and political systems, our environmental and social problems, and our unstable international situation – these are all interconnected with one another. They can only be understood from a *whole systems* perspective. We don't have a list of individual problems to solve – rather we have a *dysfunctional system* that needs to be somehow reconfigured, i.e., *transformed*.

We – the people of the world – are like the owner of an old automobile that has been repaired many times, and which can no longer be repaired: we must begin thinking seriously about a new vehicle – a transformed basis for society. And indeed, the new transformational genre has moved quite a bit beyond critique of the 'old automobile.' Serious thought and research have been devoted to understanding how our global food supply can be produced sustainably and without harmful pesticides, how we can reduce our energy usage, and how we can develop sustainable and non-polluting sources of energy and modes of transport.

Similarly, new models of currencies and economic exchange have been developed, which can enable a more functional kind of economics, based on useful productivity, as measured by benefit to people – rather than being based on the accumulation of wealth by a few. From considerations of both sustainability and economics has emerged a systems perspective oriented around decentralization, and moving decision-making toward the local: local control makes for efficient economic operations and facilitates effective stewardship of natural resources.

The technical problems involved in making our world more sensible are not insurmountable. *If the societal will existed*, we could create functional and sustainable systems, put an end to war and poverty, live peacefully and happily ever after – and we could fund the conversion project with a small fraction of the resources now devoted to military budgets. It would be an immense project, but none of it is rocket science. The major obstacles to social transformation are not technical but political; they are bound up in the question: *What is our societal will?*

In fact, our societal will is the will of our political and economic elites. If they decide to invade Iraq, for example, then the media propaganda, the resources of our society, and our men and women in uniform are devoted to that objective – regardless of public sentiment regarding the adventure. And when it comes to transformation of the systems of our societies, these established elites are dead set against any such notion. They are irrevocably committed to holding on to the reigns of power, and maintaining the current system – regardless of the environmental and social consequences. The response of our governments to the emerging transformational paradigm has been dramatically symbolized by their brutal suppression of the various anti-globalization protests.

Of all of our societal systems, the most resistant to transformation are our political systems. So long as our political systems are controlled by wealthy elites, none of our other systems can be transformed. Revitalization of democracy turns out to be the critical factor in social transformation. And yet, revitalization of democracy is the least developed part of the emerging transformational paradigm. We can find complete treatments of sustainable economics, healthy agriculture, and appropriate technologies, but when it comes to the nature of genuine democracy – or how to achieve it – we find only partial solutions.

My purpose in writing this book is to weave together the various emerging ideas into a comprehensive tapestry of social transformation – with special emphasis on the problem of achieving democratic societies. The book is self-contained and it begins from first principles. I refer to the existing literature, and I have built on the work of others, but the synthesis is my own.

The first four chapters present an analysis of our current systems, their historical origins, and the various attempts of people throughout history to reform those systems by means of social movements and revolutions. The next two chapters describe a non-violent process by which I believe lasting social transformation can be achieved on a global scale. The final three chapters describe how that process can lead to a transformed world culture based on local empowerment, human liberation, participatory democracy, sensible economics, and cooperation for mutual benefit. At the end there is an annotated bibliography and online resources section where I offer a selection of sources that I've personally found to be useful in my quest to understand these complex issues.

At one level, in terms of the substance of its analysis, this book is intended for global audiences: it is about global transformation, not just the transformation of a single society. At another level, in terms of the style of its presentation, the book is aimed primarily at Western audiences, and in particular the reader will detect a distinctly American perspective in the material. Partly this is a result of my own background, having grown up in California. More importantly however, the Western and American orientation is intentional. It is Western governments, in particular the American government, which have the preponderance of military and economic power in the world. Unless transformation occurs in America and the rest of the West, it is unlikely to be achieved anywhere – at least not in a way that can last.

There are certain terms that are used differently in America, Britain, and continental Europe, which I should probably clarify in advance. In America, the term *liberal* refers to a person who in Europe would probably be known as a Social Democrat or perhaps a Green, and who in Britain might be a Labour or Lib-Dem voter. The term *neoliberalism*, used commonly in Europe but less so in America, refers to free-trade economics and the globalization agenda. The term *neocon*, short for neoconservative, refers to the extremist ideological clique, which at the time of writing dominates Washington politics, as personified by Donald Rumsfeld and Dick Cheney.

As a final note of introduction, I'd like to say something about my own ideological prejudices, and what 'kind of person' this book is intended for. For most of my life I would have put myself squarely in the liberal camp, in the American sense. I hated racists and bigots, thought guns and capital punishment should be outlawed, that abortion should be freely available, and that religion was a particularly dangerous form of mental illness. When I first started writing, about ten years ago, I was hoping to 'educate' those on the right, and convert them to my enlightened, rational, liberal thinking.

As it turns out, my prejudices have not really changed much, but my attitude toward 'those on the right' has changed considerably. In my attempts to debate conservative thinkers on the Internet and in person, I found that I was learning as much from them as they were learning from me. Their views on the evils of big government, their emphasis on self-reliance and local solidarity, and their skepticism regarding the mainstream media impressed me as being very sensible perspectives. I began to see that we liberals had blind spots and prejudices every bit as objectionable as those we criticized in our right-wing brothers and sisters. I began to see that ideological labels are divisive, and that underneath the skin we are all real people with sincere contributions to make to our societies.

I will not be able to hide my liberal biases in this material; they come out in the language that I use and in my choice of examples. But I hope this will not deter those of you who are of a conservative persuasion from giving consideration to what I have to say. Ultimately, social transformation depends on our ability, as human beings, members of an allegedly intelligent species, to get beyond our superficial differences and realize that we are all in this together. A better world for all of us is a better world for each of us! I invite you to join me in the quest to find a path to such a world.

Richard Moore
Wexford, Ireland
October 2005

I

The Matrix

One cannot separate economics, political science, and history. Politics is the control of economies. History, when accurately and fully recorded, is that story. In most textbooks and classrooms, not only are these three fields of study separated, but they are further compartmentalized into separate subfields, obscuring the close interconnections between them.
—J.W. Smith, *The World's Wasted Wealth II*

Are you ready for the red pill?

If you would be a real seeker after truth, it is necessary that at least once in your life you doubt, as far as possible, all things.
—René Descartes, *Principles of Philosophy*

The defining dramatic moment in the film *The Matrix* (Warner Bros., 1999) occurs just after Morpheus invites Neo to choose between a red pill and a blue pill. The red pill promises "the truth, nothing more." Neo takes the red pill and awakes to reality – a reality utterly different from anything he or the audience could have expected. What Neo had assumed to be reality turned out to be only a collective illusion, fabricated by the Matrix mainframe and fed to a population that is asleep, cocooned in grotesque embryonic pods. In Plato's famous parable about the shadows on the walls of the cave, true reality is at least reflected in perceived reality. In the Matrix world, true reality and perceived reality exist on entirely different planes.

The story is a kind of multi-level metaphor, and the parallels that drew my attention had to do with political reality. This chapter offers my own perspective on what's really going on in the world – and how things got to be that way – in this era of globalization and post 9/11 hysteria. Our everyday media-consensus reality – like the Matrix in the film – turns out to be a fabricated collective illusion. Like Neo, I didn't know what I was looking for when my investigation began, but I knew that what I was being told didn't make sense. I read scores of histories and biographies of important figures, observing connections between them, and began to develop my own understanding of the roots of various historical events.

When I started tracing historical forces, and began to interpret present-day events from a historical perspective, I could see the same dynamics still at work and found a meaning in unfolding events far different from what official pronouncements, and the media, proclaimed. Such pronouncements are, after all, public relations fare, given out by politicians who want to look good to the voters. Most of us expect rhetoric from politicians, and take what they say with a grain of salt. But as my own picture of present reality came into focus, *grain of salt* no longer worked as a metaphor. I began to see that consensus reality – as generated by official rhetoric and amplified by mass media – bears very little relationship to actual reality. *The Matrix* was a metaphor I was ready for.

Imperialism and the Matrix

> We must find new lands from which we can easily obtain raw materials and at the same time exploit the cheap slave labour that is available from the natives of the colonies. The colonies would also provide a dumping ground for the surplus goods produced in our factories.
> —Cecil Rhodes, "founder" of Rhodesia

> When they arrived, we had the land and they had the Bible and they told us to close our eyes to pray. When we opened our eyes, they had the land and we had the Bible.
> —Desmond Tutu

From the time of Columbus to 1945, world affairs were largely dominated by competition among Western nations seeking to stake out spheres of influence, control sea-lanes, and exploit colonial empires. Each Western power became the *core* of an imperialist economy whose *periphery* was managed for the benefit of the core nation. Military might determined the scope of an empire, and wars were initiated when a core nation felt it had sufficient power to expand its periphery at the expense of a competitor. This competitive game came to be known as *geopolitics*.

Economies and societies in the periphery were kept backward – to keep their populations under control, to provide cheap labor and resources, and to guarantee markets for goods manufactured in the core. Imperialism robbed the periphery not only of wealth and resources, but also of its ability to develop its own societies, cultures, and economies in a sensible way for local benefit. The third world is relatively poor and backward today only because the West has intentionally kept it that way.

The driving force behind Western imperialism has always been the pursuit of economic gain, ever since Queen Isabella funded Columbus on his first entrepreneurial voyage. The rhetoric of empire concerning wars, however, has typically been about other things – the *White Man's Burden*, bringing *true religion* to the heathens, *Manifest Destiny*, defeating the *Yellow Peril* or the *Hun*, seeking *lebensraum*, or *making the world safe for democracy*. Any fabricated motivation for war or empire would do, as long as it appealed to the collective consciousness of the population at the time. The propaganda lies of yesterday were recorded and became consensus history – the fabric of the Matrix.

> Kings had always been involving and impoverishing their people in wars, pretending generally, if not always, that the good of the people was the object.
> —Abraham Lincoln

While the costs of territorial empire (fleets, colonial administrations, wars, etc.) were borne by Western populations generally, the profits of imperialism were enjoyed primarily by private industrialists, bankers, and investors. Government and wealthy elites were partners in the business of imperialism: corporations and banks ran the real business of empire while government leaders fabricated noble excuses for the wars that were required to keep that business going. Matrix reality was about patriotism, national honor, and heroic causes; true reality was on another plane altogether: that of big money. While in the Matrix we chose our national direction democratically, in reality we were being sold noble-sounding agendas that masked the expansionist projects of wealthy elites.

Industrialization, beginning in the late 1700s, created a demand for new markets and increased raw materials; both demands spurred accelerated expansion of empire. Wealthy investors amassed fortunes by setting up, or funding, large-scale industrial and trading operations, leading to the emergence of an influential capitalist elite. Like any other elite, capitalists used their wealth and influence to further their own interests however they could.

> People of the same trade seldom meet together... but the conversation ends in a conspiracy against the publick, or in some contrivance to raise prices.
> —Adam Smith, *The Wealth of Nations*

Thus capitalism, industrialization, nationalism, warfare, imperialism – and the Matrix – coevolved. Industrialized weapon production provided the muscle of modern warfare, and capitalism provided the appetite to use that muscle. Government leaders pursued the policies necessary to expand empire while creating a rhetorical Matrix, based around nationalism, to justify those policies. Capitalist growth depended on empire, which in turn depended on a strong and stable core nation to defend it. National interests and capitalist interests were inextricably linked – or so it seemed for more than two centuries.

World War II and **Pax Americana**

1945 will be remembered as the year World War II ended and the bond of the atomic nucleus was broken. But 1945 also marked another momentous fission – the breaking of the linkage between capitalism and national expansionism. After every previous war, and in many cases after severe devastation, European nations had always picked themselves back up and resumed their competition over empire, their geopolitical game. But after World War II, a *Pax Americana* was established. U.S. planners had worked out a new blueprint for world order, in a series of studies carried out by the Council on Foreign Relations (CFR):

> Recommendation P-B23 (July, 1941) stated that worldwide financial institutions were necessary for the purpose of "stabilizing currencies and facilitating programs of capital investment for constructive undertakings in backward and underdeveloped regions." During the last half of 1941 and in the first months of 1942, the Council developed this idea for the integration of the world.... Isaiah Bowman first suggested a way to solve the problem of maintaining effective control over weaker territories while avoiding overt imperial conquest. At a Council meeting in May 1942, he stated that

the United States had to exercise the strength needed to assure "security," and at the same time "avoid conventional forms of imperialism." The way to do this, he argued, was to make the exercise of that power international in character through a United Nations body (Shoup, 148)[1]

After 1945 the U.S. began to manage all the Western peripheries on behalf of capitalism generally, while preventing the communist powers from interfering in the game. Capitalist powers no longer needed to fight over investment realms, and *competitive* imperialism was replaced by *collective* imperialism. International financial stability was provided by the Bretton Woods agreements, which established fixed exchange rates among the major currencies, all pegged to the dollar, which was in turn backed by gold. Bretton Woods also established the World Bank and the International Monetary Fund (IMF), both intended to provide loans for development projects in the third-world.

The new blueprint thus had two parts, one geopolitical and one economic. Pax Americana was the geopolitical part, and it stabilized geopolitics by eliminating armed conflict among the Western powers. The Bretton Woods system was the economic part, and it stabilized the global financial environment.

Opportunities for Western investors were no longer linked to the military power of their nations, apart from the power of America. In his *Killing Hope: U.S. Military and CIA Interventions Since World War II*, William Blum chronicles hundreds of covert and overt interventions, showing exactly how the U.S. carried out its imperial management role.

The postwar blueprint was aimed at promoting development and economic growth on a scale never seen before. The investment opportunities were immense, with much of the industrialized world in ruins from the war – in urgent need of rebuilding. And with the new Bretton Woods institutions, the stage was set for unprecedented levels of investment and development in the periphery, the third world.

This development agenda promised great returns for investors and banks, huge new markets for manufacturers and entrepreneurs, and unprecedented prosperity for Western populations. As in the pre-1945 days, primary manufacturing

---

1. See the References section, where sources are in order by author's name; references are indicated by (author name, page number).

industries were to be concentrated in the core nations, providing there good employment, strong national economies, and content populations. For the third world there was the hope of modernization and improving living conditions, but the terms of trade and development continued to be exploitive, vis a vis the core and the periphery – the West and the third world.

In the postwar years Matrix reality diverged ever further from actual reality. In the postwar Matrix world, imperialism had been abandoned and the world was being "democratized"; in the real world, imperialism had become better organized and more efficient. In the Matrix world the U.S. "restored order," or "came to the assistance" of nations which were being "undermined by Soviet influence"; in the real world, the U.S. was *"maintaining effective control over weaker territories."* In the Matrix world, the benefit was going *to* the periphery in the form of countless aid programs; in the real world, immense wealth was being extracted *from* the periphery, by *"programs of capital investment…in backward and underdeveloped regions."*

These growing *glitches* (anomalies) in the Matrix weren't noticed by most people in the West, because the postwar years brought unprecedented levels of Western prosperity and social progress. The rhetoric claimed progress would come to all, and Westerners could see that myth being realized in their own towns and cities. The West became the collective core of a global empire, and exploitative development led to prosperity for Western populations, while generating immense riches for corporations, banks, and wealthy investors.

Popular rebellion and the decline of the postwar blueprint

A Jewish folk tale relates the story of a mute child who had never said a word despite all the efforts of the doctors. Then one day, at the ripe age of ten, he dropped his spoon and cried out, "The soup is too salty!" His parents asked him in amazement why he had kept silent for years, and the child replied, "Until now, everything was all right."

The postwar development-centered blueprint served as an effective governing paradigm for the first two postwar decades, providing both domestic passivity and good returns for wealthy investors. But in the 1960s large numbers of Westerners, particularly the young and well educated, began to notice the glitches in the Matrix. In Vietnam imperialism was too naked to be successfully masked as something else. A major split in American public consciousness occurred, as millions of anti-war protesters and civil-rights activists punctured the fabricated consensus of the 1950s and declared the reality of exploitation and suppression both at home and abroad. The environmental movement arose, challenging even the exploitation of the natural world. In Europe, 1968 joined 1848 as a landmark year of popular protest:

> In 1968, the entire post-war order was challenged by a series of insurrections from Berkeley to London, from New York to Prague. Oddly enough, the challenge was not successful, at least not in the period in which it actually took place. The true effects of the student protest movement were felt well after 1968.
>
> 1968 was a year of revolution. That's the year that John Lennon sang *Revolution*. It's the year that Grace Slick and the Jefferson Airplane sang, "Now it's time for you and me to have a revolution" from their album *Volunteers*. In a period of unprecedented material prosperity and cultural activity, the sons and daughters of the most privileged sections of the United States and of Europe decided to make their own revolution. They were the sons and daughters of the Left, better yet, the Old Left. Their parents, many of them at least, were either pink or red, that is, many of them were communists, socialists, Trotskyites, feminists, pacifists or just plain liberals. Their sons and daughters began to refer to themselves as the New Left (Kreis).

These developments disturbed elite planners. The stability of the postwar blueprint was being challenged from within the core: the formula of Western prosperity no longer guaranteed public passivity. A report published in 1975, "The Crisis of Democracy" (Crozier), provides a glimpse into the thinking in elite circles. Alan Wolfe discusses this report in Holly Sklar's eye-opening anthology, *Trilateralism* (Wolfe, 35–37). Wolfe focuses particularly on the analysis Harvard professor Samuel P. Huntington presented in a section of the report entitled "The United States." Huntington is an articulate promoter of elite policy shifts, and contributes pivotal articles to publications such as the Council on Foreign Relations' *Foreign Affairs*.

Huntington tells us that democratic societies "cannot work" unless the citizenry is "passive." The "democratic surge of the 1960s" represented an "excess of democracy," which must be reduced if governments are to carry out their traditional domestic and foreign policies. Huntington's notion of "traditional policies" is expressed in a passage from the report:

> To the extent that the United States was governed by anyone during the decades after World War II, it was governed by the President acting with the support and cooperation of key individuals and groups in the executive office, the federal bureaucracy, Congress, and the more important businesses, banks, law firms, foundations, and media, which constitute the private sector's "Establishment" (Wolfe, 37).

In these few words Huntington spells out the reality that electoral democracy and the will of the people have little to do with how America is run, and summarizes the kind of people who are included within the elite planning community.

The postwar blueprint was failing in its mission of providing public passivity, but it was already in trouble for another reason as well: it was costing too much. That is to say, its profitability to investors had reached the point of diminishing returns. By the early 1970s – due to higher labor costs, taxes, and regulatory restrictions in the West – investments in industrial development had become far more profitable in the *"under developed"* world. It no longer made financial sense to continue investing capital to maintain a strong Western industrial base. If people were no longer pacified by economic prosperity, why should investors continue paying for that prosperity with unappealing investments?

The essential bond between Western national interests and the interests of capitalism was broken in 1945, with the advent of Pax Americana and collaborative imperialism. Nonetheless, those interests continued to be aligned in the postwar era – with its emphasis on Western industrialization and stability, growth and development, and popular prosperity. But this postwar alignment was one of convenience only, on the part of investment capital: the arrangement continued only as long as it was profitable. As the 1970s unfolded, and investments were increasingly moved out of the West, the postwar system of economic stability was undermined by the elite investment community, and we begin to see the establishment of a new and quite different economic blueprint.

A definitive step in this undermining process occurred on August 15, 1971, when President Nixon, on the advice of an elite group in his Treasury Department, took the dollar off the gold standard. In one fell swoop, the entire basis of financial stability in the postwar blueprint was undermined.

> When Nixon decided no longer to honor U.S. currency obligations in gold, he opened the floodgates to a worldwide Las Vegas speculation binge of a dimension never before experienced in history. Instead of calibrating long-term economic affairs to fixed standards of exchange, after August 1971 world trade was simply another arena of speculation about the direction in which various currencies would fluctuate (Engdahl, 129).

London banking elites and the strategy of oil-based dominance

> History teaches by analogy, not identity. The historical experience is not one of staying in the present and looking back; rather, it is one of going back into the past and returning to the present with a wider and more intense consciousness.
> —Daniel Estulin, investigative journalist

The postwar blueprint had been developed during the war by the Council on Foreign Relations, on behalf of the U.S. government, and that blueprint was in fact the paradigm by which the world was run for three decades. Presidents came and went; Cold War confrontations came and went; squabbles between America and Europe came and went – yet the blueprint carried on. Who was behind the Council on Foreign Relations? Who has the power to choose agendas for the globe and then ensure that the course be followed for decades? Who decided, by 1971, that the time had come for a change?

Let us now step back from our story, leaving it for now in the mid 1970s, with the postwar economic blueprint collapsing, and take a fresh look at the past century from another perspective. We'll be peeling another layer off the Matrix onion, to find the man behind the man behind the curtain, so to speak. Is there in fact some singular elite group that has essential power in the world today? If so, who are they and how did they get their power?

Not to hold you in suspense, we're going to be talking about bankers, and the power of finance. In particular we'll be looking into the most exclusive banking circles in New York (Wall Street) and London (the City of London – "The City"), and see how this fraternity has come, putting it baldly and honestly, to rule the world.

> The world is not, in fact, ruled by global corporations. It is ruled by the global financial system.
> —David Korten, *When Corporations Rule the World*

Let's begin our fresh look by briefly considering the role of London banks during the heyday centuries of the British Empire. One of the innovations of this empire was that payments for purchases were not carried around in ships in the form of gold bullion. Instead, when sales or purchases occurred anywhere in the empire, that simply resulted in numbers being moved from one account to another in a pair of London banks, where both buyer and seller would maintain accounts.

This was a safer and cheaper way to settle transactions, and it meant that the London banks had the use – for their own investment purposes – of everyone else's reserve funds, from throughout the empire. Over the centuries of empire, returns on these invested reserves mounted up: the wealth and power of the banks grew ever stronger. The City became the unquestioned financial capital of the world, and the Pound the world's most trusted reserve currency. This gave The City great power: the banks could manipulate world markets by such simple measures as adjusting interest rates and controlling credit availability.

British supremacy in manufacture was the economic engine behind the Victorian-era Empire, enabling London banks to achieve their dominance over global finance. But with that dominance established, the banks found there were more lucrative investments to be found in foreign markets than in Britain itself. With no apparent regard for the fate of the British economy or the industrialists who had made their wealth possible, the London banks proclaimed a doctrine of "free trade" and simply moved their money to where they could get the greatest returns. We of course can see this same scenario today on a global scale, where again free trade is the rhetoric, and again disinvestment in Western domestic economies is the reality.

But behind her apparent status as the world's pre-eminent power, Britain was rotting internally. The more the British merchant houses extended credit for world trade, and City of London banks funneled loan capital to build railways in Argentina, the United States and Russia, the more the domestic economic basis of the United Kingdom deteriorated. Few understood how ruthlessly lawful was the connection between the two parallel processes [i.e., *free trade* and *domestic disinvestment*] at the time (Engdahl, 1).

If we consider the wealth of big banks, in comparison to the wealth of industrial corporations – or nations for that matter – we find a scenario much like that in a poker parlor. The corporations and nations are the players, and the banks are the house. Players go up and down; some get rich, some go into debt, and some go broke – and they all suffer when economies experience recession or depression. But the house never loses, always takes its share of every pot, always collects its debts – and can change the rules of the game whenever it sees fit.

Besides the power derived from its wealth and financial control, The City gained additional power from a secret relationship with government, and in particular with the British intelligence services.

Rather than the traditional service providing data from agents of espionage in foreign capitals, Britain's secret intelligence services operated as a secret, Masonic-like network which wove together the immense powers of British banking, shipping, industry and government. Because all this was secret, it wielded immense power over credulous and unsuspecting foreign economies. In the Free Trade era after 1846, this covert marriage of private commercial power with government was the secret of British hegemony (Engdahl, 8).

Britain is famous for the 'old-boy' networks that emerge out of its elite 'public school' system. In that cultural tradition of personal loyalty and honor-bound discretion, a particular informal 'fraternity' was assembled that became the covert guiding force behind British strategy – a fraternity that one might fairly call a secret government. This fraternity was, and still is, a secret network of key players from the London banks, the intelligence services, and the leading British oil companies – with The City, as usual, being the prime mover in the arrangement, the party with the broadest strategic agenda.

The constituencies of this fraternity – banking, intelligence, and oil – reflect a particular strategy of geopolitical dominance, a strategy that was adopted by Britain prior to the outbreak of World War I, and which continues operating to this day, although now under the leadership of the big Wall Street banks. This strategy is simple and effective:

1) Gain control of oil sources.

2) Control the price of oil and the currency in which oil is traded.

3) Maintain this control, by overt and covert means, and leverage it into the geopolitical and financial domination of world affairs.

We can see the effectiveness of this strategy today, where the Anglo-American oil companies dominate global petroleum trade, and where oil can only be purchased with dollars. In order to ensure a reliable energy supply, each nation must accumulate dollars with which to fulfill its petroleum purchase contracts. These dollars are then typically parked in U.S. Treasury securities until they are needed – thus subsidizing U.S. deficits and Pentagon budgets. These immense reserve funds are called *petrodollars* and they are redirected to the Wall Street banks, where they can be invested for profit – just as with the London banks in the heyday of the British Empire. These petrodollars then find their way to London, where they are called *Eurodollars*, and are invested in unregulated global markets. By such means control over oil finance leverages into global financial hegemony for an Anglo-American banking fraternity.

World War I and the House of Morgan

In Matrix history books, World War I is presented as an unfortunate accident, caused in part by German expansionism, and in part by unwise entangling alliances – alliances that caused a local conflict in the Balkans to escalate unexpectedly into a major war between the European powers. In reality, World War I is best understood in the context of Britain's strategy of oil-based financial dominance.

In the lead-up to World War I, German productivity in technology, industry, and commerce had eclipsed that of Britain – in large part due to The City's domestic disinvestment policy. In addition, Germany was building a modern fleet that threatened Britain's supremacy at sea. London and the Pound continued to dominate global finance, but German banks were beginning to exercise increasing financial power. Furthermore, Germany was eagerly pursuing the construction of a rail system, connecting Berlin with Baghdad, which if completed would give Germany direct access to oil supplies, and would also open up an inland trading network that would seriously undermine Britain's dominance in trade and shipping.

Germany was certainly within her rights as a sovereign nation to pursue these policies – but she was also on a course to unseat Britain from her position of dominance in European affairs and global finance. And with her own oil supplies, Germany would put an end to Britain's strategy of oil dominance before the strategy could be established. Such a course of events was not acceptable to London's elite banking fraternity, nor was it acceptable to the British establishment generally, with its traditional balance-of-powers perspective on European geopolitics. Desperate measures – if British supremacy was to be preserved – were called for.

> In April 1914, King George VII and his foreign minister, Sir Edward Grey, made an extraordinary visit to meet French President Poincaré in Paris. It was one of the few times Sir Edward Grey left the British Isles. Russia's ambassador to France, Iswolski, joined them and the three powers firmed up a secret military alliance against the German and Austro-Hungarian powers. Grey deliberately did not warn Germany beforehand of its secret alliance, whereby Britain would enter a war which engaged any one of the carefully constructed web of alliance partners she had built up against Germany.
>
> Many in the British establishment had determined well before 1914 that war was the only course suitable to bring the European situation under control (Engdahl, 29).

Whereas in the Matrix we had "unfortunate entangling alliances," in reality we had a trap secretly set by the British, intended to ensnare Germany into a war with all of her neighbors – in typical British balance-of-powers fashion. It was a war in which millions would die and from which Britain would emerge with a dominant position in the Middle East, and able to pursue its new strategy of oil-based financial hegemony.

> While France was occupied with Germany, in a bloody and fruitless slaughter along the French Maginot Line, Britain moved an astonishingly large number of its own soldiers, more than 1,400,000 troops, into the eastern theatre.
>
> …The angry French feebly protested that while millions of their forces bled on the Western Front, Britain took advantage of the stalemate to win victories against the weaker Turkish Empire… (Engdahl, 40-41).

At one level, with World War I, we see yet another geopolitical engagement among Western powers in the centuries-long game of competitive imperialism: Britain and France were able to extend their peripheries into the former Ottoman Empire, at the expense of German hopes for her own periphery, based on the Berlin to Baghdad rail system. But at another level, as regards Britain's new oil strategy, World War I represents a singular shift in world affairs, establishing a new basis for geopolitical dominance that survives to this day.

Of particular significance was the role played by New York banks in financing the war, and the Anglo-American banking alliance that emerged from the war. The City was to be eclipsed by Wall Street, but the strategy of oil-based dominance was to be carried forward, in what eventually became a firm but covert Anglo-American alliance.

This was to be a comprehensive alliance, bringing the Anglo-American oil companies into a potent cartel (the Seven Sisters), bringing the London and New York banking elites into strategic collaboration, and creating a special relationship between the American and British intelligence and diplomatic communities.

The visible cooperation today between President Bush and Prime Minister Blair, as regards Iraq and other matters, is but the tip of the iceberg of a broad and long-standing alliance. And in the relationship today between Wall Street, the CIA, and the Anglo-American oil companies, we see an American version of Britain's secret fraternity at work, guiding the course of the world from behind the scenes, according to the principle of oil-based dominance, under the strategic guidance of New York and London banking elites.

By 1914, returning now to developments prior to the outbreak of war with Germany, Britain had her trap well set. Only a spark was needed to start the inferno: the entangling alliances were powder kegs ready to go off. But there was one fly in Britain's ointment.

One of the better kept secrets of the 1914-18 world war was that on the eve of August 1914, when Britain declared war against the German Reich, the British Treasury and the finances of the British Empire were in effect bankrupt (Engdahl, 35).

In order to fight the war, Britain would need credit – lots of credit. No one was more aware of this than the banking fraternity that was planning the war, and they had been hard at work making appropriate arrangements. The credit was to come from America, with the help of J.P. Morgan and other New York bankers who had intimate ties to London. But as the U.S. lacked a central bank, it would be difficult and risky to raise the immense funds that would be required.

On the night of November 22, 1910, a group of newspaper reporters stood disconsolately in the railway station at Hoboken, New Jersey. They had just watched a delegation of the nation's leading financiers leave the station on a secret mission. It would be years before they discovered what that mission was, and even then they would not understand that the history of the United States underwent a drastic change after that night in Hoboken.

   The delegation had left in a sealed railway car, with blinds drawn, for an undisclosed destination. They were led by Senator Nelson Aldrich, head of the National Monetary Commission. ...Accompanying Senator Aldrich at the Hoboken station were his private secretary, Shelton; A. Piatt Andrew, Assistant Secretary of the Treasury, and Special Assistant of the National Monetary Commission; Frank Vanderlip, president of the National City Bank of New York, Henry P. Davison, senior partner of J.P. Morgan Company, and generally regarded as Morgan's personal emissary; and Charles D. Norton, president of the Morgan-dominated First National Bank of New York. Joining the group just before the train left the station were Benjamin Strong, also known as a lieutenant of J.P. Morgan; and Paul Warburg, a recent immigrant from Germany who had joined the banking house of Kuhn, Loeb (Mullins, 1).

The participants in the Jekyll Island conference returned to New York to direct a nationwide propaganda campaign in favor of the "Aldrich Plan." Three of the leading universities, Princeton, Harvard, and the University of Chicago, were used as the rallying points for this propaganda, and national banks had to contribute to a fund of five million dollars to persuade the American public that this central bank plan should be enacted into law by Congress.

Woodrow Wilson, governor of New Jersey and former president of Princeton University, was enlisted as a spokesman for the Aldrich Plan. During the Panic of 1907, Wilson had declared, "All this trouble could be averted if we appointed a committee of six or seven public-spirited men like J.P. Morgan to handle the affairs of our country" (Mullins, 10).

Thus, by secret intrigue, was America's Federal Reserve System born – a central bank in all but name. The prominent and well-funded backers of the plan were able to get Wilson elected President, and on December 23, 1913, when most Congressman had gone home for Christmas, the Federal Reserve Act was snuck through Congress and Wilson signed it the next day.

In theory, the Federal Reserve system was to be under the control of Congress, but it in fact this new central bank was owned and controlled, albeit indirectly, by members of the Anglo-American banking fraternity. Britain had secured her line of credit for the planned war in Europe. Four months later, in April, Britain set up its alliances with France and Russia, and three months after that hostilities began, sparked by a suspicious assassination.

The House of Morgan took on the task of supplying the British war chest with funds, and Morgan was granted the exclusive right to procure provisions in the Americas for Britain and her allies. This was strictly against international law, as Woodrow Wilson was maintaining an official policy of American neutrality in the European conflict.

Morgan, with its franchise as sole purchasing agent for the entire Entente group, became virtual arbiter over the future of the U.S. industrial and agricultural export economy. Morgan decided who would, or would not, be favored with very sizeable and highly profitable export orders for the European war effort against Germany.

Firms such as DuPont Chemicals grew into multinational giants as a result of their privileged ties to Morgan. Remington and Winchester arms companies were also favored Morgan 'friends.' Major grains trading companies grew up in the Midwest as well, to feed Morgan's European clients. The relations were incestuous, as most of the Morgan loans raised privately for the British and French were raised through the corporate resources of DuPont and friends, in return for a guarantee of the huge European munitions market (Engdahl, 52).

Despite this invaluable help from Morgan, Britain and France were unable to win the war, particularly after Russia, under the new Bolshevik regime, withdrew from the conflict. In order to ensure a British victory – and to save the House of Morgan from financial ruin – America would need to enter the war.

Morgan and his wealthy backers then undertook a propaganda campaign aimed at arousing U.S. public opinion against Germany. Germany played into their hands by unleashing its U boats against American ships that were ferrying supplies to Britain. Top American officials were convinced to support American entry into the war because the collapse of the Morgan syndicate threatened to bring down the whole American economy. Once America did declare war, Germany's defeat was assured.

> We have come to be one of the worst ruled, one of the most completely controlled and dominated Governments in the world – no longer a Government of free opinion, no longer a Government by conviction and vote of the majority, but a Government by the opinion and duress of small groups of dominant men.
> —Woodrow Wilson

In Matrix history books, the postwar Versailles peace conference was dominated by the personalities of Clemenceau, Wilson, and the other diplomats: it was their vindictiveness, ineffectiveness, or short-sightedness that were the cause of the disastrous postwar debt regime – leading to decades of economic stagnation in Europe. In reality, these arrangements were simply a matter of Morgan collecting his debts. The House of Morgan, through its agents and connections, was the architect of the repayment regime.

> ...Britain and the other allied powers owed the United Sates $12,500,000,000 at 5 per cent interest. Britain, France, and the other Entente countries, in turn, were owed by Germany, according to the Versailles demands, the sum of $33,000,000,000. The figures were beyond the scale of imagination at that time (Engdahl, 56).

The Anglo-American alliance

London's banking elite accomplished much by its World War I project. Germany was eliminated as a major competitor, and Britain gained a dominant position in the Middle East, making her strategy of oil-based dominance in Europe viable. But London had paid a high price for these gains: Britain, along with the rest of Europe, ended up in deep debt to the House of Morgan, and America rather than Germany had become Britain's chief rival for global supremacy – in both oil and finance.

Britain had positioned herself well, but there was no way she could maintain for long her time-honored position of global supremacy. America, in particular Wall Street elites, had gained too much out of the war, from the debts that were owed, and from the economic development enabled by Europe's immense wartime purchases. America's financial and business elites had tasted global power, and they were no longer going to play second fiddle to anyone. Britain's elite fraternity accommodated itself to this new situation by pursuing a dual strategy: in the short term London competed vigorously with America for control over oil sources, and for the long term British elites planted the seeds of a strategic collaborative arrangement between the two powers.

> During the course of the Versailles talks, a new institution of Anglo-American coordination in strategic affairs was formed. Lionel Curtis, longtime member of the secretive Round Table or 'new empire' circle of Balfour, Milner and others, proposed organizing a Royal Institute of International Affairs.
>
> ...The same circle at Versailles also decided to establish an American branch of the London Institute, to be named the New York Council on Foreign Relations, so as to obscure its close British ties. The New York Council was initially composed almost entirely of the Morgan men, financed by Morgan money (Engdahl, 55).

The Council on Foreign Relations, as it eventually was called, was to become the primary vehicle of U.S. elite planning, with close ties to London. In the interim, however, America found itself locked in a bitter battle with Britain over oil fields and the control of markets. Despite its tremendous advantages of scale and financial resources, the U.S. found itself out-maneuvered on front after front, including even the petroleum resources of Latin

America, where Britain managed to get hold of two-thirds of the developed oil fields.

Eventually, however, both powers decided that cooperation would be more productive than further competition. By 1928, they had agreed to combine their forces, as regards oil and geo-political polices. Thus was born the 'Seven Sisters' oil cartel.

> Their secret pact was formalized as the 'As Is' agreement of 1928, or the Achnacarry agreement. British and American oil majors agreed to accept the existing market divisions and shares, to set a secret world cartel price, and to end the destructive competition and price wars of the previous decade. The respective governments merely ratified this private accord the same year in what became the Red Line agreement. Since this time, with minor interruption, the Anglo-American grip over the world's oil reserves has been hegemonic. Threats to break that grip have been met with ruthless responses, as we shall later see (Engdahl, 74-75).

We can now see the basic patterns that continue to character-ize this alliance to this very day: the constant use of secrecy and deception, the utter ruthlessness of these people who plan wars for their own enrichment, and the effectiveness with which they achieve their major objectives. We see this alliance operating to-day in Iraq, where both parties lied about weapons of mass de-struction and invaded Iraq, in the latest venture in their oil-dominance strategy.

> The war is not only being carried out with a view to taking over Iraq's oil reserves, it is intended to cancel the contracts of rival Russian and European oil companies as well as exclude France, Russia and China from the region (Chossudovsky).

Let us next consider the role of the Anglo-American alliance in promoting fascism, and in World War II. In November 1925, Benito Mussolini's government worked out an agreement with the U.S. and Britain to repay Italy's war debts. One week later J.P. Morgan & Co., Italy's financial agents in America, loaned Italy $100 million, stabilizing Mussolini's regime. The fascist model provided the necessary 'discipline' to ensure repayments.

If we see that Germany is winning we ought to help Russia and if Russia is winning we ought to help Germany and that way let them kill as many as possible, although I don't want to see Hitler victorious under any circumstances.
—Harry S. Truman, *New York Times*, June 24, 1941

Adolf Hitler was even more attractive to Anglo-American interests. Besides offering the same 'disciplinary repayment' advantage that fascist Italy provided, along with lucrative investment opportunities as Germany rearmed, the British and Americans sought to play Germany and the Soviet Union off against one another, in typical balance-of-powers fashion. By withholding credit, the London and New York banks were able to bring about the financial collapse of the Weimar Republic, and create the conditions for the Nazis – who had been secretly financed during their rise by Western capital – to come to power.

Germany's war effort, both before and after America and Germany were officially at war, was a collaboration between German and American industrialists and bankers. Ford, General Motors, and many other American firms built factories in Nazi Germany, produced planes, tanks, and the other weapons needed by the Reich, and continued operating throughout the war. In some cases critical supplies needed by Allied forces, were instead routed to German industries. Prescott Bush, grandfather of President G.W. Bush, acted as an American agent for Nazi interests during the war.

Both Dulles brothers were partners in Sullivan and Cromwell which handled the legal affairs of American IG (the U.S. subsidiary of IG Farben). The Dulles brothers were also deeply involved in a number of U.S. and German firms and banks or their subsidiaries that contributed to the Nazi build-up and in U.S. firms which later traded with the enemy during World War II (such firms as the Chase Bank, Ford, ITT, General Aniline and Film, and Standard Oil) (Fresia, 108).

President Franklin Roosevelt knew that these corporations were trading with the enemy, there was little he could do. "Roosevelt was blackmailed," states Higham. "You can't run a war without Chase Bank, or Standard Oil of New Jersey, or ITT" (Fresia, 109).

By carefully coordinating its assistance to both Germany and the Soviets, U.S. elites were able to maximize those nations' mutual devastation. After entering the war officially, America had the additional lever of military action against the Axis, so as to further manipulate the progress of the war, in collaboration with British forces. America emerged from the war with its industry intact, with 40% of the world's wealth and industrial capacity, a monopoly on nuclear weapons, and control of the seven seas. Never before had one nation held such a degree of hegemony over world affairs.

The balance of power had quite clearly shifted from London to New York by this time, but the Anglo-American alliance continued, with an even firmer grip on global oil supplies. Winston Churchill declared the existence of the "Iron Curtain," and the Cold War was launched in order to inhibit the non-capitalist powers from interfering in, or benefiting from, the Anglo-American postwar blueprint of economic growth and popular prosperity.

Our 'fresh look' at the previous century has brought us full circle back to the point where it began: the era of the postwar blueprint. My purpose in this review has been to show how the largely covert Anglo-American alliance – of banking, intelligence, and oil interests – has come to dominate the world. While in the Matrix banks stay mostly out of the limelight as regards geopolitical affairs, in reality the top banks in New York and London are the prime movers in this alliance, and hence the prime movers in world affairs generally.

> The ten largest bank holding companies in the United States [today] are firmly in the hands of certain banking houses, all of which have branches in London. They are J.P. Morgan Company, Brown Brothers Harriman, Warburg, Kuhn Loeb and J. Henry Schroder. All of them maintain close relationships with the House of Rothschild, principally through the Rothschild control of international money markets through its manipulation of the price of gold. Each day, the world price of gold is set in the London office of N.M. Rothschild and Company (Mullins, 47-48).

In Matrix reality nations go to war for noble causes. When we peel away the first layer of the Matrix, we find that nations go to war as part of a geopolitical struggle over dominance and empire. When we peel away the next layer, we find that for the past century even competitive imperialism has not been the full story: geopolitics itself turns out to be a rigged game, with nations being manipulated from behind the scenes by an elite financial clique for its own private benefit.

Abandoning Bretton Woods: the petrodollar scam

The abandonment of the postwar economic blueprint, signaled by the end of the gold standard in 1971, can be seen as a replay of the decision by London's banking elite, a century before, to disinvest in the British economy, beginning the decline of Britain's economy and industry from their imperial position of global dominance. Once again the reason was the same: there was more to be gained in international markets – from investments and by financial manipulations – than there was in further domestic investment. And once again, disinvestment led to the economic and industrial decline of what had once been the world's greatest industrial power, in this case the USA.

There is however a fundamental difference between these two parallel scenarios. Britain had never attained quite the same level of global military hegemony that America did, with its postwar Pax Americana regime. Britain may have ruled the waves, but it was relatively weak in land warfare. It could only maintain its strong geopolitical position by playing a shrewd balance-of-powers game – within the traditional context of competitive imperialism. When Britain declined industrially, its ability to win at this game depended on its use of covert intrigue and financial manipulations, and eventually on its strategy of oil-based dominance.

America – with its Pax Americana regime and its Bretton Woods scheme – had actually transformed the global game itself, establishing what I have called a system of 'collaborative imperialism,' as part of a 'postwar blueprint.' While Britain chose effective strategies within a given game, the U.S. had actually set up a whole new game.

Similarly, as Wall Street decided to abandon the economic aspects of the postwar blueprint, it was once again setting up a whole new game, another blueprint for some new kind of world economic order. Not only was it now seeking its rewards in global markets, as did The City a century before, but it was setting out to change the nature of those global markets to its own advantage.

The postwar economic blueprint had been based on global economic growth and development, Western industrialization, financial stability, and relatively full Western employment. New York and London banks sought their rewards by investing in this immense global growth boom, and they favored stability and low inflation so as not to dilute the value their eventual returns from their investments. As it turns out, the abandonment of this economic blueprint was to be total: every single one of its foundations was to be cut away.

August 15, 1971 stands as a pivotal date in this transition: that is when the Bretton Woods accords were officially repudiated, as regards the dollar gold standard, and that is when we begin to see the emergence of a new blueprint for the global economy. But in fact, the process of disinvestment in the U.S. domestic economy had begun much earlier, in the wake of the recession of 1957. The U.S. industrial base was aging by 1957, and in need of major investment and modernization. This was not an attractive proposition to the big New York banks, who saw much more promising opportunities in foreign investments, as did the London banks a century before.

As dollars began to flow out of the U.S., into credit-hungry markets in Europe and around the world, the U.S. economy slid into further decline, and its industry became increasingly uncompetitive, while the recipient nations of the outward investments were able to modernize their own industrial infrastructures. Profits from these foreign investments were not returned to the U.S., but were reinvested again in foreign markets. This growing pool of expatriated U.S. capital was the beginning of what came to be known as the 'Eurodollar market'.

Whereas normal investments in the U.S. economy were not considered desirable by the elite banking community, investment in a build-up in the high-profit military sector could offer significant returns – and provide military muscle for geopolitical management. As the 1960s began, banking and defense industry forces combined to encourage intervention in Vietnam.

A young President Kennedy went along with this advice, as with much of the advice he got from influential circles. But as he became more confident in his leadership role as President, he increasingly began to follow his own vision of the national interest – which not surprisingly diverged with the interests of banking elites. Among other transgressions against the interests of this behind-the-scenes elite power center, Kennedy had decided, just a few days before his highly controversial assassination, to withdraw from Vietnam. Johnson, on assuming office as President only several days later, promptly reversed that decision.

John Judge, a life-long Washington D.C. resident, and a serious researcher into covert operations, relates an anecdote told to him by his mother – who at the time of Johnson's assuming office was a secretary to the Joint Chiefs of Staff. Kennedy was assassinated on a Thursday, and Judge's mother was called in to do some typing the following Sunday, three days later. The memo she was asked to type declared that military planners should plan on the basis of a war that would last ten years and cost 50,000 American lives. She thought there must be some error in the figures, and called a member of the Joint Chiefs to confirm. He replied, in essence, that she should shut up and type. Ten years and 50,000 GI's lost turned out to be a very accurate prediction of the actual outcome of the Vietnam project.

> The Vietnam war strategy was deliberately designed by Defense Secretary Robert McNamara, National Security Advisor McGeorge Bundy, with Pentagon planners and key advisers around Lyndon Johnson, to be a 'no-win war' from the outset, in order to ensure a prolonged buildup of this defense component of the economy (Engdahl, 114-115).

This strategy of militarization and conflict offered lucrative investment opportunities for Wall Street capital, but the Vietnam War could only be pursued by means of deficit spending on the part of the U.S. government – a situation reminiscent of Britain's predicament during World War I. While Britain solved its funding problem with credit from the House of Morgan, the U.S. solved its Vietnam funding problems simply by printing money, in the form of Treasury bond issues. By the terms of Bretton Woods, these printed dollars became real: they could be exchanged at a fixed rate with any other major currency. No one doubted America's ability to stand behind its bonds, so these printed-money bonds became a profitable place to park excess dollars. In this way Europe financed America's deficits during the Vietnam War.

While the Bretton Woods accords gave America this advantage – it could literally print money and force the rest of the world to share the inflationary effects – the accords also brought an accompanying disadvantage: dollars could be exchanged for gold from the U.S. Treasury at the rate of $35 per ounce. Given the decline in the American economy, this exchange rate had become entirely unrealistic, significantly overvaluing the dollar in real economic terms. As a consequence, the U.S. experienced a dangerous drain not only of Eurodollar capital, but also of gold stocks. By 1971 decisive action was called for – the American economy, and the whole global financial system, was approaching meltdown.

There was an obvious and simple solution available for this crisis, a solution that could have been expected to restore financial stability: revaluing the dollar more realistically with respect to gold. This solution, however desirable it would have been for the American and global economies, was not acceptable to elite banking interests. They wanted to retain the power that an overvalued dollar had given them. As a stopgap, while they made arrangements for a new financial blueprint, they decided to abandon the fixed exchange rate system, in order to stem the drain of U.S. gold reserves. This is the context in which they advised Nixon, through their agents in his administration, to take the dollar off the gold standard.

The new blueprint, for a new kind of global economy, was to be based on the time-honored strategy of oil-based dominance, but applied more drastically than ever before. A scenario was presented by State Department economist Walter Levy, at a secret Bilderberger meeting in May 1973 in Saltsjobaden, Sweden. The meeting was attended by David Rockefeller (head of Chase Manhattan Bank), Robert O. Anderson (head of ARCO), Zbigniew Brzezinski, Henry Kissinger, and others with close ties to oil and banking interests. The scenario addressed the question: "What if OPEC oil revenues were to increase by 400%?"

Besides offering windfall profits to the Anglo-American oil cartel, the scenario was also very appealing to the bankers. Since oil was priced in dollars, a sharp increase would lead to a demand for dollars, creating once again a strong-dollar regime, and ensuring the continued financial dominance of the Anglo-American banking elites. In addition, such an increase would greatly curtail industrial growth globally, shifting the balance of power even more towards the dollar and Anglo-American interests. Here was the core of a new financial blueprint, and it showed real promise. As so often before (e.g., World War I,

World War II, Vietnam), an engineered war was to provide the vehicle for implementation of this elite agenda.

Nixon's national security advisor, Henry Kissinger, with his secret, high-level diplomatic contacts in Israel and the Arab states, was in a perfect position to stir up the necessary trouble. By misrepresenting each side to the other, and blocking intelligence reports from reaching normal U.S. diplomatic channels, he was able to ensure the outbreak of war, and a predictable Arab oil embargo – since the U.S. would be forced to come to Israel's aid. The Yom Kippur war began on October 6, 1973, some five months after the pivotal Bilderberger meeting. By January 1974, three months later, the 400% rise in petroleum prices was a fait accompli (Engdahl, 130-138).

Thus began the petrodollar era. Instead of being over-valued by virtue of a fixed exchange rate and an unrealistic gold valuation, dollars were now overvalued because they were needed to pay for high-priced oil. Once again dollars could be printed, and the rest of the world would be forced to finance American deficits. This petrodollar wealth would then find its way to London's unregulated Eurodollar market, where it could be invested in global markets, taking full advantage of the speculative opportunities created by fluctuating currency exchange rates.

The whole Bilderberger scheme had been a brilliant coup, and the Arab states took the blame for it all, just as Germany earlier was forced to take the blame for World War I. Bretton Woods stability had now been replaced by petrodollar volatility, and the postwar blueprint of growth and prosperity had been sabotaged by an engineered oil shock. The stage was now set to establish an entirely new blueprint for the global economy, based on a radical 'free trade' agenda. Not only would this agenda transform the nature of the global economy, it would also undermine the principle of national sovereignty itself – a principle that had been the foundation of world affairs ever since the Treaty of Westphalia was signed in 1648.

The neoliberal project

In the late 1800s – the era of 'Robber Barons' like J.D. Rockefeller, Andrew Carnegie, and J.P. Morgan – the economic philosophy of *laissez-faire* prevailed in America and Britain.

> The laissez-faire school of thought holds a pure capitalist or free market view, that capitalism is best left to its own devices; that it

will dispense with inefficiencies in a more deliberate and quick manner than any legislating body could. The basic idea is that less government interference in private economic decisions such as pricing, production, and distribution of goods and services makes for a better economy.
—Wikipedia

In America, this era marked a period of economic growth and industrialization, and the laissez-faire polices enabled the Robber Barons to dominate this process and amass great fortunes by monopolizing markets and establishing trusts and cartels – unfettered by government interference.

In Britain on the other hand, where laissez-faire was combined with free-trade policies, this was an era of economic decline and de-industrialization, as the London banks moved their investments into global markets – again unfettered by government interference. For ordinary people in both nations, this was an era of sweatshops, the exploitation of child labor, the suppression of workers generally, widespread poverty, and early mortality for mine and factory workers, and in Ireland, a famine that could have been readily prevented – but that would have been 'government interference.'

In the twentieth century laissez-faire thinking fell into general disrepute. After the Great Depression of the 1930s, Keynesian economics in Britain and the New Deal in America ushered in an era of selective government intervention in economic affairs, aimed at providing greater economic stability, higher employment levels, and better working conditions. Monopolies were broken up and corporate regulations were introduced to curb the worst excesses of the laissez-faire era. This trend toward progressive reform culminated in the postwar blueprint, with its emphasis on general Western prosperity.

The abandonment of Bretton Woods stability, and the establishment of the petrodollar era, began a process by which all of the twentieth century economic reforms were to be undone. The next major step in this retrograde process came in 1980, with the programs of Ronald Reagan in America and Margaret Thatcher in Britain. These programs were in fact the re-introduction of discredited laissez-faire economics, but disguised by new packaging.

Whereas in the laissez-faire era people were told that government should not interfere with *capitalism*, with Reagan and

Thatcher we were told that government should stop interfering with *us* – ordinary people: the new policies were allegedly aimed at 'getting government off *our* backs.'

> Government is not the solution to our problems; government is the problem.
> —Ronald Reagan, Inaugural Address, 1981

But packaging aside, Thatcherism and Reaganomics were nothing more than warmed-over laissez-faire economics. While the rhetoric was about individualism, the reality was about reducing corporate taxes, giving corporations free reign, exploiting workers, suppressing unions, and selling off public assets at below-value prices – in a scam called 'privatization.' Every family knows that owning a home is better than renting one, and yet Reagan and Thatcher were able to convince most people that publicly-owned infrastructures were a bad idea, and that we would be better off renting our infrastructures – forevermore and at whatever price – from private corporations. The farm was being sold out from under us, and most of us were believing that we were being somehow liberated. Such is the power of the Matrix.

Economists, being academics, needed an esoteric term for this new-old economics, and they couldn't use *laissez-faire* because it had been discredited. *Neoliberalism* is the label they generally adopted, referring to the reintroduction of 'economic liberalism,' which was another label they used in the 1900s for laissez-faire economics. This not-very-deep verbal disguise was sufficient to distract most observers from noticing the retrograde reality – that we had regressed a full century in a few short years, under the cover of Reagan-Thatcher propaganda, as designed by Milton Friedman and his 'Chicago School' of 'economists.'

In the 1900s, as mentioned above, there were two versions of laissez-faire. In Britain it was combined with free trade, in order to allow domestic disinvestment and de-industrialization, while in America it was combined with a considerable degree of protectionism, in order to facilitate industrialization. Like laissez-faire, neoliberalism initially also encompassed both protectionist and free-trade policies, and still does today as regards, for example, Western farm subsides. But by the end of the Reagan-Thatcher era, in the early 1990s, it became clear that 'free trade' was to be a core element of the neoliberal project.

In 1995, the series of treaty conferences known as GATT (General Agreement on Tariffs and Trade) was transformed by the creation of the World Trade Organization (WTO). Whereas in the earlier GATT conferences the representatives of sovereign nations reached agreements, and then went home to seek ratification, the WTO is a permanent institution, with a big headquarters in Geneva, and a large staff. Not only does the WTO provide a forum for treaty negotiations, but it also has the power to adjudicate trade disputes between member nations, and to prescribe sanctions for violators of WTO decisions.

The powers that have been granted to the WTO by so-called 'free trade' treaties extend a great deal beyond any reasonable definition of the term *free trade*. The legitimate scope of free trade, as articulated by economist David Ricardo in the early 1900s, was limited to policies regarding tariffs and import quotas: the free trade doctrine was mainly about eliminating protectionism. If Portugal can produce wine more efficiently than Britain, and Britain can produce fabrics more efficiently than Portugal, Ricardo argued that it would benefit both nations to allow those goods to be traded without tariffs or quotas. Even this strict version of free trade is open to considerable criticism – when all economic factors are taken into account – but the neoliberal 'free trade' treaties have expanded the notion of free trade beyond all reason.

> Restrictions on goods must be the least-trade-restrictive possible and the restrictions must be "necessary." To prove that a regulation is "necessary," a country must prove that there is a world-wide scientific consensus on the danger, and a WTO tribunal of corporate lawyers must agree that the proposed regulation is a reasonable response to the danger. Furthermore, any regulation must be the "least trade restrictive" regulation possible. Obviously, this puts an almost-insurmountable burden of proof on any government that wants to protect its citizens and its environment from harm (Montague).

In one case, California had a law prohibiting certain cancer-causing additives in gasoline. A Canadian manufacturer claimed this law was "protectionist" and the WTO agreed, forcing California to rescind its law. There is no appeal from such absurd WTO decisions, nor is their any reasonable kind of due process involved when the decisions are made. Under the guise of 'free trade,' the WTO provides a forum in which corporate representatives can arbitrarily eliminate national regulations aimed at protecting the environment or public health, or ensuring safe working conditions, whenever those regulations reduce corporate profits.

Each new round of WTO negotiations is aimed at extending still further the power of the WTO over nations, and many third-world members of the WTO have, quite understandably, resisted this process and have managed to slow it down – encouraged to some extent by the energy of the anti-globalization movement. Not to be deterred, the neoliberal project has proceeded outside the official WTO process, with initiatives like NAFTA (North American Free Trade Agreement). As with neoliberalism generally, such initiatives are sold on the basis of promised benefits to individuals, while in reality they are nothing more than wholesale transfers of power and wealth from governments and the people to corporations. Corporate profits go up as a result, while the promised individual benefits seldom materialize, and worsening conditions for people generally are instead the typical outcome.

Privatization is a central agenda of the neoliberal project, and it is being pursued on several fronts. With Thatcher and Reagan we saw examples of the national political process being used to advance the agenda. The 'free trade' agreements, and the WTO, also contribute to the agenda by declaring an increasing number of government-provided services as being 'unfair competition,' and seeking to open up these 'markets' to private operators. Perhaps the most effective vehicle for moving the privatization agenda forward, at least in the third world, has been the IMF. By setting conditions on nations seeking critically needed loans, the IMF has been able to carry privatization to extreme lengths.

In some cases water itself has been privatized, making it illegal for someone to dig a well in their own backyard – that would be 'stealing from the company.' Water becomes just another commodity, to be sold at all the market will bear, or to the highest bidder. If a wealthy multinational agribusiness operator buys a lot of the water, the local population can be left without enough to survive. When famines result, the Matrix media tells us the cause was something else, like low rainfall. They don't mention that the available water went for commercial purposes, rather than being used to enable people to survive.

Neoliberal claims about 'more efficient services' under privatization are dubious at best, as exemplified by a comparison of Britain's deteriorating and accident-prone privatized rail network with Europe's excellent state-run systems. Flawed as our governments frequently may be, government-provided services are for the most part aimed at serving the needs of the public, and there is some degree of public accountability. Privatized services, on the other hand, are subject to little or no accountability, and their aim is always to maximize operator profits.

> Few trends could so thoroughly undermine the very foundation of our free society as the acceptance by corporate officials of a social responsibility other than to make as much money for their shareholders as possible.
> —Milton Friedman, *Capitalism and Freedom*

Free trade, as envisioned by Ricardo, is aimed at improving national economies by means of mutually beneficial trade. 'Free trade' as interpreted by the WTO is aimed at maximizing corporate profits by removing the ability of nations to enforce sensible and necessary regulations. Rather than being beneficial, the effect of 'free trade' on national economies, and on public health and welfare, is more likely to be disastrous.

Privately run businesses can be a very good idea when there is real competition, leading to good products and services at fair prices. Neoliberalism's privatization agenda, however, is aimed more at taking over industries and infrastructures that are natural monopolies, such as energy and transport networks, prison systems, schools, etc. In pursuit of maximum profits, costs are cut, maintenance is deferred, prices are set at whatever the market will bear, and there is no incentive to provide quality of service beyond minimum acceptable levels. Furthermore there is 'cherry picking': in the case of rail this means that investments are more likely to be made in the most profitable urban routes, leaving outlying areas with inadequate service or no service at all.

As adverse as the economic and human-welfare consequences of the neoliberal project may be, perhaps even more alarming are the political implications. What the neoliberal project is really about, at the most fundamental level, is the transference of economic sovereignty from elected governments to the globalist institutions (WTO et al.) that represent elite corporate and financial interests. While neoliberalism is generally considered to be an economic philosophy, the neoliberal project is at its core a political project, aimed at undermining the sovereign nation state, and replacing it with an institutionalized form of global corporate governance.

> Mussolini said, "Fascism should more properly be called corporatism, since it is the merger of state and corporate power."
> —*Harper's Magazine*, January 2002

The essential bond between capitalism and nationalism was broken in 1945, with the establishment of the Pax Americana regime. The postwar blueprint nonetheless provided stability and prosperity in the West, artificially preserving the nation state system by means of the Bretton Woods framework. As a consequence, the broken bond was not noticed by most observers.

When the Bretton Woods framework was fatally undermined in 1971, with the abandonment of the dollar gold standard, the stage was set for the broken bond to manifest itself, for capitalism to pursue its own path independent of the destabilized nation-state system. The neoliberal project has accelerated this destabilization process with a frontal assault on the nation state, and has established a system of global governance, under elite control, to replace the sovereign-nation-state system that has prevailed since 1648. The WTO, IMF, and World Bank can be seen as the 'Department of Finance and Commerce' of an emerging corporatist world government.

This leaves the system of world order in a bit of a lop-sided condition. Are nation states sovereign or not? They still have the trappings of political sovereignty, and yet that is little but an empty shell with no power over economic and regulatory matters. Under such conditions, how can nations be adequately governed?

The neoliberal economic regime can be expected to lead to discontent and unrest among Western populations, as we've already begun to see with the anti-globalization movement. That movement, however, represents only the activist tip of a larger political iceberg. As conditions continue to worsen, the base of discontent is likely to broaden considerably. Stripped of its economic and regulatory sovereignty, the disempowered nation state will have few resources available to alleviate this discontent. The seeds have thus been sown for a crisis of governance in the West, a crisis of policing and public order.

As it turns out, the neoliberal project represents only part of the elite blueprint for world order in the new millennium. In subsequent developments we shall see that the full new-millennium blueprint will complete the process of disempowering the nation state, transferring political sovereignty as well to centralized, elite-controlled institutions. The full blueprint also includes new schemes for maintaining public order and geopolitical order – both of which were launched upon the world under the banner of the 'War on Terrorism.'

9/11 and the New American Century

> The great masses of the people in the very bottom of their hearts tend to be corrupted rather than consciously and purposely evil...therefore, in view of the primitive simplicity of their minds, they more easily fall a victim to a big lie than to a little one, since they themselves lie in little things, but would be ashamed of lies that were too big.
> —Adolf Hitler, *Mein Kampf*

> Why, of course, the people don't want war. Why would some poor slob on a farm want to risk his life in a war when the best that he can get out of it is to come back to his farm in one piece. Naturally, the common people don't want war; neither in Russia nor in England nor in America, nor for that matter in Germany. That is understood. But after all, it is the leaders of the country who determine the policy and it is always a simple matter to drag the people along, whether it is a democracy or a fascist dictatorship or a Parliament or a Communist dictatorship...[V]oice or no voice, the people can always be brought to the bidding of the leaders. That is easy. All you have to do is tell them they are being attacked and denounce the pacifists for lack of patriotism and exposing the country to danger. It works the same in any country.
> —Hermann Goering, interview during the Nuremberg Trials, April 18, 1946

The world changed on September 11, 2001, with the attacks on the World Trade Center and the Pentagon. The changes were profound, affecting each of our lives, our attitude toward 'security,' and the whole context of international relations. Let us first trace these developments within the world of the Matrix, and after that we'll seek to understand what's really been going on. Here's the basic story, as told inside the Matrix:

American officials at all levels were caught completely off guard on 9/11 by a terrorist attack that used totally unexpected methods; our standard defenses were unequipped to deal with it. The government responded quickly to this new kind of threat, realizing that it could come in many forms, including dirty bombs and biological weapons. A Patriot Act was passed, giving the government the power it needs to track would-be terrorists and prevent them from getting around our security procedures. Civil libertarians say these measures threaten our civil liberties, but they are intended only for terrorists, and we need the measures for our security.

A general *War on Terrorism* was declared, with Homeland Security on the domestic front, and a general warning to terrorist-supporting nations that they might be liable to attack. The government soon followed up on these warnings with an attack on Afghanistan, and later Iraq. Our leaders will leave no stone unturned in their effort to ensure our security. When they believed that Saddam Hussein was preparing to threaten us with terrorist weapons of mass destruction, they wisely invaded, intending not only to protect us, but also to bring the blessings of freedom and democracy to the suppressed Iraqi people.

Since the attacks of 9/11, our nation has been on the defensive. We are discovering threats all over the world, and we are stretching our resources in order to respond adequately to them. We have no designs of our own regarding conquest or empire; we are simply doing our best to make the world safe from terrorism and weapons of mass destruction. It is regrettable that our allies do not give us more support.

In order to understand the reality of these developments, we can begin by looking at the goals and the agenda of those who, at the time of this writing, occupy the White House – those who were responsible for our security and defenses on 9/11 and who have subsequently made the decisions about how to 'respond' to those events. Donald Rumsfeld, Paul Wolfowitz, and crew came into the White House with a detailed agenda up their sleeves. The agenda of the new White House was written up as a report, *Rebuilding America's Defenses: Strategy, Forces and Resources For a New Century*, produced in September 2000 by The Project for the New American Century (PNAC), and now proudly displayed on their website. The report is an updated version of a classified *Defense Policy Guidance* document drafted in 1992 under the supervision of Wolfowitz. Some of the founding members of PNAC include Wolfowitz, Rumsfeld, Dick Cheney, and Richard Perle, a group who are frequently referred to as *neocons* (neoconservatives). Here are some excerpts from their written agenda for the New American Century, with emphasis added.

[T]he United States has for decades sought to play a more permanent role in Gulf regional security. While the unresolved conflict with Iraq provides the immediate justification, the need for a substantial American force presence in the Gulf *transcends the issue of the regime of Saddam Hussein* (PNAC, 14).

Further, these constabulary missions are far more complex and likely to generate violence than traditional 'peacekeeping' missions. For one, they demand American political leadership rather than that of the United Nations, as the failure of the UN mission in the Balkans and the relative success of NATO operations there attests (PNAC, 11).

Despite the shifting focus of conflict in Europe, a requirement to station U.S. forces in northern and central Europe remains. The region is stable, but a continued American presence helps to assure the major European powers, especially Germany, that the United States retains its long-standing security interest in the continent. This is especially important in light of the nascent European moves toward an independent defense 'identity' and policy; it is important that NATO not be replaced by the European Union, leaving the United States without a voice in European security affairs (PNAC, 16).

Since today's peace is the unique product of American preeminence, a failure to preserve that preeminence allows others an opportunity to shape the world in ways antithetical to American interests and principles. *The price of American preeminence is that, just as it was actively obtained, it must be actively maintained* (PNAC, 73).

To preserve American military preeminence in the coming decades, the Department of Defense must move more aggressively to experiment with new technologies and operational concepts, and seek to exploit the emerging revolution in military affairs (PNAC, 50).

Further, the process of transformation, even if it brings revolutionary change, is likely to be a long one, absent some catastrophic and catalyzing event – *like a new Pearl Harbor* (PNAC, 51).

It is ironic, and perhaps intentionally so, that the neocons chose 'a new Pearl Harbor' as their metaphor. Recently released documents are now revealing that America had broken the Japanese codes, that President Roosevelt knew precisely when and where they were going to strike, and that he felt he needed such a dramatic incident in order to bring (then strongly isolationist) America into the war and stop the Nazis. It was no accident that the strategically important aircraft carriers were safely away at sea when the attack on Pearl Harbor came.

Much new light has been shed on Pearl Harbor through the recent work of Robert B. Stinnett, a World War II Navy veteran. Stinnett has obtained numerous relevant documents through the Freedom of Information Act. In *Day of Deceit: The Truth about FDR and Pearl Harbor* (2000), the book so brusquely dismissed by director Bruckheimer, Stinnett reveals that Roosevelt's plan to provoke Japan began with a memorandum from Lieutenant Commander Arthur H. McCollum, head of the Far East desk of the Office of Naval Intelligence. The memorandum advocated eight actions predicted to lead Japan into attacking the United States. McCollum wrote: "If by these means Japan could be led to commit an overt act of war, so much the better." FDR enacted all eight of McCollum's provocative steps – and more.

While no one can excuse Japan's belligerence in those days, it is also true that our government provoked that country in various ways – freezing her assets in America; closing the Panama Canal to her shipping; progressively halting vital exports to Japan until we finally joined Britain in an all-out embargo; sending a hostile note to the Japanese ambassador implying military threats if Tokyo did not alter its Pacific policies; and on November 26th – just 11 days before the Japanese attack – delivering an ultimatum that demanded, as prerequisites to resumed trade, that Japan withdraw all troops from China and Indochina, and in effect abrogate her Tripartite Treaty with Germany and Italy.

After meeting with President Roosevelt on October 16, 1941, Secretary of War Henry Stimson wrote in his diary: "We face the delicate question of the diplomatic fencing to be done so as to be sure Japan is put into the wrong and makes the first bad move – overt move." On November 25th, the day before the ultimatum was sent to Japan's ambassadors, Stimson wrote in his diary: "The question was how we should maneuver them [the Japanese] into the position of firing the first shot..." (Perloff).

Prior to 9/11, the neocons were facing precisely the same predicament Roosevelt had faced: they had a momentous agenda they were eager to pursue, and it was an agenda that the domestic population would be strongly opposed to. And like Roosevelt, the neocons had the means to bring about a sufficiently dramatic incident to shift public opinion. In Roosevelt's case he simply needed to wait for Japan to respond to his provocations; in the neocons' case, they needed only to arrange the events of 9/11. They were certainly in a much better position to do so than was the ragtag bunch Al Qaeda allegedly sent over to do the job – and the neocons had a much more understandable motive as well.

We'll probably never know for sure what really happened on that day, but the number of glaring anomalies in the Matrix version of 9/11 are countless, from the failure to follow standard intercept procedures in the case of hijacked aircraft, to the mysterious collapse of a third WTC building that was not hit by a plane, to the numerous urgent warnings U.S. intelligence had received from around the world – warning of precisely such an attack by Al Qaeda, to several FBI investigations into Al Qaeda prior to 9/11 that were mysteriously quashed from Washington, to an exercise being carried out on the very day regarding hijacked airliners attacking buildings, to the fact that some of the alleged terrorists had been secretly trained by U.S. security forces. That part of the Matrix is riddled with glitches.

> NEW YORK CITY, NY (Oct. 26, 2004) An alliance of 100 prominent Americans and 40 family members of those killed on 9/11 today announced the release of the 9/11 Truth Statement, a call for immediate inquiry into evidence that suggests high-level government officials may have deliberately allowed the September 11th attacks to occur. The Statement supports an August 31st Zogby poll that found nearly 50% of New Yorkers believe the government had foreknowledge and "consciously failed to act," with 66% wanting a new 9/11 investigation.
> —http://www.911truth.org/article.php?story=20041026093059633

Whether they had a hand in the events of 9/11 or not, those events provided precisely the *new Pearl Harbor* that the neocons believed was necessary so that their path to pursuing their PNAC agenda would not *be a long one.* Regardless of who was responsible for the dramatic incident, it has led us to a Matrix world where a *War on Terrorism* is being pursued, and a real world where the U.S. is grabbing for global hegemony, and the infrastructure has been put in place to turn the USA – by virtue of the 'Patriot Act' – into a fully regimented society, under military administration. According to 50% of New Yorkers, at least, these glitches in the Matrix are becoming rather transparent.

This agenda, which has been cherished by the neocons for at least twelve years, casts a different light on American 'responses' to the events of 9/11. In terms of the Matrix construct, the driving motivations for invading Iraq – evidence of weapons of mass destruction and support for terrorism – have turned out to be untrue. But in terms of the PNAC agenda, the invasion of Iraq is clearly called out as an important early initiative. The invasion of Afghanistan seems to have done little to curtail the alleged activities of Bin Laden or Al Qaeda, but it goes a long way toward projecting American force into South Asia and extending "*American military preeminence*," as recommended in the PNAC report.

Although the report does not mention economics or mineral resources specifically, it can be taken as obvious that control over petroleum sources and pipelines is a primary element of "*military preeminence*." Besides, we need to keep in mind the Anglo-American elite's time-honored strategy of oil-based dominance, which the PNAC agenda clearly serves.

While in the Matrix the USA is defending itself against terrorism around the world, we can see that in reality America is pursuing an aggressive, expansionist campaign, following the recipe outlined in the neocons' own PNAC agenda.

With the PNAC agenda being expressed both in word and deed, we can now see how geopolitical order is to be managed in the new-millennium blueprint. Not content to remain merely the global policeman, the U.S. is striking out to be the outright global dictator. The term 'Pax Americana' is of course a reference to *Pax Romana* – the internal peace of the Roman Empire. In the new blueprint this reference becomes all the more apt, with the Pentagon now taking on the role of the invincible Roman Legions, and with Washington as the new Rome.

The hidden hand of the market will never work without a hidden fist –
McDonald's cannot flourish without McDonnell Douglas, the builder of
the F-15. And the hidden fist that keeps the world safe for Silicon Val-
ley's technologies is called the United States Army, Air Force, Navy and
Marine Corps.
—Thomas L. Friedman, *New York Times*, March 28, 1999

The management of discontented societies

"It is also a fact that America is too democratic at home to be autocratic
abroad. This limits the use of America's power, especially its capacity for
military intimidation. Never before has a populist democracy attained
international supremacy. But the pursuit of power is not a goal that
commands popular passion, except in conditions of a sudden threat or
challenge to the public's sense of domestic well-being. The economic self-
denial (that is, defense spending) and the human sacrifice (casualties, even
among professional soldiers) required in the effort are uncongenial to
democratic instincts. Democracy is inimical to imperial mobilization."
—Zbigniew Brzezinski, *The Grand Chessboard*, p.35

If the PNAC agenda provides the new-millennium blueprint
with a scheme for geopolitical order, we are still left with the
problem of how to maintain public order in discontented societies. It turns out that preparations to deal with this problem have
been underway for some time, since the very beginning of the
neoliberal project in the early 1970s. Let us step back and review
this process, beginning with the postwar era.

The postwar years, especially in the United States, were characterized by consensus politics. Most people shared a common
understanding of how society worked, and generally approved
of how things were going. Prosperity was real and the Matrix
version of reality was reassuring. Most people believed in it.
Those beliefs became a shared consensus, and the government
could then carry out its plans as it intended, 'responding' to the
programmed public will.

The 'excess democracy' of the 1960s and 1970s attacked this
shared consensus from below, and elite planners decided from
above that ongoing consensus wasn't worth paying for. In deciding to pursue the neoliberal project, circa 1971, they could easily
foresee that new means of social control would need to be developed. Ultimately of course, there was always the brute-force fascist solution: the outright police state, which we are now

beginning to see as part of the War on Terrorism. But back in the 1970s such a regime would have been infeasible politically, and was not yet necessary: the neoliberal project was just beginning.

By examining shifts in Matrix propaganda over the past three decades, along with other kinds of shifts in official policy, and observing how these shifts have affected society and public sentiments, we can in retrospect see how we have been gradually conditioned to accept a creeping police state. Perhaps the most obvious of these conditioning programs has to do with our attitude toward police forces, the limits on their powers, and the importance of civil rights and liberties. We must recall here that a strong respect for civil liberties had always been a proud and cherished principle of Western democracies, particularly in America, with its long-hallowed Bill of Rights.

I suppose the Matrix attack on this civil-liberties mindset began in earnest with the film *Dirty Harry*. Here we had a noble cop, of incorruptible integrity and dedication, who was being prevented from dealing with a heinous crime in progress by senseless bureaucratic interference 'from above.' In order to save a helpless, abducted young girl, he was forced to defy his superiors, employ his own heavy-handed police methods, and heroically save the day – to eventual praise. The perpetrator, just to complete the story, was a sadistic sociopath, totally undeserving of any compassion from the audience.

This pioneering film served as a template for a whole genre of films and television dramas, continuing up to this very day. Time after time we see a noble cop, or perhaps a duo, and always they must defy the system in order to bring a worthless sociopath to justice. Frequently, in this genre, an obviously guilty perpetrator is left at large because of a 'technicality' – some silly thing about 'rights.' As the genre has evolved, even the mention of 'rights' leads to a snicker, not only from the cops in their patrol car, but from most viewers as well. The message: cops need to be 'freed' to do their jobs.

As a result of this conditioning campaign, the concept of civil liberties was reframed in the public mind: rather than being seen as protector of law-abiding citizens from government abuse, 'rights' were being perceived as a serious hindrance to law enforcement. This perception was not supported by criminological evidence, but who listens to criminologists? Certainly not scriptwriters. Most people's 'experience' of crime is what they see on television, and when the same scenario is reinforced time after time, Matrix reality is taken on board as reality perceived.

The contrast between the noble cop and the depraved perpetrator is also important in this conditioning process. In particular, we need to look at the kind of perpetrator images we are presented with. There are certain stock images, such as the young black gang member, the older black drug dealer, the Italian mobster, the helpful ghetto resident who reveals 'what's goin' down on the street,' etc. Rather than law enforcement being about solving crimes, this genre invites us to see the noble cop in the role of 'civilized man' maintaining control over certain anti-social elements of society. Cops aren't dealing with individual crimes; rather they are protecting 'us' from 'them.' Why shouldn't we give more power to these brave guardians of our tranquility?

Drugs and drug-related violence have played a very important role in this conditioning process, in both reality and in the Matrix. In reality the U.S. government, in particularly the CIA, is very much involved in the drug trade, and in the promotion of drug-related violence. During the Contra hearings it was revealed that part of the Contra's funding came from the sales of crack cocaine and automatic weapons to L.A. Latino street gangs. The role of the CIA's Air America airline in ferrying drugs became so widely known that a Hollywood film was produced, which tried to explain the matter away as 'understandable rogue corruption.' More recently in Afghanistan the Taliban had put a halt to opium growing; after the American invasion the opium growers were back in business. Here's just one example of the many reports that have come out in several well-referenced books by various investigators, in this case regarding Southeast Asia some decades ago:

> I, for example, had reason to gather evidence based on talking to American officials in my own inquiry that the Chief of Staff of the Royal Laotian Army and the commander of the CIA secret army was involved in drugs. What happened when I made this allegation? The CIA did everything to discredit my allegations. They attacked me. They didn't attack Vang Pao who was operating a heroin ring. They didn't go after General Owen Radicone who had the world's biggest heroin operation – they went after me! They tried to suppress my book, they threatened to murder my sources, they spent $25 million in staging a massive opium burning by the Nationalist Chinese

forces in northern Thailand announcing they were retiring from the drug trade. I mean, they went through all kinds of hoops to discredit me and my allegations. They protect these guys. While you're working with the agency, you are protected (McCoy).

While on the one hand the U.S. government is involved in supplying and profiting from drugs, on the other hand it declared a 'War on Drugs,' and over the years the severity of the penalties, the arbitrariness of policing procedures – and the degree to which the Bill of Rights is being ignored – have steadily increased. These real-world developments combine with their Matrix representations to effectively move forward the conditioning agenda. In addition, very real precedents have been set regarding seizure of property, severity of sentences, permissibility of evidence, access to parole, etc.

Another relevant genre, of more recent vintage than the noble cop scenario, involves courtroom and law-firm dramas, as exemplified by *The Practice* and *Ally McBeal*. The focus in these dramas is not on so much on winning noble cases, but rather on law as a cynical game: the technicalities and legalities, and how to manipulate them, are what it's all about, along with what kind of deals can be cut. Realistic or not, the overall effect of this genre serves to undermine one's faith in the legal system as it currently operates, and again encourages us to consider important rights to be 'technicalities.'

Cruising along beside this genre is the very popular *CSI* (crime scene investigation) television multi-series. Here we learn how terribly unreliable witnesses and obvious evidence can be. Only sophisticated forensics is capable of solving crimes, and forensic teams always have incorruptible integrity and highly professional competence. (This despite well-publicized cases of FBI forensic labs falsifying results in order to achieve convictions.)

Taken together these two genres, regarding lawyers and forensics, convey a subliminal message: trial by jury is defective. If you were an innocent accused, wouldn't you rather have the *CSI* squad investigating the scene, rather than put your trust in Ally McBeal, unreliable witnesses, and some random jury and prosecutor? In fact, trial by jury is the oldest institution in the evolution of British and American democracy, preceding parliaments, and is one of the only forums in our societies where ordinary people actually have power, and can apply their own best judgment.

> I consider trial by jury as the only anchor yet devised by man, by which a government can be held to the principles of its constitution.
> —Thomas Jefferson

In this regard we need to keep in mind the very real campaign by corporate lobbyists to 'do something' about all those big corporate lawsuits. One of the core objectives of this lobbying campaign is to eliminate juries from the corporate liability process. If juries can be eliminated from criminal trials as well, then the state will have additional tools with which to maintain civil 'order' under the neoliberal regime. These two television genres do not go very far in this direction, but they do serve well as softening-up conditioning.

All of the genres we've considered, along with the War on Drugs and similar developments, turned out to be softening up conditioning for the big event: one wholesale frontal assault on the whole civilized notion of citizens' rights. That assault came in the form of one of the 'responses' to 9/11.

> The illegal we do immediately, the unconstitutional takes a little longer.
> —Henry Kissinger, cited in *New York Times Magazine*, October 28, 1973

There have been two primary 'responses' to 9/11 by the U.S. government, both under the banner of the War on Terrorism. The first 'response' has been the vigorous campaign of military aggression and conquest, as outlined beforehand in the neocons' PNAC agenda. The second response has been a campaign to achieve unlimited powers of civil control, including arbitrary arrest, unlimited detention without charges or evidence, denial of outside contact, and the use of torture, murder, rape, and other 'inhuman' practices against detainees. Every one of these things has in fact occurred and been admitted publicly, in some cases involving American detainees, in some cases at the hands of U.S. personnel, and in some cases contracted out to foreign governments such as Egypt, where torture is common.

Such practices are in fact encouraged by policy documents released by Vice President Cheney, and despite official apologies regarding certain publicized incidents, the practices continue while a few low-level sacrificial lambs have been the victims of token and well-publicized prosecutions for 'abuses.'

I don't use the term fascist lightly, but we are looking here at images right out of Nazi Germany: the raid in the night, the disappeared-forever neighbor, the sadistic Gestapo – even the slave labor camp, in the form of a massive prison-labor industry and the world's highest rate of incarceration, as a result of the hypocritical War on Drugs.

So far the full force of the new police-state legislation has been unleashed mostly on marginalized groups, in particular Muslims. But there's nothing ethnic in the written legislation. Anyone who is 'suspected' of being involved in a group which is 'suspected' of being involved in 'terrorism' in any way, direct or indirect, can be arrested and held indefinitely without charges or evidence – even if the suspicion itself is not genuine. This state of affairs became official with the recent decision in the well-publicized Padilla case, where a Federal Court ruled in favor of the Bush administration, which claimed that it had the right to indefinitely imprison an American citizen without charging him with a crime.

The various precedents that are being set, regarding the Patriot Acts and extended police powers, are affirming that this draconian legislation is here to stay, and that it is enforceable. This is very ominous, because so far we've only seen the tip of the iceberg as regards the full scope of this legislation.

We've seen a few isolated domestic cases, all allegedly related to violent terrorism, and we've seen maltreatment of non-citizen prisoners. But in fact this legislation defines terrorism very broadly, and it applies to all citizens. If you send a donation to an environmental group, and if someone associated with that group commits an act of sabotage, as did Earth First! members, you could conceivably be charged for contributing to terrorism.

This doesn't imply that we are likely to see lots of prosecutions of individuals, but it does imply that environmental advocates in general might be designated as a 'terrorist group,' making a considerable segment of the population subject to arbitrary detention. Environmentalism is only one example. Any cause or movement that sometimes engages in civil disobedience would be equally vulnerable. Even sending email messages could designate you as a terrorist if you express support for some group you believe to be fighting a just cause, but where Homeland Security feels differently.

The main point here is that the new police powers are unlimited, and could be applied in any number of ways, depending only on the will of the Federal Government. 'Suspicion of terrorism' can be applied to any person or group that meets with government disfavor, since no evidence or charges need to be produced. America is now officially a police state, the necessary legislation and precedents having been carefully established. There has been no need as yet for the iron fist to be widely brandished, but it is available whenever needed to maintain 'order' under the neoliberal, New-American-Century regime.

> We are fast approaching the stage of the ultimate inversion: the stage where the government is free to do anything it pleases, while the citizens may act only by permission, which is the stage of the darkest periods of human history, the stage of rule by brute force.
> —Ayn Rand, "The Nature of Government"

Although it has received little public attention, the fact is that the situation in the rest of the West, as regards police-state powers, is essentially the same as in America. As part of the War on Terrorism, Washington has pushed other governments to adopt 'adequate security measures,' so that they can 'play their role' in 'fighting global terrorism.'

Incidents such as the Madrid and London rail bombings, and the Omagh bombing in Northern Ireland, have served to move this agenda rapidly forward – each being promptly followed by the adoption of 'anti-terrorist' legislation. Like 9/11 itself, these incidents have all been suspicious, in that they each were unprecedented in their scale, were characterized by a variety of anomalous circumstances, and made no sense in terms of terrorist motivation. From any conceivable terrorist perspective, these incidents have all been entirely counter-productive. Regardless of who has been responsible for these incidents, the primary outcome has been the adoption of draconian 'anti-terrorist' legislation granting essentially unlimited police powers to Western governments.

In the EU legislation, for example, 'terrorism' is defined very broadly indeed. If a public demonstration is aimed at "changing the economic system," and if property damage occurs during the demonstration, then everyone involved in the demonstration can be charged with terrorism. In Britain, in the aftermath of the July 11 subway bombings, a shoot-to-kill policy has been adopted, and can be applied to anyone who is 'suspected' of being a suicide bomber. The first time this policy was applied an innocent Brazilian was the victim, and he was wearing or carrying nothing that could possibly have concealed a bomb. Nonetheless, the policy remains, the precedent stands, and no one has been punished for the wrongful killing – while a whistleblower in the case was suspended from his job.

As in America, these iron-fist powers are being mostly kept hidden in a velvet glove, and given as little publicity as possible. But they are available whenever the need for them might arise. In addition, U.S. security forces are staking out a direct role for themselves in the domestic affairs of other Western nations.

Milan – A radical Egyptian cleric known as Abu Omar was walking to a Milan mosque for noon prayers in February 2003 when he was grabbed on the sidewalk by two men, sprayed in the face with chemicals and stuffed into a van. He hasn't been seen since.

…Italian authorities suspect the Egyptian was the target of a CIA-sponsored operation known as rendition, in which terrorism suspects are forcibly taken for interrogation to countries where torture is practiced.

—*Washington Post*, March 13, 2005

US INVESTIGATORS, including CIA agents, will be allowed to interrogate Irish citizens on Irish soil in total secrecy, under an agreement signed between Ireland and the US last week.

—*Irish Examiner*, July 21, 2005

The UN and the new-millennium blueprint

The last stage but one of every civilisation, is characterised by the forced political unification of its constituent parts into a single state.

—Arnold Toynbee, *The Study of History*

Today Americans would be outraged if U.N. troops entered Los Angeles to restore order; tomorrow they will be grateful. This is especially true if they were told there was an outside threat from beyond, whether real or promulgated, that threatened our very existence. It is then that all peoples of the world will plead with world leaders to deliver them from this evil. The one thing every man fears is the unknown. When presented with this scenario, individual rights will be willingly relinquished for the guarantee of their well being granted to them by their world government.

—Henry Kissinger speaking at Evian, France, May 21, 1992 Bilderbergers meeting. Unbeknownst to Kissinger, his speech was taped by a Swiss delegate to the meeting.

Most of the new elite blueprint has now come into focus. The principal elements are the continued dominance of the Anglo-American clique and oil cartel, neoliberal economics, the establishment of centralized corporatist institutions (WTO et al.) to manage financial and regulatory affairs, the use of police-state methods to keep populations under control, and the use of the Pentagon to manage geopolitical affairs in support of this blueprint for world order in the new millennium.

The one element that remains out of kilter in our picture so far is that of political governance. The relic of official national sovereignty makes little sense in a world where essential decision-making is being moved to centralized global institutions. The blueprint would be much more balanced with the establishment of a centralized political institution that is in harmony with the elite agenda, and that has the charter to deal with legislation and administration on a global basis. The UN, as Kissinger suggests above, would be the natural entity to groom for such a role.

In order for the UN to serve elite interests in this role it would need to be 'reformed' in various ways. In terms of its internal operations, the UN would need to be made more centralized, so that it can be more directly controlled by elites. In terms of its authority, it would need to be established as a governing body with powers of enforcement and taxation. We can see the beginnings of such a 'reform' agenda in the UN's recently published "Draft Outcome Document."

The language of this document, as we might expect, is couched in terms of venerable principles, such as advancing human rights and the cause of peace. Embedded in this language, however, are certain key phrases that indicate the direction the 'reform' effort is heading. In the excerpts below, such key phrases have been emphasized.

In the following excerpts we see laid out the basic agenda of enhancing the authority of the UN, and we see a foot-in-the-door regarding taxing authority:

V. Strengthening the United Nations

117. We reaffirm our commitment to strengthen the United Nations with a view to enhancing its authority and efficiency as well as its capacity to address effectively the full range of the challenges of our time. We are determined to reinvigorate the intergovernmental organs of the United Nations and to adapt them to the needs of the twenty-first century.

119. We emphasize the need to *provide the United Nations with sufficient and predictable resources* with a view to enabling it to carry out its mandate in the fast changing and complex and challenging world (UN 27).

Security Council

125. We reaffirm that Member States have conferred on the Security Council primary responsibility for the maintenance of international peace and security, acting on their behalf, as provided by the Charter (UN 28).

Global Governance and Systemic Issues

28. We further reaffirm the need for the United Nations to play a *more decisive and central role* in international development policy and in ensuring coherence, coordination and implementation of development goals and actions agreed by the international community (UN 7).

Here we see executive power being centralized in the office of the Secretary General, with only an annual responsibility to report back to the General Assembly:

Management reform

136. We commit to ensure that the Secretary-General has sufficient authority and flexibility to carry out his managerial responsibility and leadership; we support granting broad authority to the Secretary-General to redeploy posts and resources from lower to higher priority areas, under relevant rules and regulations established by the General Assembly, and invite him to report to the General Assembly each year on outcomes (UN, 31).

Just as the fear of crime and drugs was used to increase police powers in the U.S., we see here similar means being used to support greater UN authority, and the creation of a permanent UN military force:

Impunity

112. Recognizing that justice is a vital component of the rule of law, *we commit to end impunity for the most serious crimes of concern to the international community,* such as crimes of genocide, crimes against humanity and war crimes, by cooperating with the International Criminal Court, the existing ad hoc and mixed criminal tribunals and other mechanisms for international justice (UN, 26).

Transnational crime

93. We express our grave concern at the negative effects on development, peace and security and human rights posed by *transnational crime,* including smuggling and trafficking of human beings, *narcotic drugs,* and small arms and light weapons, and at the increasing vulnerability of States to such crime. We reaffirm the need to work collectively to *combat transnational crime.*

96. We decide to *strengthen the capacity of the United Nations Office on Drugs and Crime* to provide assistance to Member States in those tasks upon request (UN, 23).

Use of force

74. We reiterate our commitment to refrain from the threats or use of force in any manner inconsistent with the purposes of the United Nations. We reaffirm that one of the Purposes and Principles guiding the United Nations is to maintain international peace and security, and to that end to take *effective collective measures for the prevention and removal of threats to the peace,* and for the suppression of acts of aggression or other breaches of the peace, and to bring about by peaceful means, and in conformity with the principles of justice and international law, adjustment or settlement of international *disputes or situations which might lead to a breach of the peace* (UN, 19).

Peacekeeping

56. Recognizing that peacekeeping plays a vital role in helping parties to conflict end hostilities and commending the contribution of UN Peacekeepers and other personnel in that regard, noting improvements made in recent years to United Nations peacekeeping, including the deployment of integrated missions in complex situations, and stressing the need to mount *operations with adequate capacity to counter hostilities* and fulfill effectively their mandates, we urge further consideration of the proposal for the *establishment of a strategic military reserve capacity to reinforce UN peacekeeping missions* in times of crises and endorse the creation of a *standing capacity for*

rapid deployment of United Nations civilian police in peacekeeping (UN, 16).

Here we see enshrined the principles of neoliberalism and 'free trade':

Global partnership for development

Implement regulatory frameworks and commercial laws that encourage business formation and build public confidence in private markets through a clear definition of property rights, protection of those rights, transparent rulemaking, enforcement of contracts and general respect for the rule of law (UN, 4)

Trade

24. We recommit to promote a *universal, rules-based, open, non-discriminatory and equitable multilateral trading system*, recognizing the *major role that trade can play* in promoting economic growth, employment and development for all... (UN, 6).

Next we see the beginnings of a taxing authority for the UN, under the cover of 'helping poorer nations:'

UNITED NATIONS, Sep 27 (IPS) – Less than two weeks after the much-ballyhooed U.N. summit meeting of some 170 political leaders, the world's 132 developing nations want to sustain the pressure on rich donor nations to deliver on their promises.

The summit process, Annan pointed out, "clearly created stronger support" for 0.7 percent of gross national product as official development assistance from rich to poorer nations. As a result, Annan said, there will be tens of billions of dollars earmarked for the fight for development.

Additionally, "innovative sources of financing" – including a *tax on airline tickets* – should begin to come on stream by next year.

—Inter Press Service News Agency

—http://ipsnews.net/news.asp?idnews=30433

Helping poorer nations might be a very good thing, if that was actually intended. In this regard we might consider the 'debt forgiveness' program announced at the recent G8 summit (July, 2005). Contrary to public perceptions, this program will make things worse rather than better for the indebted nations. The program is really a scheme by which Western taxpayers will reimburse the IMF for uncollectible loans to the third world. These reimbursements will then be subtracted from national aid budgets, yielding no net gain to the 'forgiven' nations. Not only that, but debtor nations that subscribe to this program must submit to additional, harmful, privatization measures. When we read about funding the "fight for development" we need to keep in mind that this kind of aid is typically earmarked for projects that benefit Western corporations more than the recipient nations.

John Bolton, long known to be highly critical of the UN, has recently been dispatched to the UN to push this reform process forward:

> Washington – The recent 2005 U.N. World Summit agreement was an important first step in what will be a long process of reform of the United Nations, U.S. Ambassador John R. Bolton says.
> —http://usinfo.state.gov/is/Archive/2005/Sep/29-300799.html

With the U.S. taking the leadership role in this UN 'reform' campaign, and with the indicators we've already seen of where that campaign is headed, it does indeed appear that the UN is being groomed to become the political branch of a world government, as Kissinger suggested. This is a project that is likely to find widespread support from the people of the world, because it will be sold on the basis that it will reduce poverty, fight terrorism, and bring world peace. Those who point out that this garden path is leading directly to global tyranny will most likely be dismissed as 'conspiracy theorists.'

The political process will appear to have changed only slightly in the West, with one more level of government added – as the EU level has been added in Europe. All important decisions, such as those regarding finance, 'security,' budget allocations, taxation, environmental policy, corporate regulations, migration of populations, the use of genetic-engineering and nuclear technologies, etc., will be made by the remote UN world government.

People will feel totally detached from this centralized process, just as today's Europeans feel detached from the decisions made in Brussels. People will be encouraged to focus their attention on their disempowered local governments, as in the EU today, and as in Britain, with its phony devolution regime. Whatever suffering the centralized government might impose on Westerners will be blamed, as it is today in the EU and Britain, on 'mismanagement' by these disempowered local governments. Political parties will take turns claiming they can 'better manage' if they win the next election.

The role of national governments under this new-millennium blueprint will be reduced primarily to collecting taxes and keeping its citizens under control, so that corporations and banks can pursue their neoliberal agenda unmolested by popular unrest. This basic situation is not really that different than how things are today, except that the regime will be even more remote, even less democratic, and quite a bit more extreme in its measures.

While the UN will have official political sovereignty, and will have sufficient armed forces to enforce its will in most cases, we can be sure that the U.S. will retain for itself an independent role, and that the Pentagon will continue to be the predominant military force. Consider these words, penned recently by Newt Gingrich and George Mitchell, again with emphasis added:

> The United States pursues its interests in international affairs, including issues of peace, stability, trade, and national security, in collaboration with others wherever possible. Our actions are usually more effective when they are taken in concert with others. *At the same time, the United States can, and sometimes must, act independently if collective efforts cannot be achieved or are ineffective.* The United States *advances its interests* through a range of multilateral arrangements, with both established organizations and ad hoc coalitions. *A strong and effective United Nations can be an important instrument for the pursuit of the American goals* of freedom and security (USIP vi).

We can now see the entire outline of the new-millennium blueprint. Sovereignty is to be transferred from nation states to a world government made up of the UN, the WTO, and various other centralized global institutions. While the trappings of democracy are likely to be retained, popular sentiment will have little relevance to essential policy, as is already the case today in most nations. The neoliberal economic regime will give free reign to elite corporate and financial interests, and any attempt at popular rebellion will be brutally suppressed.

Behind all of these developments can be found the hidden hand of the elite Anglo-American financial clique, subtly but effectively orchestrating national agendas, global markets, and the establishment of the new global regime. The ongoing relationship of the elite clique to the new world government will be much like its traditional relationship with the American and

British governments: the tail will be wagging the dog. Public criticism will be focused on the visible globalist institutions, on corporations, or on national governments, while the bankers behind the curtains will be merrily counting their takings.

Capitalism and the Matrix

Capitalism is usually considered to be an economic philosophy. Apologists typically talk about the virtues of a free market, and refer back to the theories of people like Adam Smith and David Ricardo. Critics then point out the tendency to monopolization, exploitation, and imperialism – arising from the actual operation of the marketplace in the real world. In our age of environmental awareness, critics focus increasingly on capitalism's relentless pursuit of economic growth, and point out how that kind of growth is destroying our life-support systems.

In this context – capitalism as economic philosophy – the treatment I have found most useful is David Korten's, in *The Post-Corporate World: Life After Capitalism*. He points out that Adam Smith's notion of a market economy actually makes a great deal of sense – but it has nothing to do with capitalism.

Smith's model can be seen operating in the real world in the realm of small businesses, where competition typically does lead to a beneficial and self-optimizing marketplace. Smith's model includes all-important constraints, the primary one being that no buyer or seller, or clique of same, is big enough to significantly influence market prices. Real-world capitalism violates this and every other of Smith's constraints.

I found Korten's observation – obvious once it is pointed out – to be liberating. It opened up the vista of economic possibilities, as regards alternatives to capitalism. Contrary to Marxist doctrine, there's nothing really wrong with private property and profit seeking. As even communist regimes have eventually all needed to concede – for their own survival: the pursuit of private profit often leads to efficient economic functioning.

From an economic perspective, the problems of capitalism have to do with lack of balance, and lack of limits. We might say that capitalism is all yin and no yang, all push and no repose. The profit motive is fine, but it must be counter-balanced with something else, with some other equally powerful dynamic principle. Trying to put arbitrary leashes on growth – simply legislating Smith's constraints – doesn't work; that just creates a challenge to be overcome by the ever-so-clever entrepreneur and his lobbyists. Economies of scale are real, and profit as the only principle leads inevitably to monopoly capitalism, as it always has in every real-world case.

As I suggested in the foreword to this book, our problems as a society are all interconnected: we can't deal with them piecemeal. Economics cannot be addressed in isolation. We need to look at things in a broader context, a context in which there are more dynamic forces operating, and in which it is possible to find some kind of overall balance.

The conclusion I have reached – and I'll be expanding on this in the rest of the book – is that *culture* is the context we need to be looking at. Culture is the container, the system, in which politics, economics, and social relationships generally, all interact with one another. If we want to change our societies in any significant way, we need to make changes at the level of culture.

This observation may not at first seem to be very useful. How, you might reasonably ask, can we hope to change our cultures? This question is a deep one, and I won't try to offer a brief answer at this point. I will however say that there is light at the end of this tunnel, and we will be seeking that light as our narrative proceeds. For now, I simply want to introduce culture as a focus in our investigations.

Korten, like many observers who are looking at the problems of our society, focuses on capitalism, and corporations, as being the primary forces in our societies, the forces that need somehow to be tamed. I agree with this, to a large extent, and yet our discussion in this chapter has not talked much about capitalism, or at least it has not seemed to. But in fact, from a broader perspective, we have indeed been talking about capitalism.

The fact is that capitalism is not really an *economic* philosophy at all; rather it is a *political* philosophy. Capitalism is basically the belief that those who have the most spare money – the most capital – should decide how our societies develop. This is a political belief, a belief about who should make the important societal decisions. It is an entirely undemocratic belief; in fact it is a belief in the virtue of *plutocracy* – rule by the wealthy.

> Capitalism is the astounding belief that the most wickedest of men will do the most wickedest of things for the greatest good of everyone.
> —attributed to John Maynard Keynes

From an economic perspective, there is no particular capitalist economics. In today's political climate we are invited to identify capitalism with free trade and neoliberalism. But in fact every major capitalist economy was developed under a regime of protectionism. Britain in the early 1800s, America in the late 1800s, Japan in the postwar era: when these mighty industrial engines were being created they each depended on sufficient protectionism to enable their fledgling industries to get off the ground unimpeded by already-established foreign competitors.

The American Civil War, for example, was primarily about the North's industrialists overcoming the South's insistence on a free trade regime, which was well suited to maximizing cotton exports. The North got its protectionism, and that led to the growth of America's great industrial economy. This growth would have been much more difficult to accomplish in a free-trade regime, where Britain's more established industries would have retarded American industrial development.

From this broader perspective, our discussion of the Anglo-American clique and its manipulations has been very much a discussion about capitalism. If those who have the most capital – those who control the biggest banks – are in charge of setting society's agenda – which is what capitalism is about – then they will do so according to their overall perceived best interests, not by following any particular economic doctrine. A war or depression can be more useful, at times, than economic growth, while protectionism and free trade are simply tools for different jobs.

In terms of the Matrix, the biggest myth about capitalism is the belief that capitalism is a branch of economics. When the Chairman of the Federal Reserve announces a change in interest rates, we are supposed to believe that he is striving to 'tune the engine' as best he can, according to the latest economic data. In reality he is simply exercising arbitrary power over our personal and collective lives, acting as high priest of a self-serving financial elite, issuing unchallengeable edicts from on high – without revealing what secret agendas are being facilitated.

Aristocracy is one kind of plutocracy, and capitalism is another. It is in this realm of political systems that capitalism is most appropriately considered. While aristocracy favors inherited wealth, and is characteristically land-based and conservative, capitalism tends to favor wealth accumulation, and is characteristically development-based and change-oriented.

Of the two, aristocracy is typically more stable and more compatible with economic sustainability. When I've visited, as a tourist, family estates of the old British aristocracy, I've always been impressed by the walls full of portraits – generation after generation of the same family governing the same domain from the same house.

When we look at the elite Anglo-American banking clique, with its inter-connecting family trees, we are seeing a hybrid of these two kinds of plutocracy. On the one hand we get the worst of capitalism, with its economic instability, its environmentally destructive practices, and its constant destabilization of our cultures and societies. On the other hand, at the very top of the power pyramid, we are faced with the inheritance-based political stability of aristocratic rule, although this aristocracy is based not on land wealth, but rather on control over global finance. In a very real sense, we can see the elite financial clique as being the successors of the linked families that occupied the thrones of Europe in the centuries that preceded the advent of republics. The Enlightenment was the process by which the reins of rule passed from one elite to another.

Civilization in crisis

> Only after the last tree has been cut down
> Only after the last river has been poisoned
> Only after the last fish has been caught
> Then will you find that money cannot be eaten.
> —Cree Prophecy

I've always been fascinated by the story of Pompeii. Why didn't everyone leave? They could see the volcano beginning to erupt, and they were directly in its path of destruction. When the ashes began to rain down, many stayed: they covered their heads and went about their business, right up until it was too late to escape. How do we explain this kind of behavior? Were these people in denial or what?

Our civilization has brought us to the point where we have all become like the stragglers of Pompeii. In our case, however, there isn't a single threat to our survival – as individuals and as a civilized society – but a whole collection of them. Perhaps the most obvious is the total dependence of our societies on a finite oil supply. Instead of addressing this problem, our leaders strive to keep the energy economy growing, paving over the countryside with motorways, and increased automobile sales are always seen as a 'good economic indicator.'

On the environmental front we have global warming, melting ice caps, ozone depletion, acid rain, soil loss and desertification, fishing stock depletion, disturbances to the dynamics of the all-important Gulf Stream, increasing ferocity and frequency of hurricanes, and the pollution of our air, water, and food supplies. Like the people of Pompeii, we can see these ashes of destruction beginning to fall, and yet we, individually and as societies, go on about our business as usual.

Rapidly increasing population levels pose another threat, stressing global food, water, and available-land resources. These resources are further stressed by the operation of the global economy, whereby, for example, America, with 5% of the world's population, consumes 20% of the world's energy resources. In fact, increasing population is by far the lesser of the two stress factors: it is the resource-hungry 'advanced' nations that are the primary reason why our civilization has become unsustainable.

Unsustainability is the term that probably best sums up our predicament as a civilization. We simply cannot continue much longer on the path we are following. If we don't do something to change things, the realities of a finite Earth will change them for us. If we don't change our agricultural methods, our soil bank and water tables will be ruined, and we'll be faced with mass starvation. If we don't convert to a sustainable energy regime, declining fuel supplies will cause our essential infrastructures to collapse, leading once again to mass starvation. In each aspect of our economy, we find systems of utilization that are unsustainable.

I described this situation in the Foreword, where I talked about our global society, as a system, being *dysfunctional*. The system can't be fixed; it needs to be transformed – or it will bring transformation upon us, by the collapse of our civilization. I also suggested that the technical problems involved in transforming our societies are not insurmountable – if we turned our full attention, as societies, to addressing those problems. The more insurmountable problem seems to be our political systems, which act not in the interests of people generally, but act rather on the behalf of self-serving elites.

If we were to diagnose the ills of our civilization, using medical terminology, the diagnosis would be that civilization is suffering from both a chronic disease and an acute, life-threatening infection. The acute infection is the unsustainability of our modern societies; the chronic disease is rule by elites – a disease we've been suffering from ever since the days of the first Mesopotamian kings, some 6,000 years ago. We've never been able to shake that disease, but unless we find a way to do so soon, we'll die from our acute infection.

Elite responses to the crisis

It is not as if today's ruling elites were unaware of the crisis civilization is facing. In fact they are well aware, and it is that very awareness that provides urgency to the PNAC agenda – which is aimed at seizing scarce resources, and gaining control over global affairs, in anticipation of the emerging crisis. That awareness likewise provides urgency to the establishment of the new-millennium blueprint – which provides for the control of populations in troubled times, and which centralizes administrative and military functions in an elite-serving world government.

I earlier cited neoliberalism, and the anticipation of its consequences, as being the motivation for most of these agendas. In a short-term sense that was true, but from our current perspective we can see that neoliberalism merely adds to the more fundamental crisis of unsustainability. Even if the worst excesses of neoliberalism were to be eliminated, the crisis would not be significantly postponed. The new-millennium blueprint, seen from this perspective, provides a means of enabling elites to deal with the crisis as they see fit, with full control over resources and their distribution.

We now need to peel back another layer of the Matrix onion, and examine the various responses of the ruling clique to the obvious unsustainability of civilization – as it currently operates, and at current population levels. Although public awareness of global warming, peak oil, and sustainability has come relatively recently, our elite rulers, having the vision to plan and create whole blueprints of world order, while managing global finance – and with their think tanks and access to intelligence information – have certainly been aware of the impending crisis for some considerable time.

Let us reconsider, for example, the oil shock of 1973, which ushered in the petrodollar era, and curtailed development in the third world. From the perspective of oil marketing, the 400% price increase can be seen as a decision to 'go for the premium market.' Instead of fueling the world's wholesale demand for development, at a generally affordable price, the decision was to sell less oil, at a higher price, to those who could afford to pay. As a business decision, this evidently made sense: oil company profits have soared with every price increase.

From the perspective of the crisis of unsustainability, this 'marketing decision' had the consequence of dividing the people of the world into two classes: those who could afford to continue participating in the unsustainable system, and those who were being left by the wayside. In the first class we find the wealthier nations, and in particular those individuals who can command high salaries in service to the corporate machine. In the second class we find the poorer nations of the third world, the residents of our impoverished ghettos, and the homeless and unemployed in our modern cities and towns.

There are many motivations for the neoliberal agenda, but one of the primary outcomes of that agenda has been to accelerate this two-class-division of global populations. Officials and the media admit that the gap between the haves and the have-nots is rapidly widening, and they try to explain that away in various ways, or else they promise us that things will get better eventually. But they won't get better: they'll get worse.

In economic terms, the essence of neoliberalism is *monetization* – everything being measured in terms of its value as a commodity on the market. If you're not employed, that's your fault: you need to get retrained so that you will have value on the employment market. If a nation's economy is deteriorating, that's because it is not *competitive* enough, i.e., it is not offering enough value to the all-powerful 'investment community.' Such a nation needs to lower its corporate taxes, relax its regulations, and cut back on public services, so that it will have more 'value' to offer on the investment market, particularly as regards privatization opportunities. The Matrix conditions us to accept this state of affairs with shows like *The Weakest Link*.

The neoliberal agenda does not include a safety net for those left by the wayside. As we can see today in Europe, existing so-cial-welfare structures, long part of the postwar blueprint, are under frontal assault as the free-trade neoliberal program advances. All over Europe we have seen, and are seeing, mass protests as job-protection measures are eliminated, services are cut back or privatized, and industries are destroyed by foreign competition.

Safety nets of all kinds are being systematically destroyed all over the world, even as employment declines, and energy-fueled inflation increases. In the third world, the IMF has wholesale destroyed whole social infrastructures, casting millions into abject poverty, and leading directly to mass starvations. In America, the Social Security pension system is under threat, which is likely to mean the safety net will be removed for the elderly. America never did have many of those safety nets that Europeans are now vainly struggling to preserve.

Farm subsidies, which have provided a safety net for farmers under the pressure of free trade, are under threat as the free-trade agenda moves ever forward. The welfare dole system acts currently as a safety net for many in the West – far too many – but that safety net is nothing we can count on. Providing a dole offers little value as a capital investment, other than as a means of pacifying the population, and that kind of value doesn't count for much in the neoliberal marketplace – particularly if other means of social control are available.

What happens to those left by the wayside as the remaining safety nets disappear? What happens when human life is treated entirely as a commodity, its welfare provided for only to the extent that it returns value to the neoliberal marketplace? We can see part of the answer to this question in the mass famines and genocidal civil wars that have plagued Africa. The media shows us the pictures, and bemoans the fact that the attention of the 'international community' is elsewhere. In the actions of the 'international community' we see reflected the priorities of those who are running our societies. Untold billions are available for military campaigns to secure oil supplies, but African people, who contribute little to the global economy, and have no political clout in the West, can just be left to die.

> Depopulation should be the highest priority of foreign policy towards the third world, because the US economy will require large and increasing amounts of minerals from abroad, especially from less developed countries."
> —Attributed to Henry Kissinger, "National Security Study Memorandum 200: Implications of Worldwide Population Growth for U.S. Security and Overseas Interests", April 24, 1974

A search on Google reveals hundreds of hits citing the above quotation. However, on downloading and reading the memo, NSSM 200, I was unable to find that particular passage. Perhaps the quote is a hoax, or perhaps it was deleted before the memo was declassified and made public. I've nonetheless featured the alleged quote, because genuine or not it serves as a very good summary of what the full NSSM 200 document is actually about, if you read between the lines. Consider this passage, which explains why U.S. planners are so concerned with population levels:

> The real problems of mineral supplies lie, not in basic physical sufficiency, but in the politico-economic issues of access, terms for exploration and exploitation, and division of the benefits among producers, consumers, and host country governments (NSSM, 40).

That is to say, the U.S. wants to ensure its own access to resources, and it wants that access to be on favorable terms. The document explains in great detail why high population levels interfere with such access, and is therefore a threat to U.S. "security and overseas interests." The actual policy proposals in the public NSSM document are not extreme; they emphasize voluntary measures. However those voluntary measures have clearly not been successful, nor were they likely to be. The following passage suggests that stronger measures, not fully specified, were being anticipated:

> There is an alternative view which holds that a growing number of experts believe that the population situation is already more serious and less amenable to solution through voluntary measures than is generally accepted. It holds that, to prevent even more widespread food shortage and other demographic catastrophes than are generally anticipated, even stronger measures are required and some fundamental, very difficult moral issues need to be addressed (NSSM, 14).

This language is a bit evasive. It is suggesting that measures "stronger" than "voluntary" may be required. In straight talk that means, "imposed measures may be required." And in the context of the document, it is third world governments we are talking about, which may or may not "voluntarily" adopt depopulation policies. So, once again in straight talk, the passage is saying, "We may need to impose depopulation measures on populations, against the will of their governments."

If we consider this elite line of thinking, expressing a need for 'imposed depopulation,' and if we look at the mass starvation in Africa, accelerated by the IMF and ignored by the 'international community,' we cannot avoid considering the hypothesis that intentional genocide may be part of the elite agenda for dealing with civilization's crisis: those left by the wayside are 'useless feeders,' a waste of space, undeserving of capital investment: why not just quietly get rid of them?

Such an hypothesis, if taken seriously, amounts to a very serious accusation against elite planners, and is not to be undertaken lightly. On the other hand, as these people regularly manipulate whole nations into wars, with millions killed, why should we put anything past them? In this case, as regards genocidal intentions, we might take into account the role of the CIA in African genocide episodes, episodes that were allegedly being ignored by the 'international community.'

> By December, 1996, U.S. military forces were operating in Bukavu amid throngs of Hutus, less numerous Twa refugees, Mai Mai guerrillas, advancing Rwandan troops and AFDL–CZ rebels. A French military intelligence officer said he detected some 100 armed U.S. troops in the eastern Zaire conflict zone.
>
> Moreover, the French intelligence service, DGSE, reported that Americans had knowledge of the extermination of Hutu refugees by Tutsis in both Rwanda and eastern Zaire and were doing nothing about it. More ominously, there was reason to believe that some U.S. forces, either Special Forces or mercenaries, may have actually participated in the extermination of some Hutu refugees.
>
> …It was known that the planes that the U.S. military deployed in eastern Zaire included heavily armed and armored helicopter gunships typically used by the U.S. Special Forces. These were fitted with 105 mm cannons, rockets, machine guns, land mine ejectors and, more importantly, infrared sensors used in night operations.

U.S. military commanders unabashedly stated the purpose of these armed gunships was to locate refugees to determine the best means of providing them with humanitarian assistance.

Towards the end of 1996, U.S. spy satellites were attempting to ascertain how many refugees escaped into the jungle by locating fires at night and canvas tarpaulins during the day. Strangely, every time an encampment was discovered by space based imagery, Rwanda and Zaire rebel forces attacked the sites (Madsen).

We now have quite a bit of evidence to suggest that the 'genocide hypothesis' deserves serious consideration. To begin with, we have the basic economic context: the combination of radical neoliberal economics, together with the systematic removal of safety nets, creates a situation where increasing millions of people, globally, will be in abject poverty, and will be playing no role in the global economy. A world is being intentionally created in which millions, even billions, will have no place.

Next, there is the attitude of elite planners to population growth: for them it is a matter of strategic importance to reduce population levels, using imposed measures if necessary, so as to make resources readily available to the advanced economies.

Next, there is the elephant in the kitchen of actual mass die-offs in Africa: the systematic tolerance of these events by the 'international community' is lacking any acceptable explanation. What we do know is that this tolerance must reflect the priorities of leading governments, particularly the U.S., which typically takes the lead in UN interventionist activities.

Finally, there is the actual participation by Western intelligence agencies in genocide. Overall, I think we have a rather strong case for the genocide hypothesis. If the globally enforced neoliberal regime is going to be established, and if it is not to include safety nets, then what *does* one do with those who don't have a place in the system?

If we were setting up this new blueprint for a new millennium, we couldn't just ignore this problem. Rather than having starving people on every street corner, wouldn't it make more sense to have some more organized and less publicly visible way of culling redundant populations? If you find this notion unthinkable, recall that little more than a century ago the native populations of Australia and North America were being openly and systematically exterminated: they were redundant to the development plans of the colonizing governments.

Consider how die-off episodes, e.g. starvation in the Sudan, are treated in the media: we are shown the wretched faces, we are given some shallow explanation of why this is happening, and then we are given a number to call to make a contribution. The subliminal message: governments can't solve these problems; it's up to you and me.

In this vein, we can also note the increasing reliance on NGOs (non-governmental organizations) to take the lead in relief efforts. Overall, we are seeing a passing of the buck – regarding responsibility for responding to human tragedy – from governments and the UN to individuals and NGOs. If these people fail; it's their fault; they don't care enough. Realistically, they – individuals and NGOs – have no chance of responding in any significant way to the impending scale of impoverishment. Those who are passing the buck are well aware of this.

Let's step back now, and review what this section on civilization's crisis has been about, looking from a broad perspective.

The first observation was about *sustainability*: the way our civilization uses resources is simply unsustainable; drastic changes are inevitable, of one kind or another, not too long in the future, with or without our help. That is the crisis we face, as a civilization.

The second observation was about *transformation*: we can't just fix our current systems; they are inherently unsustainable. We need a comprehensive, bottom-to-top, reinvention of our economies, taking into account the hard reality of sustainability – and this is not beyond our technical capacity, if our societies were so motivated.

The next observation was about *elite rule*: civilization's actual response to its crisis is being decided by a clique of behind-the-scenes manipulators who have little regard for anyone's welfare other than their own. This clique is showing no signs of responding to the crisis in any kind of acceptable way, as regards the welfare of most of humanity. It is worth noting, as well, that civilization has been characterized by elite rule for some 6,000 years, and most of that was based on slavery.

Next came a *diagnosis*: our civilization is plagued by both a chronic illness (elite rule), and an acute infection (unsustainability). Until we cure our chronic illness, we can't do anything about our acute infection.

Our next observations were about the *elite responses* to the crisis: the new-millennium blueprint, with its elite-controlled world government, enables a small clique to 'manage' the unfolding of the crisis and to decide how resources will be allocated and distributed, and who will be left out. By use of police-state methods, and with military forces centrally controlled, the means will be available to deal with any unrest, or to enforce any extreme measures, that may accompany this 'management' process.

Under neoliberalism, and with safety nets eliminated, the world is being divided into those who are part of the system, and those who have no place in the system. The homeless in our towns and cities, and the recent mass die-offs in Africa, can be seen as symbols this division.

As the realities of our unsustainability crisis begin to take effect, the ranks of those 'left by the wayside' can be expected to swell to into the many millions, even billions. There is considerable evidence to suggest that organized genocide may indeed be part of the blueprint for this neoliberal world. But even without that, there will be the same mortality result, except the deaths will be distributed more randomly.

After this review, let's update our diagnosis: our civilization has a chronic illness (elite rule), an acute infection (unsustainability), and it is being subjected to a treatment (the neoliberal world system), that aims to 'cure' the infection by discarding excess population (those left by the wayside) – so that remaining resources can be used by those for whom the system has a use.

Unless we want to simply bemoan our fate and watch all this come to pass – until the day we too are among those dying by the wayside – we need to face this crisis, and view it as a challenge and an opportunity. We need to figure out how we can take command of our destinies, end elite rule, and go on to transform our societies and economies, responding intelligently to our crisis of unsustainability.

You might be wondering what I mean by *we* when I say "*We* need to face this crisis, etc." In that regard, permit me to repeat here the words of Lappé, as featured in the opening pages of this book:

> We've lived so long under the spell of hierarchy – from god-kings to feudal lords to party bosses – that only recently have we awakened to see not only that "regular" citizens have the capacity for self-governance, but that without their engagement our huge global crises cannot be addressed. The changes needed for human society simply to survive, let alone thrive, are so profound that the only way we will move toward them is if we ourselves, regular citizens, feel meaningful ownership of solutions through direct engagement. Our problems are too big, interrelated, and pervasive to yield to directives from on high.
> —Frances Moore Lappé, *Time for Progressives to Grow Up*

When I say *we*, in this context, I mean *we the people*, ordinary people, regular citizens – as expressed so eloquently by Lappé. But does this make sense? Do *we* really have the 'capacity for self governance'? What kind of 'direct engagement' can enable us to feel 'meaningful ownership of solutions' to our problems? What would self-governance look like? How would it function? How, indeed, can *we* even exist: how can we ordinary people somehow come together and agree on what we want and how we're going to proceed toward achieving it? What does *we the people* look like, in terms of political arrangements?

These are by no means easy questions to answer, but answer them we must if we want to live to see a better future than the one that has been mapped out for us by our elite rulers. The rest of this book can be seen as a quest, in search of answers to these questions. To get our bearings, in preparation for this quest, let us go back to before the Matrix existed, and look at how human societies evolved. If we can understand how we got to where we are as a civilization, we may gain some perspective on how we might go about shifting our course.

2

A brief history of humanity

As man advances in civilization and small tribes are united into larger communities, the simplest reason would tell each individual that he ought to extend his social instincts and sympathies to all the members of the same nation though personally unknown to him. This point being once reached, there is only an artificial barrier to prevent his sympathies extending to the men of all nations and races.
—Charles Darwin

Natural evolution: competition within a cooperative web

When I first learned in school about Darwin and evolution, the lesson could be summed up in the phrases, *the survival of the fittest* and *the law of the jungle*. The strong lion lived; the weak lion died. The strong caveman got the nice cave and beautiful woman; the weak caveman got the leftovers. With the strongest surviving and having the most offspring, in a constant competitive struggle, the quality of species kept improving, and eventually the level of Homo sapiens was attained.

I never thought to question this simplistic characterization of Darwin's ideas, because it seemed to make perfect sense. It turns out, however, that this just isn't how things work. For example, lions in a pride work together as a team: they hunt cooperatively, share their food, and they look out for one another. When male lions compete for leadership of a pride, we see the simplistic dynamics of genetic competition operating – but that is only one part, an occasional episode, in the life of a lion pride. In fact, it is the cooperative and social nature of the pride that in part explains the widespread success of the lion.

It was not until the latter part of the twentieth century that scientists began to study environments as a whole – as ecosystems – and to look at biology generally from a systems perspective. Once scientists looked at the real world, rather than just theorizing around the presumption of competition, they found that nature is characterized much more by cooperation than by competition. Indeed, if we seek a simple phrase to characterize our new understanding – to contrast with *survival of the fittest* – it might be *survival of those who fit in best*.

In the case of the lion pride we see an obvious example of co-operation – conscious collaboration among sentient mammals – whose shared thrill on making a kill is perhaps not that different than that of a soccer team on scoring a goal. But the principle of cooperation in nature goes much deeper, involving the relation-ship between plant and animal species within the context of their environment. Those species that *fit in best* – within the overall system of biological exchange – are the ones that have the best chance of surviving. If a predator species is too greedy for ex-ample, and kills off its prey, then it won't survive.

A colorful example of cooperation can be found in the case of an orchid, *angraecum sesquipedale*, which is pollinated only by the *predicta* moth, which in turn can only survive if it has access to that plant. They are each other's life support system – the two species have a mutually beneficial *symbiotic relationship*. Another interesting example has to do with the relationship between deer and their predators. Predators always go for the weakest or slowest individual, and this selective culling serves to maintain the health of the herd. When deer are free of predators, as when they live in some kind of protected area, the herd soon begins to deteriorate through disease.

An ecosystem is in some sense an invention of the observer. We can look at the whole Earth as one ecosystem or we can focus our attention on just a pond in a forest, or anywhere in between. But at whatever scale we might look, we find interplay among species that can in many ways be compared to the economy of a community.

In a community people occupy different economic niches, some producing what others consume, and their collective ex-changes are the economy of the community. We may only occa-sionally feel like we are "cooperating," as we go about our daily business, but every time we go into a shop and find it open and stocked as usual, we are participating in a symbiotic relationship with the shopkeeper – and both of us are cooperating in the larger endeavor of "keeping our community operating."

Similarly, in an ecosystem, species occupy different ecological niches, some being consumed by others, and their collective "exchanges" are the life-flow of the ecosystem. The ways in which cooperation occurs are not always so simple as that between a shopkeeper and customer. There can be a whole loop of exchanges, all of which together make up a symbiotic system. This is what we are referring to when we talk about the *food chain*.

Richard Dawkins invites us to look at evolution at the level of the "selfish gene" (Dawkins). Most of us are more accustomed to thinking of evolution in terms of evolving species. Those are both useful perspectives, but what may actually be more illuminating is to think in terms of evolving *ecosystems*. In a rainforest, for example, there are thousands of species of plants, animals, birds and insects – with countless and complex interconnecting relationships – all of which add up to a vibrant, vital flow of life. Such a complex system evolves over many eons, each species co-evolving along with it, prey species getting faster, predator species getting more cunning, fruit species becoming more tasty to the seed-spreading creatures, etc.

When we think in terms of species, the "goal" (i.e., tendency) of evolution seems clear: a species evolves toward being more successful, more able to obtain its food, more able to care for its young, etc. But what is the "goal" of ecosystem evolution? In what "direction" does an ecosystem tend, as it gets more refined and complex?

There are perhaps different measuring rods that might be relevant to this question, but there is one that seems to be most fitting. The tendency of an ecosystem, assuming no drastic changes in environmental conditions, is toward *maximizing the overall life activity within the system*. As an ecosystem evolves over time, the amount of life activity going on per acre tends to increase, limited only by the life-support resources available. When the right combination of sunshine, water, and soil are available – as in a rainforest – then we see how far this evolutionary process is able to go.

The rainforest can be seen as a pinnacle of ecosystem evolution. Similarly, in terms of the evolution of commerce, we might say the economy of New York City is a pinnacle. Both are examples of very complex systems, with all sorts of cooperative synergies and interconnections operating, all of which co-evolved over time. And just as a large city achieves a maximum in the quantity of economic exchanges per acre, so a rainforest achieves a maximum in life activity per acre.

As each system, the rain forest or the large city, evolved, both cooperation and competition played a role. The big wheel of evolution is cooperation: the evolving web of mutually beneficial interactions and niches, enabling ever-greater productivity per acre. The smaller wheel of evolution is competition: where players compete to occupy the most desirable niches in the evolving system. The overall tendency in both cases is toward greater cooperative efficiency. Competition, in each case, plays a supplementary tuning role, rewarding favorable adaptations within the evolving cooperative system – i.e., rewarding those who 'fit in best.'

The nature of primordial societies

Although life systems are pervaded by webs of cooperation, some species exhibit more overtly cooperative behavior than others. A cheetah lives and hunts alone; lions and dogs live and hunt in family groups. Among the most social and cooperative of the animal kingdom are the monkeys and apes. Thus our ancestors had been highly social and cooperative for millions of years prior to becoming distinctly human. We started out as cooperative bands, much like chimpanzee or baboon troops today. As we began to find our own evolutionary path, we developed increased capacities for cooperation. Perhaps the most significant of these new capacities was that for complex language. As intelligence and linguistic capacity increased, enabling more complex languages to develop, early humans could plan out hunting expeditions, discuss strategy and compare experiences, talk over the pros and cons of migrating to a new territory, etc. Language, as an adaptive trait, can be seen as a tool designed to maximize the effectiveness and flexibility of cooperation within the band.

We can perhaps now see how thoroughly wrong is the simplistic Darwinian characterization of evolution, as expressed in the common phrases, "survival of the fittest," or "law of the jungle." A *jungle*, in fact, is just another name for a rain forest – a pinnacle of *cooperative* synergy.

Based on archeological evidence, in particular skeletal and DNA remains, it seems that we have been fully human for something like 100,000 years, although as usual, experts differ over the precise dating. In any case, people were just like us for a very, very long time before any kind of civilization came along.

If a human infant could be brought across time from that far back, and be adopted into a modern family, he or she would grow up speaking today's language and be in every way a typical modern person. We can be sure there have been many individuals – throughout the span of this whole period – with the same capacity for genius as a Mozart or Einstein.

Archeological evidence conclusively indicates that for almost all of these 100,000 years – excepting only about the past 10,000 – we have all lived in small, hunter-gatherer bands. From artifacts and burial sites, archeology can tell us a lot about how we lived, what tools we used, what we ate, etc. In order to get a fuller picture of what our societies must have been like, we need to look elsewhere. History is no help, because written language was not invented until a society had already reached the early stages of civilization. We can learn a lot, however, by looking at those hundreds or perhaps thousands of indigenous societies that have been observed and studied over the past few centuries of European expansionism.

Anthropologists have surveyed the many indigenous societies that have been observed and written about by witnesses, and they have gone out and studied still-existing societies in the field directly. They have found an amazing diversity and variety of languages, cultures, systems of beliefs, diets, and economic lifestyles. By combining these observations with what we can learn from archeological investigations, anthropologists have found that societies tend to evolve through certain predictable stages as they adopt new technologies, and as they become larger and more complex.

In some cases, as with the Incas in Peru, the Europeans found complex civilizations that had evolved independently from Europe or Asia, and had gone through the stages of chiefdom, kingship, and finally emperor-divinity. In other cases they found agricultural and herding-based societies, operating under various social systems, usually based on tribal and clan relationships. And in many cases they found societies that were still operating on a hunter-gathering basis – living examples of primordial societies.

Anthropologists have observed a large number of universally shared characteristics in these remaining primordial societies (although they have needed to make allowances when looking at cases where such societies engage in exchange with more 'advanced' societies.) Every such society has a complex language, capable of abstract and imaginative expression. Every such society has its own culture, supported by mythologies, beliefs, taboos, and stories which are passed down orally from generation to generation. In this way mores, history, discovered knowledge, and adaptive behaviors are preserved and reinforced in the culture. Frequently poetic, rhythmic, and musical forms are employed – which aid greatly in preserving intact the oral cultural heritage through the generations. Typically there is a creation story in which some kind of spirits or gods lay down the foundation of the cultural beliefs and explain the society's place in the world.

Every such society, except those going through some kind of adaptive transitional phase, lives sustainably in its environment. Although the observed mythologies are very diverse, they all place humanity within the context of nature, as part of nature, with a kind of spiritual responsibility to live in harmony with nature. The members of every such society cooperate systematically in their economic endeavors – mostly hunting, foraging, and territorial defense – with culturally specified roles for different ages and sexes. Every such society is egalitarian, and decisions tend to be made by consensus based on open dialog – with no individual or clique being given the power to decide for the group. There may be 'chiefs,' selected for their wisdom and knowledge, but they hunt and gather along with everyone else, and they have no authority to command others.

Such societies exhibit territorial behavior, each group typically wandering over a particular area, following the diet opportunities as the seasons change and local areas become depleted. Although communication and exchange occur among neighboring groups, territories are defended against intruders and a pattern of relatively stable territorial niches is generally maintained. These patterns shift from time to time, as changing conditions cause some groups to migrate – and more aggressive groups sometimes displace other groups – but on a day-to-day basis each group has its own territory, within which it finds its collective livelihood.

We know that people have been basically the same for 100,000 years, in terms of their innate capacities and tendencies. We know that all observed hunter-gatherer societies share certain characteristics – and the 'sample size' of such societies is large. With this knowledge, I suggest that we can reasonably assume that for nearly all of the past 100,000 years, apart from the past 10,000, all humans have lived in societies with these same characteristics.

If there is any meaning at all in the notions of humanity's *natural state* or of *human nature*, then surely we must look for that meaning in the context of these primordial societies and their social structures. For most of our time as humans we have lived in cooperative, egalitarian bands; we have been collectively responsible for our own survival on a local basis, and we have inherited shared belief systems that have sustained our cultures and reinforced our successful environmental adaptations. To some extent such an existence is *home* for us; it is our native *comfort zone*. This is why we experience so much anxiety and stress in our gigantic modern societies where we are anonymous cogs in a machine, where we have mostly lost any sense of being part of a supportive community, and where our cultures are fragmented into competing religions and ideologies.

Cultural evolution: stability within adaptability

Animals are born with most of their behavior patterns already hard-wired in. Humans, on the other hand, learn their behavior patterns – and their culture generally – as they grow up in their society. Just as a fox or lion inherits instincts that make them efficient hunters, instincts that evolved over the eons, so early humans inherited a culture that enabled them to efficiently use their territory – a culture that had evolved over many generations. A primordial culture is finely tuned to its own local environment – as are the instincts of an animal species to the requirements of its evolved niche.

But whereas animal behaviors typically change only on a time scale of millions of years or more, human cultures can evolve over thousands or even hundreds of years. This ability to adapt to new circumstance enabled early human societies to spread out from their original primate habitats and occupy a wide variety of niches. We soon left the other species behind like so many frozen statues in a pastoral tableau. Lions are still doing exactly what they were doing before humans came along. Meanwhile, humans spread out over whole continents, from tropical deserts to the Polar Regions, evolving complex, specialized cultures suitable to each kind of environment that was encountered.

The loss of innate specialization, as a biologically inherited characteristic, represents one of the most significant genetic distinctions between humans and other species – ranking right up there with complex linguistic capacity. On the one hand, despecialization enabled us to inhabit nearly the whole globe, aided by our ability to discuss and share our discoveries and experiences. On the other hand, it has made us particularly dependent on our societies and inherited cultures for our survival. Whereas a mixed group of lions from different prides could be released into an available territory – and they might be expected to form successful new prides – a mixed group of humans from different primordial groups would find it very difficult to spontaneously organize themselves and survive in a strange environment – even if they could communicate in some common language.

Although from a long-range perspective cultural evolution is characterized by its adaptability, primordial cultures tend to exhibit remarkable stability over very long periods – when environmental conditions don't change much and there are no significant intrusions by other societies. Cultural stability is a desirable survival trait: it serves to preserve the adaptive knowledge the group has gained over the generations.

This cultural stability is facilitated by the fact that children are highly impressionable. If a primordial child, or a modern child for that matter, is told repeatedly by trusted adults that a certain mountain is the home of a certain god, with a certain sacred agenda, the child will typically take that on board as absolute, literal truth. The child learns its culture not as a set of facts to remember; rather the culture is absorbed as the child's model of reality: what the world is all about, what the role of society is in the world, and how people are supposed to behave. The more this model is reinforced through social interactions, the more deeply embedded it becomes in the child's mind. When the child becomes an adult, he or she simply *knows* that the cultural beliefs are *the truth*. The adult would no more question these beliefs than a devout Christian would question the existence of God.

As a consequence, the adults of a primordial society tend to pass on their culture to their children exactly as they themselves learned it. As children, they were too impressionable to question the culture, and as adults they don't question it because they *know it's true*. In addition, coherent stories, poems, images, and songs provide a reliable mechanism for passing on cultural details unchanged. Hence primordial cultures tend to remain remarkably stable until new adaptations are required, or new opportunities arise, due to some significant change in circumstances.

Origins of civilization: inside and outside the Garden

For nearly all of the past 100,000 years, all of us humans lived in egalitarian, cooperative, hunter-gatherer societies like the ones described above. Then, about 10,000 years ago, some societies began to systematically domesticate plants and animals as a means of food production. This shift from hunting-gathering, and its aftermath, are known as the *agricultural revolution*. Rather than opportunistically harvesting what nature naturally produces, some societies were now beginning to manage the production process themselves. The eventual consequences of this revolution were profound, bringing about fundamental changes in the economies and social structures of societies, and leading eventually to the development of civilization as we know it.

The first societies to move beyond hunter gathering were in the area known as the *Fertile Crescent*, between the Tigris and Euphrates rivers in present day Iraq. These societies were more complex than their primordial predecessors, but for the first few thousand years – according to the archeological evidence – they were peaceful and their social structures continued to be egalitarian and cooperative. They worshipped nurturing, feminine deities; women had equal roles in society along with men; their art does not portray battles or conquests. Riane Eisler, in *The Chalice and the Blade*, uses the term *partnership societies* to refer to these earliest agricultural societies.

Meanwhile on the Russian steppes another kind of post-hunter-gatherer society was developing, based on nomadic herding and horsemanship. These were male-dominated warrior societies, with strong chiefs. Archeological evidence reveals that human sacrifice was practiced, warrior deities were worshipped, and that chiefs were buried with impressive caches of weapons. Eisler places these societies in the category of *dominator societies*.

These two paths both make a certain kind of sense, each in their own context. In a settled agricultural society, there is considerable incentive to maintain peace and harmony. Warlike activity would take resources away from food production, and conflicts could lead to the destruction of crops, food-stores, and dwellings, agricultural pursuits and settled communities thrive best in a climate of stability – "partnership virtues" would provide a survival advantage.

With nomadic herding, on the other hand – particularly with horses as attack vehicles – the dynamics are different. Such nomadic groups are accustomed to being on the move, rather than being settled, and they would presumably be competing regularly with other nomadic groups for the best grazing areas and water sources – and in bad years these might be scarce and hard-fought for. One might expect "warrior virtues" and "strong leadership" to provide a competitive advantage to societies in such a context.

Up until about 4400 BC it appears that these two strains of social evolution developed mostly apart from one another. While the nomadic dominator groups expanded in the steppes regions, the partnership strain spread out from the Fertile Crescent into Europe – and led to the development of the earliest civilizations. Eisler refers to these partnership societies as the *Civilization of Old Europe*:

> Between circa 7000 and 3500 B.C.E. these early Europeans developed a complex social organization involving craft specialization. They created complex religious and governmental institutions. They used metals such as copper and gold for ornaments and tools. They even evolved what appears to be a rudimentary script. In Gimbuta's words "If one defines civilization as the ability of a given people to adjust to its environment and to develop adequate arts, technology, script, and social relationships it is evident that Old Europe achieved a marked degree of success" (Eisler, 13).

The nomadic dominator groups, based on the archeological evidence, did not create any civilizations on their own. Their development involved instead the refinement of their methods of warfare, and the rise of chiefs of chiefs – the emergence of larger hierarchical social structures. What seems to have happened around 4400 BC was the same phenomenon we saw later in the twelfth century, with the rise of Genghis Khan. In both cases an unusually strong leader arose within a warlike nomadic culture, and he managed to unify under his command a sizable population behind the mission of invading and looting agricultural-based societies.

It was such a Kurgan chief from the steppes of western Asia who must have led the first invasion against the partnership-based agricultural societies in the Fertile Crescent. Some initial raids may have been limited to looting and pillaging, but eventually what happened is that the warlike tribes took command of the more civilized societies, retaining the agricultural methods, but imposing their own authority structures.

Thus hierarchical civilization seems to have arisen as a hybrid between these two cultural strains: the partnership strain contributed the civilizing technologies and the slaves to till the soil; the dominator strain contributed the ruling hierarchy and the dominator culture. The earliest hierarchical civilizations were characterized not only by hierarchy, but also by a class distinction between the conquerors and the conquered – a kind of nobility and peasantry, a warrior class and a toiler class.

From paintings on pottery, frescoes, and eventually from written records, we can trace the changes in mythologies that occurred as partnership civilizations were conquered by dominator societies. What we typically find is that the mythologies of the earlier partnership societies were not totally abandoned, but were rather reinterpreted, and overlaid with new gods and beliefs. Hybrid mythologies were developed which served the purpose of legitimizing and reinforcing the new regime. Sometimes a female goddess from the partnership pantheon would continue in the new mythology, but she would be shown in a subservient role to the new warrior male gods, one of which would typically be supreme over the whole pantheon. In this way male dominance and subservience to hierarchy were portrayed as being part of the divine order.

In the Old Testament's *Garden of Eden* story we can see an example of this process of mythological reinterpretation and cultural overlaying. The garden itself can be seen as the pre-existing partnership society, and indeed the serpent was typically a central mythological symbol in those early agricultural civilizations. In the biblical story we see the entrance of a new male god onto the stage, one who holds absolute sovereignty, and who denounces the once-revered serpent as being an agent of evil and deception. The hybrid myth 'explains' to people why they must give up their old beliefs and loyalties and adopt the new ones.

The story doesn't deny that the garden (the partnership society) was a better place to live. Indeed, the new god must officially banish the residents in order to get them to leave. The story gives a reason for the banishment – disobedience and sinfulness – and it prescribes a new mission for humanity – to go forth and dominate the Earth and all its creatures.

Let's consider this hybrid myth from perspective of the new peasant class. The myth tells them that they were banished from the garden due to their own innate failings, and they must be obedient to the new hierarchy. It tells them that humanity's mission is to conquer and dominate nature. The net effect of the mythology is to relegate the conquered to the role of cogs in a dominator machine, a machine controlled by its ruling hierarchy. For those at the bottom, it is a mythology of oppression and exploitation mixed with self-blame.

Now let's consider the mythology from the perspective of the new rulers – the warrior chief and his lieutenants. They weren't banished from a garden; rather they gained ownership of someone else's garden. They already had their own warrior culture, in which conquest and domination were extolled as virtues. There seems to be little reason for these people to take the new mythology seriously. Its function is to legitimize their authority, and for that only the underlings need to believe – or to pretend to.

> The rich ruleth over the poor, and the borrower is servant to the lender.
> —Proverbs 22:7

One might almost imagine – based on the behavior of modern and historical elites – that the top rulers of hierarchical civilizations have maintained their original culture through the ages – as raw warriors and conquerors – never really themselves becoming civilized. Whenever I read one of those conspiracy theories about 'secret elite societies,' I always wonder: "What big secret they could be hiding?" It seems to me there's really only one big secret that such people might like to share and celebrate on special occasions: *Never forget that we run things, and we do whatever we want. Everyone else is little people, and we're going to keep it that way!*

The King of Prussia was the first to put compulsory schools into place and to make it stick. His theory, attributed to the German philosopher Fichte, was that by forcing children to attend school at a young age they would become more loyal to and afraid of the power of the state than they would be loyal to or afraid of their parents. Additionally, the King wanted soldiers who didn't question their orders but immediately did what they were told. So the Prussian school system instituted a system of "no interruptions allowed." Children could not even ask a question about the topic under discussion unless they first asked the question of, "May I ask a question?" by raising their hand and being called on. In this way they became "properly socialized" to respect and not question authority figures.

The King, however, didn't want his own children to be subject to such a treatment. They, after all, would one day become the rulers of the country. They'd be the leaders, and instead of follower-skills would have to have the skills of leadership, creativity, and independence. So he ordered the creation of a second, parallel public school system. While the first system was called "the People's School" (Volkshochschule), the second was to be the place where true education would take place. Recognizing this, it was called simply "the Real School" (Realschule). Ninety three percent of students would attend the People's School, and the seven percent who represented the elite of the nation and would be its future business and governmental leaders would attend the Real School.

—Thom Hartmann, excerpted from *The "Real" School Is Not Free*,
   http://www.thomhartmann.com/realschool.shtml

These new hybrid hierarchical civilizations enabled the rulers to engage in warfare on an expanded scale. With the production afforded by slave-based agriculture, rulers could afford to pursue conquest and expansion. Excavations reveal that their cities were repeatedly destroyed in warfare, and then rebuilt over the ruins by each wave of conquerors. Kingdoms became empires and the rest, as they say, is history.

Relationships of ownership
They whisper in the wings
To those condemned to act accordingly
And wait for succeeding kings
And I try to harmonize with songs
The lonesome sparrow sings
There are no kings inside the Gates of Eden
—Bob Dylan, *The Gates of Eden*

In the beginning we all lived in egalitarian primordial societies. Some of us then took the path to civilization, continuing our egalitarian ways, developing our arts and crafts, and creating our own partnership Eden. Others of us took the path to barbarism and warfare. The barbarians then conquered Eden, hijacking the course of civilization, and forcing us all down the war-strewn dominator path that has brought us to our current global crisis. To this day we have an exploitive kind of civilization in the domestic microcosm, and outright barbarism in the geopolitical macrocosm.

The co-evolution of conditioning and hierarchy

From the very beginning of hierarchical civilization, myths and conditioning have been used to subjugate. As civilization has evolved, the means of conditioning the masses have become gradually more sophisticated. Hammurabi was apparently the first Western ruler to reduce the cultural rules to an enumerated list, a list that was consciously designed by a known elite ruler. With the Roman Emperor Constantine we see a ruler facing a crisis of control; we see him select a religion (Christianity) to use as a conditioning tool; we see him modify the principles and censor the defining documents of that religion (Nicene Council, 325AD); we see him declare the newly re-designed religion to be the official mythology of the empire – and then we see the new regime succeed in resolving Constantine's crisis of control.

In the Western world at least, Constantine's formula continued as a primary control strategy right up until the period of the Enlightenment, c. 1800. During the intervening millennia, a partnership between the sibling hierarchies of church and throne – Constantine's formula – remained the mainstay foundation of Western dominator forms. When changing economic conditions pushed monarchs toward stronger nationalism, Protestant revolutions were encouraged, shifting the church part of the hierarchy closer to home – reducing its relative power vis-à-vis the throne – while not reducing its power to control the masses through conditioning. Indeed the pulpits now had the printing press; people could learn to read and could then condition themselves on their own time – a very effective technological adaptation on the part of elites. For many years, printing presses were used primarily for distributing biblical texts, as modified by Constantine and the early church hierarchy.

When republics were established, a radically different mythological regime accompanied them, one consciously promulgated by emerging new elites. Whereas the previous regimes had aimed to condition populations to accept the reality of their oppression – i.e., their *station* in life – the new regime proclaimed the doctrine that people can escape altogether from arbitrary rule by elites – a doctrine which may prove, someday, to be true.

But along with this appealing doctrine came a whopper of a myth: the myth told people that they had *already rid themselves of elite rule*, that *they themselves were now the sovereign rulers of society*. The schools taught, and the people came to believe, that they *lived already in democracies*. I cannot help but recall a practice they have in a certain remote village. Once a year they take the town fool, put a crown on his head, and for a day they bow down to him as king. In his case, we can forgive him if he doesn't get the joke. In our case, we should know better.

> The two greatest obstacles to democracy in the United States are, first, the widespread delusion among the poor that we have a democracy, and second, the chronic terror among the rich, lest we get it.
> —Edward Dowling, Editor, *Chicago Daily News*, 1941

Most of us are aware that our 'democracies' aren't perfect, but we generally accept the basic formula as being the 'best there is' – the problems are in the implementation, or the current leaders, or, as I have argued, behind-the-scenes elites. The basic formula is what we call a 'representative democracy': we choose among competing candidates by voting, and the winner is then expected to represent the interests of those who voted for him or her.

When this formula fails, most of us think in terms of reforming the implementation: balanced media reporting, limits on campaign spending, proportional voting, easier-access for small parties, and so on. In later chapters I will argue that the formula itself – representation as a basis for democracy – is inherently flawed. The various 'corruptions' we observe are in fact expressions of the natural dynamics of the 'game' of electoral politics. In trying to reform these systems, we are like the donkey trying to catch up with a dangling carrot, which is always just out of reach.

In a moment of insane candour, [David Boylan, a Murdoch manager], told an unvarnished truth which should be framed and stuck on the top of every television set. "We paid $3 billion for these television stations, he snapped. We'll decide what the news is. News is what we say it is."
—*The Observer*, London, July 5, 1998

In this age of mass media our illusions have become collective illusions, story-boarded by ruling elites and their PR consultants, sketched in by pre-scripted 'on-the-spot' interviews, and interpreted by cue-card-reading 'news commentators.' We see the same storyboards developed into news broadcasts and into subplots for our television shows, popular films, and our commercials. In every form of media we get the same images (e.g., Muslim terrorists, Italian gangsters, Black drug dealers, noble cops.) This is the real meaning of the Matrix metaphor: we live in a world of illusions, generated by a 'mainframe' media machine, and we don't see that in the real world our life energy is being sucked away to feed the hierarchical machine.

3

We The People and the Transformational Imperative

I say to people all the time: "If you want to know who's going to change the world, go home and look in the mirror – that's who's gonna do it!"
—Maude Barlow, National Chairperson, The Council of Canadians

A vision without a task is but a dream. A task without a vision is drudgery. A vision with a task is the hope of the world.
—Church inscription, Sussex, England, 1730

im · per · a · tive n. 1.b. An obligation; a duty: social imperative
—thefreedictionary.com

We the People and cultural transformation

In the first chapter, on the Matrix, I outlined the nature of our current societal systems and reached the conclusion that civilization is in dire crisis: our unsustainable society is in fatal collision with the limits of a finite Earth, and our political leaders are irrevocably committed to continuing on that suicidal path. In the second chapter I traced back the origins of our civilization and suggested that our early partnership societies were hijacked six thousand years ago by warrior tribes and their hierarchical, dominator cultures. It is from there that we can trace the origins of our current crisis.

Over the centuries we've seen warrior chiefs replaced by kings, and kings replaced by corporate elites, but always there have been a few who made the rules and the many who obeyed them, a few who reaped the rewards and the many who paid the taxes and fought in the wars. We've seen slavery replaced by serfdom, and serfdom replaced by employment, but always it has been a few at the top who have owned the product of our labors.

When the warrior chiefs first conquered our civilization, they found themselves in control of a more complex society than they were accustomed to, one based on systematic domestication. Animals and crops had been extracted from their natural surroundings, and installed in regimented and controlled environments, e.g., pens and gardens. By providing them with sufficient food, supplemented by appropriate restraints, certain animals could be domesticated and would acquiesce to either a long life of burden or a short life of being fattened up for the table. We can imagine the thoughts in the mind of our victorious warrior chief: "A pretty good swindle, this domestication thing, let's see if it works on people!"

And indeed, throughout the centuries domestication has been the fate of "the many": domestication to hierarchy, by means of sufficient food and appropriate restraints, and acquiescence to a long life of struggle or a short life on some battlefield. When we were still untamed, our restraints were heavy, the chains and whips of slavery. Over time we forgot what freedom was like, and fewer restraints were needed to keep us down. Today we have so forgotten the taste of real freedom that we mistake our current condition for freedom, and our own illusions have become our chains. We partake of the bread and circuses and imagine ourselves to be the sovereign rulers of Rome. We are living in a dream world, and our dream is turning into a nightmare.

> If the world is saved, it will be saved by people with changed minds, people with a new vision. It will not be saved by people with the old vision but new programs.
> —Daniel Quinn, *The Story of B*

The source of our crisis is the dominator culture itself. Environmental collapse and capitalism are merely the terminal symptoms of a chronic cancer, a cancer that has plagued us for six thousand years. No matter what dominator hierarchy might be established, or which group of leaders might be in charge, things would always evolve toward something similar to what we have now. Such is the path of domination, hierarchy, and rule by elites. There is a popular computer game called *Age of Empires*. In this game, playing the role of the ruler, you can build villages, fortify them, and set out to conquer other villages. As the game progresses, the equipment gradually advances, from bows and arrows, to medieval armaments, to tanks and artillery – but you always feel like you're playing exactly the same game with slightly different pieces. The technology has changed over the past six thousand years, but the game has always been the same, with elites at the controls putting us through our paces, down through the ages.

If we want to build a sensible society, we must base it on a different kind of culture: not a dominator culture, but a culture in Eisler's *partnership* category. We need a culture based on mutual understanding and cooperation rather than on war and conquest, a culture based on common sense rather than dysfunctional doctrine, on respect for life rather than the pursuit of profit, and on democracy in place of elite rule. After six thousand years of domestication, we sheep must finally cast aside our illusions, recognize our condition, and reclaim our identity as free human beings. In reclaiming our identities we will also be redefining our cultures.

Cultural transformation is the basis of social transformation. Social forms reflect cultural paradigms, and the dominator paradigm cannot support social forms that are capable of dealing with the crisis that faces us. Domination is the "old vision," and as Quinn points out, the world "will not be saved by people with the old vision." If we want to save the world, we must become people with a "new vision" regarding our relationships with one another as human beings, a vision based on mutual understanding and harmony.

We the People are the only hope for humanity. We are the only ones who can save the world. Domination can end only when the dominated decide to do something about it. Our own liberation, and the transformation of our societies, are two names for the same thing, two aspects of the same project. A partnership culture is a culture of liberation, as well as being a culture that facilitates social harmony and economic sustainability. Such a culture will not be given to us; we must create it by our own initiative and our own efforts. And by the very act of undertaking that initiative, we will be already expressing the essence of our new culture: liberation, empowerment, and release from the domesticating Matrix of illusions.

"That may be all well and good," you might be thinking, "but how on Earth do we go about creating a new culture and gaining a new vision? And how can that lead to the transformation of our societies?" These are very important questions, difficult questions, but I believe there are practical answers to them. Indeed, providing workable answers to those questions, insofar as I am able, is the primary mission of this book.

The basic problem is that We the People need to wake up and realize our common identity as an intelligent, aware species. As a first step in understanding what it means to *wake up*, let us review episodes in which we have woken up, in the form of social movements and revolutions. By looking at a few examples, where we have made serious attempts to transform our societies – sometimes with considerable success – there are many useful lessons to be learned.

Lessons from our long experience of struggle

Changes in society are usually initiated from the top, by elites acting through their various hierarchical institutions. In those cases where change has been initiated from the grassroots, that change has always come by the efforts of a *social movement*. "Social movements" is a broad category, including everything from polite reform organizations to armed insurrections, from labor unions to anti-globalization protests. In general, a social movement is an attempt to give voice to popular sentiment, to provide a vehicle that enables the members of the movement to act *as a whole*, to be a *collective actor* in society, to have a *coherent effect* on society.

Quite clearly the kind of transformation we are seeking will *not* be initiated by the elite establishment. If such a transformation is to be achieved, the initiative will need to come from We the People in the form of a social movement that is suitable to that task. That social movement might be quite unlike previous movements, as its objectives would be uniquely radical. But by examining various existing and historical movements, we can gain some insight as to the kind of movement that would be suitable for our needs.

> Disobedience, in the eyes of anyone who has read history, is man's original virtue. It is through disobedience that progress has been made, through disobedience and rebellion.
> —Oscar Wilde

Let's first take a look at the *anti-globalization* movement, a movement whose sentiments are largely in harmony with the kind of transformation we have been discussing. The movement understands that unbridled capitalism is destroying the world, and the movement seeks a radical shift towards democracy, justice, and sustainability. In its World Social Forum gatherings, the movement strives to develop a coherent vision and effective action strategies. The movement has many thousands of committed activists worldwide, who are willing to participate in movement events at considerable expense, and sometimes risk, to themselves. Is the anti-globalization movement an appropriate vehicle for achieving global transformation?

The movement is extremely encouraging, in that it indicates how large the constituency is for social transformation, and how committed that constituency is to thoughtful activism. And the movement provides a forum in which that constituency can build networks, learn how to organize itself effectively, and build a sense of movement coherence. But we cannot avoid the observation that the results on the ground have not been encouraging, nor is there any particular sign that outcomes will improve. The WTO and IMF continue to wreak their havoc, bio-engineered crops spread, the war machine rolls on, human rights lie shattered on the ground, and destruction of the biosphere accelerates.

The movement is being ignored politically and it isn't showing signs of developing into a truly mass movement. It is a very large choir, but it's not a quorum of the congregation. In its current form it is unlikely to have even a restraining effect on our descent into oblivion.

Nonetheless, if a transformative movement is to arise, the people in the anti-globalization movement will certainly be part of it. In that sense, we should perhaps think of the anti-globalization movement as in fact *being* our transformative movement, but still in latent form, missing some unknown element. When such a new element comes along, the potential of the anti-globalization movement is likely to be transformed. In search of such a "new element," let us move on and consider another movement, one from history.

About a century ago, just prior to 1900 in the U.S., there was a movement that provides a closer model for the kind of movement that might bring about transformation today. Its goals were not quite transformational, but they were radical, and they did represent a challenge to the ascendancy of monopoly capitalism. This movement did have a vision of a significantly re-formed system, a strategy for bringing about change, and an effective program for expanding its constituency. It began as the *Farmers' Alliance*, was later known as the *Populist Movement* and the *People's Party*, and it became a very significant actor in American society. In 1890, for example, Georgia and Texas elected Alliance Governors, and thirty-eight Alliance members were elected to the U.S. Congress (Zinn, 277–289).

The Farmers' Alliance began in 1877 as a self-help movement in Texas, organizing cooperatives for buying supplies and selling crops. The cooperatives improved the farmers' economic situation, and the movement began to spread throughout the Midwest and the South. By 1889, there were 400,000 members.

This was a thinking movement as well as an action movement. Howard Zinn, in *A People's History of the United States* (which I've been paraphrasing in this section), writes: "The Populist movement also made a remarkable attempt to create a new and independent culture for the country's farmers. The Alliance Lecture Bureau reached all over the country; it had 35,000 lecturers. The Populists poured out books and pamphlets from their printing presses." Zinn goes on to cite from another source: "One gathers from yellowed pamphlets that the agrarian ideologists undertook to re-educate their countrymen from the ground up. Dismissing 'history as taught in our schools' as 'practically valueless,' they undertook to write it over – formidable columns of it, from the Greeks on down. With no more compunction they turned all hands to the revision of economics, political theory, law, and government." And from another source: "...no other political movement – not that of 1776, nor that of 1860-1861 – ever altered Southern life so profoundly" (Zinn, 286–287).

There is much here that makes sense for a transformational democratic movement. Our current systems are supported by cultural mythologies, and "writing it over" is a good description of what needs to be done if the Matrix illusions of the old culture are to be exposed and the culture of a new society is to be developed. The emphasis on education of the membership shows a respect for popular intelligence, and it builds a shared cultural perspective that enables a movement to act with increasing unity and coherence. The emphasis on outreach and recruitment is necessary if a movement hopes to grow large enough to bring about significant changes.

The Populist Movement arose due to economic problems that were being faced by farmers, and the movement set out to find practical ways to solve those problems. If a movement *makes demands*, then it is affirming that power resides elsewhere – in that person or agency which is the target of the demands. If a movement *creates solutions*, then it is asserting its own empowerment; it is taking responsibility for its own welfare. The emphasis on economics in particular is also appropriate to a transformational movement. Economics is the basis of most social activity, and it is in the realm of economics that solutions can be found to our social and environmental malaise.

The Populists, being largely conservative farmers, were closely connected to place, and their movement was in part an expression of localism. The movement built up its constituency region by region, rather than by seeking isolated members spread throughout the society, as does the Sierra Club or the anti-globalization movement today. To use a military metaphor, the Populists *captured territory* and then *consolidated* that territory through education and by implementing its solutions in that territory. It was an *inclusive* movement, in the sense that the Populists appealed to the great majority within their territory. They were therefore able to win elections there and gain some degree of official political power. Such a *territorial emphasis* is very appropriate to a transformational movement. Within a *captured territory* – a region in which people generally have become part of the movement – the vision and culture of the movement has an opportunity to flower and to find expression in ordinary conversation among people. The culture has a place to take root and grow, and people's sense of empowerment is reinforced by being in the daily company of those who share an evolving vision – and who are in effect collaborators in a shared project.

The Populist Movement was also an expression of localism in another way. At the core of the Populist political agenda was a set of economic reforms. Those reforms represented an attempt to stem the ascendancy of centralized big-money capitalism – and reassert the interests of locally based farms and small businesses. The Populists were calling for fundamental reform of the financial system, the debt system, and currency policies. They wanted to give local communities and regions enough economic viability to be able to take responsibility for their own welfare.

In their relationship to the political process, the Populists again have much to teach a transformational movement. They began as a grassroots organization oriented around self-help, not as a movement attempting to influence the political machine. They were successful at their self-help endeavors, and they expanded their focus to recruitment and territorial expansion. Only when they had achieved overwhelming success at the grassroots level did they turn their attention to the ballot box. In this way they were able to achieve some measure of political power without compromising their objectives in the horse-trading that characterizes competitive politics. They were able to integrate politics into their tactical portfolio and also retain their integrity and focus as a grassroots movement.

But ultimately the Populists faltered and collapsed, and we have as much to learn from that experience as from their earlier successes. They ran up against an unavoidable barrier, one that all radical movements must run up against eventually – the limit on how much can be accomplished in the face of establishment opposition. In order to promote their economic reform agenda, and encouraged by their electoral successes, they decided to commit their movement wholeheartedly to the political process. They joined forces with the Democratic Party and backed William Jennings Bryan in the election of 1896. The Populists had then placed themselves in a no-win situation. If the Democrats lost, the movement would be defeated and shattered; if the Democrats won, the movement would be swallowed up in the horse-trading of Democratic Party politics.

The reactionary capitalist establishment responded vigorously to this opportunity to put a final end to the upstart Populist movement. Corporations and the elite-owned media threw their support to the Republican candidate, William McKinley, in what Zinn calls "the first massive use of money in an election campaign." Bryan was defeated, and the Populist movement fell apart. The establishment was taking no chances: even diluted within the Democratic Party, the Populists represented too much of a threat from below, they were too successful at providing a voice for We the People. Democracy had raised its ugly head, and elites chopped it off at their earliest opportunity.

Any transformational movement that wants to go the distance must be prepared to resist the seductive siren call of electoral politics – a siren whose voice becomes even more appealing after the movement has made some significant progress. As the Populists' earlier experience showed, politics can be used successfully to consolidate gains made on the ground, particularly if the expansion program employs a territorial strategy. But when electoral politics is allowed to dominate movement strategy – before the territory of the movement encompasses the entire electorate – then the hope of ultimate success has been lost. Either the movement will be destroyed abruptly, or it will die a slow drowning death in the quicksand of factional politics. In the next chapter we'll look more closely into the nature of our electoral political system.

Any transformational movement must also eventually run up against the barrier of establishment opposition. As with the Populists, it makes good sense for a transformational movement to focus initially on what people can collectively do for themselves, without confrontation and within the constraints of the existing system. This is how the movement can be built, and how a culture can be fostered based on common sense, self-reliance, and democratic empowerment. But the movement's self-help progress will eventually be frustrated by the economic and political constraints of the established system, and that's when the movement needs to decide what it's really about.

> How well we know all this! How often we have witnessed it in our part of the world! The machine that worked for years to apparent perfection, faultlessly, without a hitch, falls apart overnight. The system that seemed likely to reign unchanged, world without end, since nothing could call its power in question amid all those unanimous votes and elections, is shattered without warning. And, to our amazement, we find that everything was quite otherwise than we had thought.
> —Václav Havel, 1975

At that point the movement can either take the *blue pill*, and settle for temporary reformist gains within the elite's political circus, or it can take the *red pill* and face the challenges of the real world – of power and engagement. As much as some of us may be enamored of a win-win, love-your-enemy approach to the universe, we must face the fact that the currently entrenched regime is determined to stay in power, ruthless in its tactics, and resourceful in its application of its many means of suppression, subversion, and co-option. Though we may carry universal love in our hearts, the strategic thinking of the movement must at some point focus on the principles of effective engagement. The Populists have little to offer us here. A better model for this phase would be the non-violent grassroots movement against British rule in India, led and inspired by Mahatma Gandhi.

Gandhi is most renowned for his non-violence and for his universal empathy for all people, including even the British oppressors. Those are wise principles for any transformational movement that must engage an armed establishment, and that seeks to create a just and democratic society. But Gandhi is also renowned for his *strategic acumen,* and we can learn much from that aspect of his work. Like a skillful *Go* player, he was able to set up situations where the British felt compelled to respond, yet any response they chose would undermine their position. They had to choose between yielding ground to the movement or else engaging in suppressive measures that could only serve to build greater sympathy and support for the movement, as exemplified in the famous 'salt march to the sea.' The point is not necessarily that a movement should emulate Gandhi's specific tactics, but rather that creative and realistic strategic thinking is absolutely essential to successful engagement.

Gandhi's movement did succeed in its immediate objective of ousting the British occupiers, but it failed to achieve Gandhi's deeper vision for a new kind of harmonious and democratic society. The leadership of the movement was concentrated too much in him personally and after his assassination his followers reverted to traditional political patterns. His movement was in the final analysis a *hierarchical* movement, with himself at the top as the benevolent guiding light.

A successful transformational movement – which seeks to establish a democratic, non-hierarchical society – would be best served by taking a non-hierarchical approach from the very beginning. Goals, means, and strategy would be better developed at the grassroots level, and the movement culture should facilitate the exchange of ideas and solutions, thus building a self-reliant and *holographically led* movement – and a movement that is not vulnerable to collapse due to leadership decapitation.

The Populist Movement too had a hierarchical leadership structure, and this limited its transformational potential in several ways. In the long run hierarchy is the bane of democracy, so in that sense the Populists were from the beginning not pursuing a path toward a transformed democratic society.

The wisdom of the Populist movement was limited by the cultural perspective and prejudices of the relatively small leadership cadre. In particular, the rural, farmer-based leadership limited the growth of the movement to what we might in some fairness call their *own kind of people*. Although movement activists sympathized with urban industrial workers, and expressed support for their strikes and boycotts, the culture of the Populist leadership did not lead them to bring urban workers into their constituency, to make them part of the Populist *family*. From an objective strategic perspective, it is clear that this was a fatal error of omission. There was a natural alignment of interests, based on mutual exploitation by monopoly capitalism, and an effective joining of forces would have propelled the expanded movement onto a new and much higher plateau of political significance.

Any movement, which aims to create a transformed and democratic society, needs to keep this in mind: *when the new world is created, everyone will be in it – not just the people we agree with or the people we normally associate with*. A movement must aim to be all-inclusive if it seeks to create a democratic society that is all-inclusive. *Is there anyone you would leave behind, or relegate to second-class citizenship?* If not, then you should be willing to welcome to the movement anyone who shares the goal of creating that new world.

The future arrives of its own accord; progress does not.
—Poul Henningsen, Danish designer and social critic

Our Transformational Imperative

We the People have found our identity and common purpose many times in the past: on the fields of Lexington and Concord, at the gates of the Bastille and the Czar's palace, in the struggle against British occupation in India, and in movements like the Populists. We have a tradition to learn from, and there are many wrong turns we must avoid. Martin Luther King used a phrase that sums up one of the most important lessons we need to take to heart, *Keep your eyes on the prize*. If we want a world that is democratic, and sustainable both economically and politically, then we must stay true to that vision. Only a thorough and radical cultural transformation can rid us of the dynamics of hierarchy, domination, and elite rule.

There is no one out there, no actor on the stage of society, who can or will bring about the radical transformation required to save humanity and the world – no one that is except *We the People*. In waking up to our responsibility, we will be taking the first step in our own liberation, the first step to transforming our cultures, and the first step toward saving the world. There is no one else who will do it for us, and it is a job that must be done.

This is our *Transformational Imperative*.

4

Our Harmonization Imperative

The world needs a new, non-polarised, and non-contentious politic; one not made possible by those in situations that promote a left-right, black-white, capitalist-communist, believer-infidel thinking. Such systems are, like it or not, promoting antagonism and destroying cooperation and interdependence. Confrontational thinking, operating through political or power systems, has destroyed cultural, intellectual, and material resources that could have been used, in a life-centred ethic, for earth repair.
—Bill Mollison, *Permaculture: A Designers' Manual*

Adversarial systems and representative democracy

If We the People are to respond effectively to our Transformational Imperative, then we will need to do so by means of an appropriate social movement. In the preceding chapter I argued that a protest movement (such as the anti-globalization movement) cannot be our transformational vehicle. I also suggested that electoral politics cannot be our vehicle either, and I offered the Populist Movement as an example of a promising popular movement that finally floundered on the shoals of the political system. In this chapter I'd like to take a deeper look at our 'democratic' system, as a prelude to investigating what kind of movement could serve our needs.

Representative democracy is an adversarial system. Candidates compete for party nominations; parties compete to get their candidates elected, and elected representatives compete to get their programs adopted in parliaments. In the U.S. Constitution, adversarial dynamics are enshrined in the form of a carefully worked out *balance of powers* among the executive, judiciary, and legislature.

In the Matrix, there is a naïve democratic theory behind this system of governance. When advocates for each side present their case, there is some hope that all relevant information will emerge, enabling good decisions to be reached. When candidates and parties compete, there is some hope that their relative success will be related to the size of their following – leading indirectly to a democratic result. In a competition among people, ideas, and programs – the theory goes – the best will rise to the top.

But with any kind of system, theory is one thing and practice is another. Systems tend to have *inherent dynamics* – and the way those dynamics play out is not always consistent with the intentions or purposes under which the system is established. In the case of hierarchies, an inherent tendency toward centralization of power inevitably pushes against whatever mechanisms are set up to constrain the hierarchy. We can see this in the gradual consolidations of power by the Federal Government in the U.S. and by the creeping power of the Brussels bureaucracy in the EU. In the case of adversarial systems as well, there are inherent dynamics that we can observe wherever adversarial systems are employed.

> It's hard to make things foolproof because fools are so damned ingenious.
> —Mark Twain

An adversarial process operates as a *competitive game*. The objective of the game is to win. If you want to be a successful player in the game, you need to be better at winning than the other players. In the case of politics, winning means getting elected. According to the naïve theory of democracy, the election of a candidate should reflect general acceptance of the candidate's program. But in reality, victory in the political struggle depends on the ability to attract a constituency by whatever means prove to be effective – and selling programs isn't the means that works best in practice. More important might be the charisma of the candidate, or the vulnerability of the opponent to a smear campaign, or the ability to focus public attention on superficial but dramatic issues, or countless other propaganda games we see played out in typical campaigns. When programs are talked about, a candidate usually does best by evading questions or by telling people the lies they want to hear. The dynamics of the competitive game lead to results that have little to do with the naïve theories behind representative democracy.

In the film, *Runaway Jury*, Gene Hackman's character is a professional jury-fixer. He expresses his opinion of the ethics of the courtroom game, in a comment to the defense lawyer (Dustin Hoffman): "I'm in it to win, just like you are. Because that's what I was hired to do. Everything else is colored bubbles."

Electoral reforms can be attempted, and have frequently been implemented, but reforms are like sand castles set against the tide. The same gaming dynamics, and similar results, can be seen in every nation that uses competitive elections. Indeed, if we look back two thousand years to the Roman Republic we can see the same patterns of corruption, complete with costly campaigns, *gerrymandering* of districts, bought votes, etc. What we need to understand here is that *corruption* is the wrong word for these phenomena. They are not *corruptions* of the system; rather they are the *normal behavior* of such a system. It is the adversarial system itself that is a corruption – a corruption of democratic principles.

It's important to remember that the constitutional system was not designed in the first place to defend the rights of people. Rather, the rights of people had to be balanced, as Madison put it, against what he called "the rights of property." Well of course, property has no rights: my pen has no rights. Maybe I have a right to it, but the pen has no rights. So, this is just a code phrase for the rights of people with property. The constitutional system was founded on the principle that the rights of people with property have to be privileged; they have rights because they're people, but they also have special rights because they have property. As Madison put it in the constitutional debates, the goal of government must be "to protect the minority of the opulent against the majority." That's the way the system was set up.

—Noam Chomsky, *CorpWatch* interview, May 6, 1998

Representative democracy and elite hegemony

Representative democracy is an ideal system to facilitate rule by wealthy elites. In any adversarial game, the advantage goes to the strongest players. In the schoolyard, the game of *King of the Mountain* is naturally dominated by the biggest and strongest kids. In politics, the game of elections is naturally dominated by those with the most campaign funds and the most media support. By such means wealth can be translated directly into political power and influence – and by such means every so-called 'democracy' is in fact ruled by wealthy elites, either in office or from behind the scenes. There is an ironic truth behind the Matrix myth that capitalism and 'democracy' are closely related. In the myth the two are related by a mutual respect for human freedom; in truth they are related by their mutual friendliness to elite domination.

It is not by chance that we are governed by a system that facilitates elite rule, nor was the system established due to a mistaken faith in the naïve theory of representative democracy. The naïve theory is for school textbooks; it is part of the Matrix. The elites who set up these political systems understood very well how they function in the real world. Let's look a classic example.

When the American Revolution was over, the result was thirteen sovereign republics, collaborating under the *Articles of Confederation*. But there were problems. So much was new that unforeseen difficulties arose. There was no common agreement to protect sea-lanes, for example, and piracy became rife. The States all agreed that the Articles required amendment. A more collaborative framework was needed. The legislatures agreed to sponsor a *Constitutional Convention*, empowered to amend the Articles and bring them back for unanimous approval of the States. The delegates were supposed to represent their States, and the Constitution was to be an agreement *among the States*, an amended version of the Articles. Such was the charter under which the Convention was empowered to operate.

The legislatures, unfortunately, mostly appointed their delegates from among their local wealthy elites, their 'better people.' The delegates then ensconced themselves in secret session and proceeded to betray the charter under which they had been assembled. They discarded the Articles, and began debating and drafting a wholly new document, one that transferred sovereignty to a relatively strong central government. The delegates reneged on the States that had sent them, and took it upon themselves to speak directly for "We the People" – and thus begins the preamble to their Constitution. In effect they accomplished a *coup d'etat*. They managed to design a system that would enable existing elites to continue to run the affairs of the new nation, as they had before under the Crown – under a Constitution that *seems* to embody sound democratic principles.

At every level of the new Constitution there were safeguards against uprisings from below. The life-appointed Supreme Court Justices and the six-year Senators provided a kind of conservative flywheel against any kind of rapid change. The President was to be elected indirectly by State Legislatures, which provided a buffer from "mob" sentiments in each state. Most significantly, the strongest protections in the Constitution were granted to private property. The Constitutional sanctity of private property guaranteed that existing elites would be able to hold on to and continue developing their fortunes. Whereas in most European nations the financial system is controlled by a central government bank, in the new American republic the private sector was given a more influential role. This provided American elites with a way to influence economic affairs outside of political channels as well.

This may seem like a cynical assessment of the legacy of America's *Founding Fathers*. Have they not given us all those noble sayings?... "Give me liberty or give me death," "The price of liberty is eternal vigilance," etc. Were they not true democrats? Some were and some weren't. Even some of the best of them, like Thomas Jefferson, were slave-owning aristocrats. The worst of them, like Alexander Hamilton, would have preferred rule by an American royalty. In general the allegiance of colonial elites to democracy was tempered by their concern for their own self-interest, and their notion of how society should operate. They didn't want Royal interference in their affairs, but neither did they want interference by ordinary people – what many of them referred to as "the mob."

By the very way they carried out the secret Constitutional Convention they demonstrated how the new government was going to operate. They were delegates, chartered to represent their constituencies, and they were mostly from wealthy elite circles. When gathered in their own company they betrayed their constituencies and represented instead their own mutual interests – yet they presented their work as the embodiment of their charter. And they succeeded politically in selling their product to the people and to the States. Such has been the pattern of American politics ever since.

After the Convention completed its work, a debate raged throughout the colonies as to whether the new Constitution should be ratified. As part of this debate, a series of newspaper articles appeared that came to be known as the *Federalist Papers*. These papers reveal with considerable candor the elite reasoning behind the design of the new government.

> In Federalist Paper #10, James Madison argued that representative government was needed to maintain peace in a society ridden by factional disputes. These disputes came from "the various and unequal distribution of property." "Those who hold and those who are without property have ever formed distinct interests in society." The problem he said, was how to control the factional struggles that came from inequalities in wealth. Minority factions could be controlled, he said, by the principle that decisions would be by vote of the majority.
>
> So the real problem, according to Madison, was a majority faction, and here the solution was...to have "an extensive republic," that is, a large nation ranging over thirteen states, for then "it will be more difficult for all who feel it to discover their own strength, and to act in unison with each other...The influence of factious leaders may kindle a flame within their particular States, but will be unable to spread a general conflagration through the other States" (Zinn, 96).

The purpose of the new system, in other words, was to enable the colonial elite to retain their economic and political dominance by systematically preventing the ascendancy of any kind of popular democratic movement. The rules of the adversarial game were carefully worked out so as to enable the successful management of factionalism by the elite establishment. The system was consciously designed to facilitate elite rule and that is how it has functioned ever since.

> We have frequently printed the word democracy. Yet I cannot too often repeat that it is a word the real gist of which still sleeps, quite unawakened, notwithstanding the resonance and the many angry tempests out of which its syllables have come, from pen or tongue.
>
> It is a great word, whose history, I suppose, remains unwritten, because that history has yet to be enacted. It is, in some sort, younger brother of another great and often-used word, Nature, whose history also waits unwritten.
>
> —Walt Whitman, "Democratic Vistas"

Divide and rule: the role of factionalism

Directly after the ratification of the Constitution, two elite-led political parties were established. Madison, Jefferson, and Monroe joined the *Democrat-Republicans*, while Hamilton, Washington, and Adams joined the *Federalists*. This set the pattern for U.S. politics ever since: two mainstream parties, both controlled by wealthy elites who belonged to the same clubs and social circles, and providing the illusion of choice to voters. The two major parties had the funding to carry out major national campaigns, and then as now people were corralled into choosing between the lesser of two evils when they cast their ballots. Democracy has existed only in the Matrix.

From the beginning, the primary agenda of all mainstream parties has been to U.S. expansionism and the further enrichment of the wealthy elites who control both the economy and the government. As Madison anticipated, political stability in America has been achieved through the management of factionalism. At any given time, some sizable faction was always doing rather well under the elite-managed system of economic growth, and these more prosperous elements provided a solid base of support for government policies.

But there was always a mass of unrest boiling up from the less advantaged segments of society. Particularly with industrialization and the increasing dominance of capitalist economics, wealth was very unequally distributed, workers, women, and minorities were exploited, and there were always movements of various kinds attempting to influence the elite agenda. These movements were contained either geographically, or by pitting one faction against the other. The Populists probably came closer than any other movement to challenging elite hegemony, but they too finally fell prey to adversarial dynamics when they cast their lot in the electoral game.

Today the grassroots U.S. population is divided into two primary factions, usually known as *liberals* and *conservatives*, or *left* and *right*. This split represents a rather sophisticated version of factional manipulation. It does *not* represent any real difference of interests. It is not that grassroots liberals and conservatives are from different economic strata, or have different self-interest agendas for fundamental national policies. The divisions, though deeply felt, are not over matters of state, but over issues such as abortion, gay rights, and the like. These kinds of issues, according to the Constitution, are not even the business of the Federal Government – they are the kind that should be dealt at the state level or, as the Constitution clearly provides, "by the people themselves."

But divisiveness is so effective at controlling the population that the major parties are happy to promote such issues to the national level, where they can be exploited to generate fear and anxiety. Campaigns and rhetoric are focused on these peripheral issues, and fundamental issues of national policy never even come up for discussion. Campaigns have no more relevance to national policy than do high school debates, and as in high school debates the winners are decided more on the style of their presentations than on the validity of their positions. In the Matrix we have democracy, in the real world we have divide and rule.

Our Harmonization Imperative

> It ain't left or right. It's up and down. Here we all are down here struggling while the Corporate Elite are all up there having a nice day!
> —Carolyn Chute, author of *The Beans of Egypt Maine* and anti-corporate activist

For two reasons, the pursuit of a progressive victory via the electoral system is a no-win idea. The first reason, a tactical one, is simply that such a project *cannot succeed*. The divisive power of the establishment media and political machines are too powerful. Elites have refined the management of factionalism into a science. We all know this intuitively, and that is why most progressives don't want to 'waste their vote' on a Nader-style candidacy.

There is also a more strategic reason why a progressive victory is a no-win idea – even if it were achievable. Such a victory would *perpetuate hierarchy and the adversarial game*. The progressives would be on top for a while, but society would remain divided. Progressive legislation would presumably be enacted, but it would be enacted and enforced by a centralized government. Those in opposition would rankle under what they perceived to be a *leftist dictatorship*. The forces of reaction would exploit this divisiveness and there would always be a danger that the political pendulum would swing back to the right. This is in part how Reagan was able to come to power – an eventuality that would have seemed inconceivable during the euphoric progressive resurgence that followed the shame and resignation of Richard Nixon.

In order to escape from the trap of factionalism, we need to find a way to get beyond the superficial issues that divide us. Underneath our political and religious beliefs we are all human beings who want a better and saner world for our families and our descendants. Instead of focusing on what divides us, and struggling to prevail over the *other*, we need to find a way to focus on what unites us – and learn how to work together to achieve the kind of world we all want.

We face a common crisis as neoliberal capitalism destroys our societies and threatens our life support systems. This crisis presents us with an unprecedented opportunity for all of us to find a common ground, for there is no sizable segment of the population that will benefit from the direction in which the establishment is taking us. Factionalism no longer has any *economic teeth* – the regime keeps us divided not by appealing to our self-interest but by means of manufactured and sensationalized fears and anxieties.

If We the People are to respond effectively to our Transformational Imperative – to save the world and humanity from this crisis – we need first to actualize our common identity as We the People. We need to learn to see one another as human beings rather than as *us* and *them*. We need to learn how to *harmonize* our deep common interests instead of accentuating our superficial differences. In order to respond to our Transformational Imperative, we must first respond to this *Harmonization Imperative*.

Fortunately, there is a proven means by which we can move effectively toward cultural harmonization and overcome cultural factionalism. That means goes under the simple name of *dialog*, and the next chapter is devoted to examining the remarkable results that been achieved by appropriate kinds of dialog – and exploring how dialog might be employed to awaken We the People and empower us together to respond to our transformational imperative.

5

The dynamics of harmonization

Meeting dynamics: collaborative & adversarial

Consider for a moment the many kinds of meetings that occur in our society. In business meetings are held regularly to make plans and coordinate people's activities. If parents feel that their children need a crossing guard on the way to school, they organize a neighborhood meeting. When a country decides to go to war, that decision is made in some meeting among high-level officials. In government one wonders if they do anything but go to meetings, whether they be official government sessions, or meetings with staff, colleagues, lobbyists, backers, or constituents. If people want to start a political movement, they begin by organizing meetings. The American Revolution was born in New England pubs, where the rebellion-minded held meetings and plotted against the King, inspired by the local brew.

Although many of us have negative feelings about meetings, and about their effectiveness, the fact is that meetings are the place where people generally make joint plans and reach group decisions. Some of these meetings are *collaborative*, and some are *adversarial*. We are all familiar with both kinds.

A typical example of a *collaborative* meeting would be the neighborhood gathering mentioned above, where the parents would like to see a crossing guard assigned to a dangerous local intersection. The people have a common goal, and they work together cooperatively to achieve it. People offer suggestions for actions that can be taken, the suggestions are discussed, and people volunteer to help with the actions that are agreed to. If the meeting is successful, everyone comes away better off – the concept of winners and losers is largely irrelevant to a collaborative meeting.

A typical example of an *adversarial* meeting would be a city council session where a controversial development project is being discussed. The developers and business community are showing slides of beautiful landscaped buildings and talking of new jobs, while neighborhood protesters are complaining about increased traffic and the loss of a children's playground. The typical outcome of such a meeting is that one side *wins* and the other *loses*. Either the development project goes ahead, and the neighborhood suffers, or else the project is rejected and the investors may suffer considerable losses.

It is very unusual for anything creative to happen at an adversarial meeting. People, or factions, come in with agendas to promote – agendas that were created somewhere else. If the meeting is unable to resolve an issue, it is typically deferred – and people are expected to go off somewhere else and create revised proposals. The *somewhere else* – where the creative activity of planning occurs – is generally a meeting of the collaborative variety.

In our city council example, the developers and promoters have been meeting collaboratively for months preparing their project plans and developing their city-council contacts. Similarly, the neighborhood protesters have held collaborative meetings to assess their feelings and to decide how best to express their concerns to the city council. The adversarial meeting – the official *decision making* meeting – is not a discussion session, but is rather a battle of strength between the two opposing sides: Which side can muster the most support among the city council members? Which side can spout the most convincing rhetoric, painting its own proposals in the colors of the common good?

Parliamentary sessions in 'representative democracies' are based on the adversarial meeting model. A chairman governs the proceedings, proposals can be introduced, time is allowed for debate, and a majority vote decides each question. The 'debate' is typically rhetorical, for public consumption, and seldom affects the outcome of the vote. This is not a system designed to solve problems or to encourage useful discussion – it is a system designed to efficiently measure the relative power of opposing factions, and to promptly assign the rewards to the strongest. Just as the floor of the stock market is designed to efficiently manage the investment transactions of the wealthy elite, so is the floor of the legislature designed to efficiently referee power transactions among elite factions.

A collaborative meeting operates according to *collaborative dynamics*, and an adversarial meeting operates according to *adversarial dynamics*.

Collaborative dynamics are about people gathering around agreed objectives, identifying means to achieve them, and planning how to pursue that agenda. Within collaborative dynamics people have an incentive to listen to one another's suggestions, and in the planning process the group typically converges toward a consensus perspective on the task at hand.

Adversarial dynamics are about people debating from their fixed perspectives in an attempt to prevail over the other side. There is little incentive to listen to the other side, apart from looking for weaknesses that can be exploited. Each side may attempt to shift the perspective of the other side, but neither side has any intention of shifting its own perspective. People learn useful things about their shared problems within collaborative dynamics, whereas the only thing learned within adversarial dynamics is how to better combat the other side. Collaborative dynamics tend to avoid internal divisiveness when it arises, while adversarial dynamics tend to reinforce and encourage divisiveness among factions.

A gap in our cultural repertoire

These two meeting models are very common in our society, and indeed they are more or less the extent of our general cultural repertoire. We know how to get together with our allies and make plans to promote our shared interests, and we know how to fight for our side in an adversarial gathering, according to whatever rules are in play. What we don't know much about, and don't have many cultural models for, is how to *resolve differences* within a group of people. We don't know how to engage in productive dialog within a group of people who express conflicting interests.

In an adversarial meeting the differences are accepted as a given, as a fixed quantity, and the business of the meeting is to enable the different factions to battle it out until a winner can be chosen. There is no attempt to resolve the differences: people go away with their perspectives unchanged, and the same factions retire to prepare for their next engagement.

When people come into a collaborative meeting, they come in with the knowledge that they are bound by common interests to the other participants. Indeed, the people come together in order to collaborate in advancing those common interests. In order to *get on with it* and *make progress*, participants tend to avoid bringing up internal differences in such meetings. At such a meeting a *good leader* will be skillful at defusing differences, articulating compromises, and keeping the meeting *on track*. Minority factions within the group are encouraged to stifle their *divisive concerns*, and join the majority in a consensus that will advance the identified common interests of the group. And in the competition between different factions, success tends to go to those that are best able to submerge their internal differences, focus on their primary interests, and adopt decisive action plans.

Under neither dynamics is there an attempt to engage in constructive dialog regarding the differences in the group. Under adversarial dynamics there is dialog over differences – but it is the dialog of *power*, expressed in the language of influence and votes. Under collaborative dynamics, discussion of differences is avoided, so that the group can focus on their identified common interests and get on with their primary business. In one case differences are expressed competitively and are *reinforced*; in the other case differences are *suppressed*. In neither case are differences *resolved*.

This gap in our cultural repertoire creates a problem for popular initiatives, particularly in a society that is already split by factionalism. Indeed, the gap can lead to difficulties whenever people attempt to work together. Here's a real scenario I observed on a recent visit to the San Francisco Bay Area. The population there is relatively progressive, and there is widespread support for an increased focus on public transport. But instead of activists getting together and coming up with a common proposal, they soon divided themselves into two camps. One camp wanted to expand the conventional rail network, while another wanted to expand the rapid-transit system. Most of the available activist energy was then devoted to a struggle between these two camps.

As I read over the two positions, as an outside observer, it seemed obvious to me that the best of the ideas could be usefully combined into a cost-effective hybrid proposal. The real solution, it seemed, would be to make strategic interconnecting links and upgrades, and coordinate fares and schedules – across all available transport systems – rather than promoting one kind of transport to the exclusion of another. Of course my own armchair proposal probably didn't take everything into account, but the main point remains: the two camps were struggling over their differences rather than trying to resolve them – and missed any opportunity to find synergy in some creative middle ground. The collaborative meeting model could not serve the two camps, because neither side was willing to stifle its ideas – so the activists adopted the only other available cultural model: adversarial engagement. As a consequence of this split in popular activism, the transport planning decisions probably ended up in the hands speculative developers and their politician cronies, and whatever their decision, they could claim it has 'public support.'

Most of us consider public meetings to be a waste of time, particularly when they attempt to deal with issues that are complex or controversial. This is because we have prior experience with the dynamics that are likely to occur. First there will be an attempt to reach a rapid consensus, most likely proposed by those calling the meeting. Then someone in the back stands up and disagrees, voicing some objection. That sparks other suggestions and objections. The meeting threatens to *get out of control* – to revert to *adversarial dynamics*. The organizers attempt to bring the dynamics back into *collaboration*. If they succeed, then some of the participants go away feeling their interests have been betrayed; if they fail, then everyone goes away with the feeling that yet another meeting has been a waste of time.

Because of these circumstances, anyone with a motivation to pursue political activism soon learns to flock with birds of the same feather. Environmentalists flock under a green banner, animal rights activists follow their drummer, other groups rally around their opposition to corporate power, or their stance in favor of or against abortion rights, etc. To get anything done, collaborative dynamics are required, and gathering together in interest groups seems to be the natural thing to do. Those gathering together already agree on what's important, and they are thus able – depending on their organizational ability – to *get on with a program*, rather than *wasting time* debating the priority of different issues. In this way the energy of popular initiatives gets sucked into the game of adversarial factionalism – a game whose rules are set down by elites for their own advantage. Just as in Las Vegas or Wall Street, this is a game where the house always wins in the end.

And did you exchange
A walk on part in a war
For a leading role in a cage?
—Roger Waters, Pink Floyd, *Wish You Were Here*

If we want to overcome factionalism in the *macrocosm*, at the level of society, we must first learn how to overcome differences in the *microcosm* – where people meet face to face. We need to extend our cultural repertoire to include gatherings of a third kind, where people neither compete to win or lose, nor submerge their differences in order to reach a shallow consensus. We need a *third* dynamics, a dynamics of *harmonization*, a dynamics that encourages us to express our concerns fully, and which enables us to work together creatively with that information – to find ways forward that benefit everyone involved. If our cultural repertoire can be extended in this way, in the microcosm, we may find that there are new ways of working together on a larger scale as well – ways that avoid the quicksand of adversarial politics.

Two promising meetings

Back in the 1980s I was working in a well-known Silicon Valley computer company. I was looking into the potential of some new technologies, and in that role I worked with people in the research groups as well as those in the engineering groups. I didn't consider myself any kind of expert on meetings, but I certainly spent a lot of time in them. One afternoon I received a phone call from one of the researchers, with some urgency in his voice, saying that I was needed in a particular meeting. I was a bit surprised at the invitation because the people involved were not working in the area I was investigating. I didn't know what they expected from me, but I was willing to attend and find out what was going on.

When everyone had gathered, I simply asked, "What's the problem, gentlemen?" It turns out that a fracas had developed between the researchers and the engineers. The engineers had made a decision regarding a new product, and the researchers felt their own relevant results had been ignored. It was not the decision itself that was challenged, but the manner in which the decision had been made – without consultation between the groups.

I asked each of the groups to explain what the problem was, from its point of view. After a few follow-up questions I began to get the picture. As an outside observer, I could see that the problem boiled down to one of trust between the groups. The engineers felt that the research group did not trust them to make their own decisions, and the researchers felt the engineering group didn't trust the relevance of their research efforts. As I knew and respected both groups of people, I had a feeling that the trust issue was really a matter of misunderstanding. Without any training in conflict resolution or group process, I decided to follow my intuition.

I first asked the engineers to explain what they expected from the research group. Then I asked the researchers to explain what they thought the relationship between research and engineering should be. I didn't express an opinion myself on either of these questions, but simply listened to what was said. As I had suspected, there really wasn't any conflict between the views of the two groups – and because the two groups had now been able to *hear* one another, the problem evaporated and trust was restored. It had all been so simple, and happened so naturally, that I felt my presence at the meeting had been unnecessary. I was quite surprised the next day to receive a copy of a memo addressed to my boss, praising my role at the meeting! I was puzzled…I felt that I *hadn't done anything* – except to listen.

It wasn't until about 20 years later that I finally understood what had happened at that meeting. The way I came to understand was by being in another meeting, only this time I was the one involved in a fracas. It was a meeting I had called, and my goal was to work through an agenda with those I had invited. They were political activists from the Berkeley area, and my agenda involved reaching consensus on a new direction for effective activism. For the first couple of hours, the meeting (of the collaborative variety) seemed to be going 'on track.' We had flip charts with points of agreement and I was quite happy with our progress.

Then a fellow raised his hand with a complaint. He didn't like the way we were spending our time and felt I was dominating the meeting. I thought he was being disruptive and I told him I wanted to continue 'making progress.' He didn't want to accept this and, in a momentary lapse of reason, I suggested that he go off and organize his own meeting. As soon as I said this I knew it was a mistake; I could feel the 'bad vibes' I had created in the room. There was a seemingly endless moment of embarrassing silence; I wished I were somewhere else.

A woman then spoke up and asked if I'd mind if she tried a bit of facilitation. Relieved to see the focus of attention shift away from myself, I readily agreed to her offer – not knowing what 'facilitation' was or how it could help. What she did was very simple. She asked the other fellow what he was expecting from the meeting and then she asked me the same thing. She was playing the same role I had played in that other meeting 20 years before! She was asking the obvious questions that needed to be asked, and then simply listening to what we had to say. The result was also similar – once the other fellow and I really *heard* what each had to say, the conflict disappeared. He understood my concern about making progress; I understood that from his point of view we were not making progress at all – and we both respected each other's concerns as being valid and relevant.

After this, everyone began sharing their reasons for coming to the gathering, and I could feel an increased energy level in the room. Everyone had become more present, as if a black-and-white movie had suddenly burst into color. I could see in retrospect that our earlier discussion had been shallow and one-dimensional, and over-managed by me. Unfortunately we had run out of time, for I believe that with our greater 'presence' we could have had a very creative and fruitful conversation about activism and strategies. The space had been opened up to share our diverse experiences, and learn from one another. The earlier emphasis on agenda had severely narrowed our channel of communication.

In each of these two meetings, a breakthrough occurred when a certain type of *hearing* took place. What we hear depends on what we are listening for. If we are in an argument (i.e., in an adversarial meeting), we are on guard for attacks and defenses, and that is what we will hear when someone makes a statement – as we can see in the care with which lawyers choose their words. If we are pursuing an agenda together (i.e., in a collaborative meeting), we are hoping for agreement and progress, and we will evaluate whatever we hear in those terms.

In both of our meetings, the intervention of the facilitators caused the people to shift what they were listening for. When I asked the engineers what they expected from the research group, that shifted attention away from the specific decision that had been made. Instead of listening for an attack or defense, the researchers were encouraged to listen in terms of, "Who are these people and how do they see things?" Attention shifted from ideas and issues to people. The same thing happened in the Berkeley gathering. By asking the fellow, "What are you expecting from this meeting?," the facilitator enabled me to hear who the fellow was, and what his concern was, rather than hearing only a disruption to my agenda.

Ideas taken literally can be good or bad, valid or invalid, but a person is always valid, and so are their concerns, as concerns. When we are listening in terms of issues, and we dismiss a comment, we are also dismissing that person's concern as invalid, and to some extent we are dismissing and disrespecting the person. When we listen in terms of people – one human to another – then we can accept all contributions as being valid concerns, even if we happen to think that the person may be confused about some issues. And after all, who isn't confused about some issues? None of us is all-knowing. And when we accept someone's concern, we are also accepting and respecting that person.

The breakthroughs that happened at the Berkeley meeting were particularly significant for me, because I have always been rather competitive and intellectual in my approach to things. And I, like many others, would typically be thinking about what I'm going to say next, rather than listening to what the current speaker is saying. And in business meetings, everything would always be evaluated relative-to-agenda. It was a new experience for me to actually be present and listening, aware of being in communication with fellow humans, rather than casting myself in some role or another, and imposing some one-dimensional evaluation filter on people's contributions.

For me this was a new kind of communication space, a three-dimensional space occupied by people rather than a one-dimensional space occupied by concepts and ideas. I refer to this as the *space of harmonization* because in such a space it becomes possible to harmonize the concerns and needs of the people who are participating. Once we accept everyone as being an equally valid, caring human being, then *each* person's concerns become *everyone's* concerns. To ignore someone's concerns would be cast that person out in the cold, and you don't do that to a fellow human being. When this space of harmonization is entered, then the attention of the group naturally turns to the question, "How can we find solutions and answers that take all of our concerns into account?"

This shift in attention releases creative, cooperative energy that was previously being constrained by unnecessary divisiveness. I felt this upsurge of energy in the Berkeley meeting, but in that case we didn't have time left to see where that energy might have been able to take us. It turns out that the creative and cooperative energy of a group, when released in such a way, can be a very powerful thing, enabling the group in many cases to find breakthrough solutions to seemingly impossible problems – solutions which at the same time take everyone's concerns into account.

In the two examples of meetings above, we stumbled into a situation where communication had broken down, and fortunately there was someone on hand in each case to offer a bit of useful intervention, as a facilitator. We entered the space of harmonization, but in neither case was time available to do very much with the creative energy that was released.

The Michigan conference

Let us now turn our attention to a gathering in which the space of harmonization was longer lasting – and where the released energy of the group could be applied to shared problems, leading to surprising outcomes and breakthroughs in mutual understanding. This conference, "Democracy in America," was held at the Fetzer Institute in Kalamazoo, Michigan, in June 2004. Mark Satin, editor of the *Radical Middle Newsletter* was a participant, and he wrote about the conference in the May–June issue of his newsletter. Except where otherwise noted, the citations in this section are all taken from that article, which is archived at:
http://www.radicalmiddle.com/x_fetzer_conference.htm

Mark quotes from the conference literature:

"The purpose of this gathering is to [initiate] a new kind of public conversation that moves us beyond polarization so we [can] effectively address the issues we care most about...

"We all share the same 'boat' called the United States of America. It is more essential now than ever [that we] begin to learn how to row with, rather than against, each other..."

The participants were from all across the political spectrum, including a former FBI agent, the National Field Director of the Christian Coalition, a founding member of the National Congress of Black Women, a board member of the National Rifle Association, the president of a left-leaning legal-issues organization, former Weather Underground supporters, and former speakers at white racist gatherings.

Clearly, the people who set up this conference share my views regarding the political importance of harmonization, and the necessity of overcoming factionalism. And they set themselves quite a challenge by bringing in such radically diverse participants. They jumped directly into the lion's den: if they could achieve a space of harmonization here, they would demonstrate that harmonization is possible with almost any group of people. From such a radically diverse conference one might expect fistfights and shouting matches to emerge, rather than any kind of agreement or consensus. Tom Atlee of the Co-Intelligence Institute, who was a participant, expressed his misgivings prior to the gathering this way:

> Using Google, I researched the people who were coming to the conversation. I read articles by the conservatives and listened to their radio talk shows – and I got triggered by what they said. I reacted with anger, frustration and rejection of who they were. I thought silent counterarguments and felt the rise of adrenaline. Friends warned me to be careful – or couldn't even imagine going to talk with such people.
>
> —http://co-intelligence.org/polarization-Fetzer.html

Mark describes the first evening's activities this way:

> On Friday night, we broke into three groups (of eight participants and one facilitator each) to discuss such questions as, "What did you understand about being an American when you were 12 years old? How have you experienced political differences and how did that affect you personally?"
>
> It was impossible to participate in that exercise without coming to see (and feel and know) that every participant, whatever their politics, was a complex and caring human being.

We can see here that from the very beginning the facilitators focused attention on people and their experiences, and we can see that a space of harmonization was reached early on. Regarding an afternoon's conversation later in the conference, Mark reports:

> Someone tried to classify participants' approaches as "left" or "right." Someone on the right took umbrage with that, feeling that the qualities cited as "right" were insulting stereotypes; and that pressed many people's buttons; and round and round and round we went, and the afternoon shadows grew longer.
>
> But the end result of that conversation is we all realized – I mean, we all really "got" – how misleading and even infantilizing the old political spectrum had become.

Here we can see the space of harmonization expanding, as people dig deeper and pull out more of their concerns. Not only are they accepting and respecting one another's contributions, but also they are beginning to understand the futility of labels and factions in general. This expansion continued in a later session, where the participants were asked to tell about each of the key decisions they'd made in their political lives:

> Everyone stared, some of us open-mouthed, as various "left"-wingers and "right"-wingers, former Weather Underground supporters and former speakers at white racist gatherings, shared the incidents that shaped their lives.
>
> And revealed without even trying that every caring person is a brother or sister under the skin.
>
> And that our values are at some deep level fundamentally the same.

At the end of the conference the group came up with a remarkable declaration:

> Before leaving, we all signed our names to a document titled "We the People." Many of us signed with flourishes, as if we were signing something akin to the Declaration of Independence. Here are the key passages:
>
> "We respect our differences and recognize America needs every one of our viewpoints, ideas, and passions – even those we don't agree with – to keep our democracy vital and alive;
>
> "We recognize that meeting here and across our land for dialogues across differences builds trust, understanding, respect, and

empowerment – the conditions necessary for freedom and democracy to live in us and around us;

"And, therefore, each still grounded in our own considered views (conscience and convictions), we commit ourselves and our communities of interest to foster dialogue across the many divides in America, in large and small groups, to build trust, insight, and inspired action toward the more perfect union we all desire."

Mark's final statement about the conference:

[F]or the first time in many years, I feel enthusiastic enough about an incipient political movement to want to put my shoulder to the wheel.

In this Michigan conference we can see examples of the kind of breakthroughs that can occur when a space of harmonization is maintained for an extended period. This diverse group of people, with radically different viewpoints and agendas, actually achieved a sense of solidarity and community, which they expressed in this "We the People" declaration. And this was not simply an intellectual experience for the participants; there is an obvious passion and commitment in the language of their declaration. They could see from their own microcosm experience that harmonization could help eliminate factionalism in the macrocosm of the larger society. And they understood that the process is about trust and dialog, not about any particular platform or program.

Consensus does not mean unanimous agreement. It means we create a forum where all voices can be heard and we can think creatively rather than dualistically about how to reconcile our different needs and visions.
—Starhawk, "Lessons from Seattle and Washington D.C."

Maclean's "empowered dialog"

Let us move on and consider another example of a facilitated conference that has produced promising results in terms of harmonization:

In 1991 the leading Canadian newsweekly, Maclean's, sponsored a dialogue about the future of Canada among twelve ordinary Canadians carefully selected for their differences. They were nurses, lawyers, teachers, musicians, company workers. They were White, Black, Native, male, female, from across Canada. Right from the start, they were passionately divided about minority rights and Quebec independence. They'd never seen the world through each other's eyes. They were arrogant, hurt, compassionate, intense. *Maclean's* brought them all together for three days of conversation facilitated by a team from the Harvard Negotiation Project, led by *Getting to Yes* co-author Roger Fisher.

After two days of ideological battles and emotional upheavals, a breakthrough happened. A peacemaking woman from Ontario listened with real compassion to a very upset woman from Quebec, and they bonded. The next morning the Quebec woman, in turn, deeply heard the Native woman. A spirit of partnership blossomed and by the end of the last day, the group had agreed on a vision for Canada that advocated more mutual awareness, connectedness, and collaborative activity. Their agreement fills five of the (amazing) thirty-nine pages of coverage provided by *Maclean's* in their July 1, 1991 issue, entitled "The People's Verdict." The event was also covered by an hour-long Canadian TV documentary (Atlee).

As in the Michigan conference, harmonization enabled this group to break through their strong differences and find heartfelt common ground. In the *Maclean's* event, the group was able to move forward from that common ground and address difficult and substantial problems. Their consensus statement included recommendations on education, tourism, economics and trade, and many other issues. Furthermore, their written recommendations reveal a perspective that embraces the principles of harmonization as a means of resolving social issues. Here are two of their joint suggestions:

Rather than trying to make binding decisions now on the precise shape of Canada's future, we work together to clarify the vision of a Canada in which all Canadians would feel fully accepted, at home and fairly treated, and with an appropriate balance between national concerns and local autonomy

A vision of Canadians working together is not simply a matter of constitutional language. We suggest that Canadians devote substantial effort to the human dimension – to understanding one another empathetically, to caring and sharing their concerns and ideas. And that they also work together to make the Canadian economy as prosperous and promising for the future as they can. On a base of human understanding and economic co-operation, constitutional questions will be far easier to resolve. We suggest that all three activities be pursued concurrently (Briars).

The Rogue Valley Wisdom Council

Let us next consider a harmonization session in a community setting, where the concerns raised involve the participants directly in their daily lives. The community involved is the Rogue Valley area of Oregon, and the facilitation technique involved is called *Dynamic Facilitation* – one of the most effective forms of facilitation for achieving harmonization in a diverse group of people. Held in November 2003, the event was billed as *The Rogue Valley Wisdom Council*. *Wisdom Council* is a concept developed by Jim Rough, the inventor of Dynamic Facilitation.

The basic idea behind a Wisdom Council is to bring together a group of randomly selected citizens, as a kind of representative microcosm of a larger population – a community, a region, or even a whole nation. If the general concerns of the larger population find expression within the microcosms of the session, then it is likely that the consensus reached in the Council session will resonate with the constituency generally. If a series of Councils are held, then Jim anticipates that a sense of We the People would arise gradually in the general population, and that ongoing Councils would become effective agents for bringing coherence to that sense of empowerment. It's an exciting idea, but it hasn't been tried yet in its full dimensionality, including a series of well-advertised Councils.

Jim facilitated the Rogue Valley Wisdom Council himself, and for him the event served as a trial run of the Wisdom Council concept. He was very pleased, perhaps even a bit surprised, by the high quality of the outcomes, as seen from a process perspective. The local activists who initiated and organized the event were equally pleased by the results, based on the sense of democratic empowerment that was awakened in the participants.

To achieve a reasonably random selection of participants, hundreds of names were picked randomly from the voter rolls for the Rogue Valley area. These people were contacted by phone, and eventually a small group agreed to participate in the event. It was a two-day session, and the group chose to look into the problem of funding for education.

That problem itself served as a kind of catalyst; it gave the group a chance to work together in a space of harmonization, and develop their sense of identity as a group. As in the Michigan conference, this *finding of identity* seemed to lead naturally to a sense of democratic empowerment, expressed again by the phrase "We the People." The event was recorded on video, and one can readily see the transformation in the participants. At the beginning they seem rather shy and don't look like they had much to say. But by the end, they are overflowing with enthusiasm about the possibility – even the necessity – of some more direct kind of participation in the democratic process.

A public meeting was held immediately following the session (a standard part of the Wisdom Council concept), and this was also recorded on video. The meeting started off with a report by the participants on their experience, and their highly articulate, heartfelt expressions were in stark contrast to their original shyness. The meeting then broke up into several roundtable discussions. There was no attempt to facilitate these discussions, and remarkably the enthusiasm of the Council participants turned out to be highly contagious. The people at the meeting were able to somehow pick up the We the People spirit without actually going through the whole experience themselves. Everyone came away from the public meeting with a great deal of enthusiasm for greater public involvement in policymaking – and for the kind of dialog that harmonizing processes enable.

Let us compare the outcomes of the Rogue Valley event with those of the Michigan event. From one perspective, we could say that neither event did any real problem solving. They achieved breakthroughs in mutual understanding, and entered a "space of harmonization," but the Michigan folks did not find breakthrough solutions to the problems of factionalism in society, and the Rogue Valley folks didn't solve the problem of adequately funding education. In that sense, the outcomes of the two events were comparable, and both to some extent limited.

But from another perspective, the Rogue Valley outcomes transcended those of the Michigan event. In the Michigan case, "mutual understanding" was expressed in general terms: "We respect our differences and recognize America needs every one of our viewpoints, ideas, and passions – even those we don't agree with – to keep our democracy vital and alive." These are abstractions about abstractions. As such, the outcomes were good ones, very much better than the abstractions we might have expected from such an oddball mix of participants at a typical conference.

In the Rogue Valley case, 'mutual understanding,' although still not moving into the level of problem solving, brought in a democratic immediacy that transcended Michigan's abstractions. The fact that the people were neighbors gave a different meaning to the sense of community that they experienced in the session. Instead of thinking about what groups of people might do somewhere someday for the benefit of democracy, they were thinking about what they together might specifically do, now or soon, right there in their own community.

When they came up with the phrase "We the People," they weren't thinking only of the immediate session feeling of solidarity, and they weren't thinking only of a social abstraction – they were tapping into the deep innate knowledge that they personally had the competence and the right to participate in making the decisions that affect their lives, in dialog with their neighbors. They were experiencing not merely a promising insight, useful as such might be, but were actually beginning to awaken their own liberation as free human beings, at a visceral level. Their exuberance in telling their stories at the public meeting was a clear expression of the empowerment and liberation that had been kindled in them and among them.

As I see it, this Wisdom Council experiment in Rogue valley ties in with the focus on localism that I mentioned in the Introduction. In terms of ecosystems and systems of economic exchange, localism offers significant benefits. Within a community, or a region, people have every incentive to use their resources wisely, and to balance economic benefit against quality of life considerations, taking into account the future of the community and their children's heritage. To the extent that planning and policy decisions can be handled locally, by an inclusive democratic process, there is a strong likelihood we could "get it right," in terms of building a sensible society at the local level. And if everywhere we get it right locally, our chances of getting it right as a global society are substantially improved. We'll continue with this localism thread in Chapter 7. I wanted to mention it briefly now because of the extra significance it brings to the Rogue Valley experience.

Based on the outcomes of that experience, particularly the infectious spirit that was picked up by the attendees of the public meeting, we have every reason to expect that a series of such Councils – if held in the same local community, and adequately advertised locally – might very well lead to a general awakening of We the People within that community, as Jim anticipates in his vision of Wisdom Councils. Furthermore, the community context seems to awaken that spirit at a particularly deep level.

I suggest there is a very strong synergy between the potential for harmonization at the community level, and the benefits of localism as regards economics and the environment. For the benefits of localism to be realized, there needs to be an adequate process of inclusive democracy. It seems to me that the serial-harmonization-session approach can provide just such a process. And in order for the results of a harmonization session to have political relevance, there needs to be some relevant population that can make use of those results. It seems to me that the community provides such a relevant population.

> Democracy is an infinitely including spirit. We have an instinct for democracy because we have an instinct for wholeness... [D]emocracy is the self-creating process of life...projecting itself into the visible world...so that its essential oneness will declare itself.
> —Mary Parker Follett, *The New State*

The role of a facilitator

There are many kinds of facilitators, appropriate to many kinds of gatherings and meetings. A schoolteacher can be seen as a facilitator, directing the attention of the class to ideas and information in a sequence that can enable their understanding and learning. A marriage counselor is a facilitator, helping direct the attention of the couple to their root problems, or perhaps toward healing exercises, depending on their needs. In general, the role of a facilitator is to focus the attention of the group in a way that is effective for the job at hand.

When we accept a facilitator, we are implicitly agreeing to pay attention when she has something to say; we are agreeing to accept her comments as valid and relevant, just as we would the comments of a teacher in a class. When she then asks someone a question, she is implicitly passing the baton of relevance and validity to that person, and we may naturally shift our attention to that person's response, and are likely to *really hear*.

When we accept someone as a facilitator, we are granting to them the potential power to control, to a certain extent, the focus of our attention and that of the group. With that power, and with any kind of skill with people, it would be very easy for a facilitator to manipulate the dialog of the group in the direction of whatever agenda that facilitator might have in mind. I'm sure we've all had the experience of getting angry with a news panel moderator on TV, when he gives lots of attention to idiots on the panel, and ignores or interrupts those sensible panelists we would like to hear from. We can see that such a moderator is abusing the power he has over public attention. Similarly, when a city government holds 'public hearings,' many of us have had the experience of seeing the discussion railroaded toward whatever decision the city staff had already reached behind closed doors.

In the case of a harmonization session, it is important that the facilitator be trusted by the participants, and that she (or he) bring no agenda to the proceedings. Her role is to help the group learn how to function coherently, in the various ways that have been described throughout this chapter. The group itself is responsible for any agenda that might be adopted, and it is the participants, not the facilitator, that engage in problem solving and come up with creative solutions. Among the skills needed by a facilitator – apart from knowledge of her particular style of facilitation – is sensitivity to the energy of a group, and particularly of energy blockages. She doesn't really *direct* the attention of the group, rather she notices where the attention naturally wants to go – or where it needs to go to satisfy the group's deep needs – and helps it along by inviting it to shift in those productive directions.

Another important skill is a basic understanding of approaches to problem solving. This helps the facilitator notice standard blockages that occur in the problem-solving process, and makes it easier for her to ask appropriate questions, or to summarize contributions in appropriate diagrams, so as to help release those blockages.

A considerable amount of dedicated time is required for a group to reach its full potential, as a harmonizing, problem-solving 'community.' Two sessions can be very useful, but three or four would be closer to optimal. The extra sessions are very valuable because, as with most processes, once it gets warmed up and into high gear, that's when the most valuable outcomes are generated. In addition, the space in between sessions is important, as it gives participants a chance to reflect, both consciously and unconsciously, on what has been said.

At the same time, it is possible to get value out of a smaller-scale process. It is even possible to approach the space of harmonization without a facilitator. The simplest such process I know about is the 'talking circle' process. Some object, a stick or teddy bear or whatever, is designated as the 'talking stick,' or 'token.' The agreement is that whenever someone has the token, he is the speaker – everyone else is silent and pays attention. The speaker then has the space to say whatever's on his mind, at his own pace, without needing to rush so as to avoid being interrupted, as so often happens in normal conversation. When he has said his piece, and perhaps taken a breath or two, the token is passed around the circle to the next person. People find it easier to listen and really 'hear' when they know that eventually the token will get around to them, and they'll have their own special uninterrupted space in which to express themselves and be heard.

In this process, the token itself is functioning as facilitator, by quietly generating order and helping people focus their attention on what has heart and meaning, and what is emerging among them. In new groups using this method, this power of the token is generated largely by how it is framed at the beginning by the convener. Indigenous peoples using this kind of process have typically considered the token to be sacred. Others frame the token as empowering us to speak the truth from our hearts.

Focus itself is what enables a group to function coherently. The path the focus follows might seem a bit random – just as the path of our own internal thoughts is a bit random, as we ponder a problem in our heads. Whatever the path might be, the important thing is that the whole group be on that same path – reading from the same page at the same time, as much as possible. That is what focus is about, and that's why it is central to the role of facilitator, or talking stick, as the case may be.

The dynamics of harmonization

There are many different styles of facilitation that can enable a group to enter a state of harmonization. The primary role of the facilitator in all of these styles is to help focus attention, and to use that focus to help bring out the latent energy of the group. When people can hear one another, and accept each other's concerns as being everyone's concerns, then the door is opened, the space of harmonization is entered. All the energy that was tied up in roles and 'positions' is then released, like a weight lifted from the group's shoulder.

In the Michigan gathering, we saw a style of facilitation that gave each person a turn to express themselves in a way that revealed their humanity, and in this way a space of harmonization was reached in a very orderly fashion. In Dynamic Facilitation (DF), rather than giving people turns, the facilitator 'follows the energy' – whichever person seems most in need of expressing themselves becomes the focus of attention. Eventually everyone is 'revealed' to the group, but the process is less orderly. At least it *appears* to be less orderly, even chaotic. In fact, 'following the energy' is a kind of ordering principle in its own right, and DF seems to be particularly effective at releasing the 'deep energy' of a group, and enabling the group to find remarkable breakthrough-solutions to very difficult problems.

Entering the space of harmonization is only the beginning. It's as if everyone had been milling around the room, and now they have finally sat down at the table to begin the meeting in earnest. Only when people have accepted one another as respected fellow humans is it possible for a certain kind of dialog to begin. When the concerns of each are accepted as the concerns of all, then the creative energy of the entire group can focus on the same shared question: "How can we find solutions which take all of our concerns into account?" When the whole group's energy is synchronized in this way, a new level of creative energy becomes available, just as the synchronized waves of a laser have a level of energy not available to normal light waves.

Let me express this notion from another perspective. We have a group that is operating in the space of harmonization. They are together seeking a solution to a problem; let's say the problem is, "How can we make our neighborhood school more effective at teaching our kids?" As the process of problem solving unfolds, what moves it forward at each step are ideas and inspirations – the creativity of the problem solver. When you have a whole group of people all focusing on the same aspect of a problem, then you have many lifetimes of experience and insights all bearing on the process – the 'pool' from which ideas and inspirations can emerge is a rich one. And that's not all.

We've all heard the expression, "Two heads are better than one," and most of us have probably had experiences where a problem became much easier to handle when we had a colleague to bounce ideas around with, each idea sparking a related insight from the other. In our everyday styles of dialog, we cannot usually extend these dynamics to a larger group of people. If several people are hovering over the same problem, the appropriate expression usually becomes, "Too many cooks spoil the broth." But in a space of harmonization, where the group is focused, the "Two heads are better than one" principle can be effectively extended to many heads, and the boost in creativity that occurs can be exponential.

The key element in the dynamics here is 'bouncing ideas around.' There is one fellow I worked with over a period of many years, each of us migrating to the same companies, always wanting to be on the leading edge of technology. We often found ourselves solving problems together, and bouncing ideas around was always the process that gave us our creative solutions. The process was very chaotic, often jumping around in problem space as seemingly random insights popped out. Frequently the best ideas would emerge when one of us misunderstood the other! In trying to make sense of the misunderstood statement, an unexpected idea would emerge. Two heads were more than twice as good as one head; the whole was greater than the sum of its parts.

Ideas stimulate more ideas, and inspirations stimulate more inspirations. It's like sparks flying around the room. When there are 10 people involved, for example, and an idea is expressed, there are 9 different minds that might 'spark' off of that idea, rather than just one as when I was working with my colleague. To put it in systems terms: there is a multiplicative creative synergy that arises when a number of minds are focused in a coherent way on a shared problem.

Collective wisdom: an ancient heritage

This *creative synergy* operates on many levels. In the introductory exercises at the Michigan conference, where people were listening to each other share some of their decisive experiences, sparks were also flying around the room – as people recognized themselves in the stories of the speaker. It was 'bouncing recognition around' rather than 'bouncing ideas around,' but it was the same kind of synergy at work, with people learning from one another.

This same kind of synergy also operates at the level of wisdom. When a group of people are listening respectfully to one another's views, in a conversation about some shared problem, something more than creativity and intelligence can be enabled: it is possible for wisdom itself to manifest.

One aspect of this arises out of the nature of the dialog process itself. When people are listening respectfully to one another in a conversation, we can say that the group is being *self-reflective*. The group is behaving like a person who has taken time out to reflect on their experiences. It is in such moments of self-reflection that each of us is likely to experience those insights and inspirations that add up to whatever wisdom we are able to gather in life – and in such moments we are best able to manifest that accumulated wisdom. Similarly, for a group of people, an atmosphere of self-reflection is highly conducive to achieving wise insights, and to learning from whatever wisdom has been accumulated by the people in the group. In the space of harmonization, the thought process of the group is similar to the thought process of a contemplative mind.

Another aspect arises out of the 'multiplicative synergy' I mentioned above, only here we are referring to the synergy of shared wisdoms, rather then the synergy of shared problem-solving talents. As we saw in the Michigan conference, as the process continued over time, people dug deeper down into their core beliefs and feelings, like the layers of an onion peeling away. It is down in the cores of our minds that we exhibit wisdom, and are open to expanding its scope. And, perhaps you will agree, the language of their "We the People" declaration did indeed contain gems of wisdom – gems that surprised the participants.

It turns out that the kinds of processes we have been talking about are part of our primordial heritage as a species. In many indigenous societies – at varying stages of 'progress' and with various social structures – we often find traditional processes in which people listen respectfully, someone plays a facilitator role, and there is a conscious intention to tap into the wisdom of the group. In the indigenous Hawaiian culture, for example, there is a process called *h'o pono pono*. Here an elder simply listens to each person in turn, allowing others to 'overhear.' This continues until 'the right answer' (to the issue in question) becomes obvious to everyone.

In the Sioux Nation, a confederation of Plains Indian tribes, wisdom was considered a primary virtue, and the culture encouraged people to develop their wisdom through self-reliance, and by facing tests of various kinds in the different stages of life. A chief was chosen largely for his wisdom; his was not a position of power nor was it inherited. The stories and legends of the tribe were intended to pass on the wisdom of the tribe. When the Sioux gathered in council, whether in their local tribe or in a powwow of tribal delegations, they listened respectfully, and they sought to awaken their best wisdom in dealing with their affairs.

Harmonization is as old as humanity. It is a way of being that is in our blood and in our bones – and it is tied in with wisdom, and with self-governance. This primordial tradition was continued in our first civilizations, based on *partnership* cultures. Since 4400 BC the barbarians – the *dominators*, the *takers* – have been trying to condition our wisdom and empowerment out of us, to domesticate us to their hierarchical regimes. Divide-and-rule tactics are as old as recorded history, pitting classes and peoples against one another, beginning with gender domination – thereby subverting our potential for harmonization. Today, divide-and-rule has been turned into a science, with each of us compelled to compete in the scramble for the crumbs left over after the corporations and elites have dined.

But all these centuries of conditioning and suppression have not destroyed our souls, our inner natures. Our free spirits have never been conquered. We can see this in the face of every child, and we have seen it in the long struggle of working people to build unions, and to win the right to collective bargaining. In Chapter 3 we examined several examples, where our inborn spirit of freedom and self-determination expressed itself in social movements, and we were able to find our identity and empowerment as We the People. We have seen that almost any group of people, with a bit of help from a facilitator, is capable of rediscovering that which centuries of civilization have tried to erase.

The red pill that Neo took revealed a lot in a very short time: once his eyes were opened to reality, the whole Matrix disappeared all at once. Harmonization is a similar red pill that can enable us to escape from the Matrix of divisiveness and powerlessness. In the relatively short sessions we have examined, we have seen the spirit of We the People emerge, along with enthusiasm for the potential of harmonization to contribute to the transformation of our cultures.

Our potential for wisdom, our ability to harmonize our concerns, and our will to govern ourselves, have not been bred out of us. We are not cattle or sheep, even though our roles in civilization have often served similar functions. As Robert Heinlein put it, and I paraphrase, we are descended from willful apes, not regimented ants, and we should be proud of that. Hierarchical civilization has failed in its evil designs: we have never been fully domesticated to slave status.

We the People

"We the People" is a sleeping giant, lying in a slumber induced by the myths and conditioning that have been refined by millennia of elite rulers and religious patriarchs. For all their efforts, and their long success, their conditioning turns out to be only skin deep. The trance, despite its longevity, is a light one. Under the right conditions, the giant has been known to awaken, and his power has been mighty. Seemingly unassailable empires have crumbled in the blink of an eye.

Hierarchical civilization is now in the final stages of its evolution. It is hemorrhaging on its own dynamics of growth and exploitation. The Pentagon is embarked on an apocalyptic final campaign, seeking to enslave the whole world under a centralized global fascist regime, in control of all strategic resources – while American citizens are to be subject to arbitrary arrest and unlimited incarceration. If ever there was a time for the giant to awaken all over the world at once, that time is now.

6

Envisioning a transformational movement

If only people could see each other as agents of each other's happiness, they could occupy the earth, their common habitation, in peace, and move forward confidently together to their common goal. The prospect changes when they regard each other as obstacles; soon they have no choice left but to flee or be forever fighting. Humankind then seems nothing but a gigantic error of nature.
—Abbé Sieyès. Prelude to the Constitution, 1789, France

In search of a path to social transformation

Let's review our quest so far...

> Chapter 1 concluded with Civilization in crisis, and the thesis that our entire society needs to be radically changed, both economically and politically. We need to rid ourselves, somehow, of elite rule, and we need to establish, somehow, democratic, peaceful, and sustainable societies.

This left with us an implicit question: "If we want a different kind of society, what models do we have that might guide us?"

> Chapter 2 looked back into our origins, and found hopeful models in the Old Civilization of Europe, and the partnership cultures that characterized the earliest agricultural civilizations. These societies prove that it is possible to have a stable, peaceful, and complex society which is egalitarian and which is based on harmony among people and with nature. The path of hierarchy was the path we eventually followed as a global civilization, but it was not the only path available.

From this we know that people are capable of living in a partnership society just as they are capable of living in a dominator society; human nature is capable of cooperation as well as exploitation. Social transformation is not a hopeless quest. The question now is not whether a better society is possible, but rather how one might be created. We next need to face the question of how transformation might be accomplished.

> Chapter 3 began with the observation that the dominator culture itself is the source of current crisis. Domination can only be ended when the dominated decide to change things: We the people, in seeking our own liberation, will at the same time be transforming our dominator culture into a partnership culture. We need to understand what it means for We the People to wake up, and as first step in gaining that understanding we examined several social movements, current and historical, and I suggested some preliminary observations. One observation is that *capturing territory* is important to any transformational movement. Another observation is that electoral politics is a quagmire that any successful transformational movement must be wary of. If such a movement is to prevail, it will need to recruit nearly the whole population to its cause, as Gandhi's movement was able to do.

We now have the basic skeleton of a transformational project: We the People need to wake up and find our identity, and we need to build a social movement aimed at transforming our cultures and our societies; our movement must avoid the political quagmire and seek to bring everyone into the movement. In order to pursue such a project, we need to understand just how deep the transformation must go: we need to know which of our existing cultural paradigms must be abandoned, as being incompatible with a democratic and equitable society.

> Chapter 4 expanded on Chapter 3's preliminary conclusions, arguing the thesis that adversarial politics – the whole basis of representative "democracy" – is a system that by its inherent nature facilitates rule by elites; it is a modern version of *divide and rule*. In reality we live in a *plutocracy* – we are ruled by wealthy elites. Only in the Matrix does democracy exist. If we want real democracy, we must invent it. Our new culture must avoid the factions and interest groups that pit us one against the other; we need to create a culture that enables us to harmonize our various needs and concerns.

Harmonization, then, turns out to be the critical factor in both our movement and our new society. In order to bring everyone into the movement we need to learn how to harmonize everyone's concerns, and we also need to base our new society on harmonization if we want it to be democratic. In order to transform our societies, we need to transform our adversarial culture into a culture based on harmonization – which is the same as Eisler's "partnership culture," but expressed from the perspective of process rather than result. But how can we go about pursuing harmonization and partnership?

> Chapter 5 argued that our culture suffers from a certain deficiency: when we gather together for discussions or to make decisions, we don't know how to go about harmonizing the various concerns and interests of the participants. We either suppress our differences in order to reach a compromise consensus, or else factions compete to impose their views on the whole group. This deficiency channels us toward participation in the quagmire of adversarial politics. As a remedy, we looked at some examples of gatherings that overcame this cultural deficiency, and discovered the dynamics of harmonization. In the microcosm of a face-to-face gathering, it is possible to find our common ground and realize our identity as We the People. The necessary facilitation techniques are proven, and with their help almost any group of people can go through this kind of experience, which is in fact already latent deep in our psyches, part of our primordial heritage. Harmonization is able to bring out the creative synergy and the collective wisdom that lie latent in any group of people.

We can now see the beginning of a path to transformation: we know how to achieve harmonization in the microcosm of a face-to-face gathering. We next need to understand how we can use this knowledge to build an inclusive movement and to transform our cultures and societies. That is the objective of this chapter.

Harmonization and cultural transformation

Let us consider for a moment, from a general perspective, how cultural transformations typically take place. One common historical example of a cultural transformation would be the adoption of a new religion by a society. In this case there is some kind of conversion experience, or a *seeing the light* experience, that transmits the cultural transformation. It is an experience that transcends words; it is an experience that causes one to see things in a different way. That *different way of seeing* is the essence of the new culture. If the shift were not so profound, beyond easy verbalization, we wouldn't call it a cultural transformation; it would be no more than the spreading of a new idea or a new fashion.

Another example of cultural transformation occurred in the 1960s and 1970s, with the hippies, drugs, rock and roll, protests, the New Left, and massive popular movements. Clearly, compared to the fifties, this period brought on a major cultural transformation in our Western societies. And again, there were experiences, not easily explainable in words, which were at the heart of transmitting this transformation. Timothy Leary said, "Turn on, tune in, and drop out." He began with "turn on," which means "take psychedelic drugs" – an experience that can't be put into words, and an experience that introduces us to a *different way of seeing*. Getting high, expanding our sexual explorations, losing ourselves in tribal rock-and-roll paganism, taking to the streets in rebellious protest, doing everything our parents disapproved of – these were all experiences of a similar character, all somehow transmitting liberation from the barren fifties background culture.

By definition, a cultural transformation involves the propagation of a shift in worldview. And a shift in worldview is not something that occurs easily. It takes some kind of special experience, as we saw in the two examples above. It requires some kind of experience that takes us out of our standard mindset, into a territory we don't have words for, and enables us to see things in a way we didn't know was possible. Such an experience is necessary for cultural transformation; such an experience provides the energy that can propagate the transformation.

Harmonization, as exemplified in the sessions we have looked at, is that kind of *special experience*. It takes people out of their standard mindset, as regards social possibilities, and enables them to see those possibilities in a way that they didn't know was possible. Participants in such a session *see the light* as regards their own empowerment, and as regards the possibility of achieving mutual understanding and consensus with their peers. This is an experience that enables people to see social possibilities *in a new way* that didn't seem possible before – as was expressed explicitly in the declaration that the Michigan group came up with. And this is an experience that our current culture doesn't really have words for. In order to give a name to the experience, I found it necessary to pick a word, "harmonization," and give it an expanded definition. In order to describe the effect of the experience, participants chose a phrase that would have had little personal meaning for them prior to the experience: "We the People."

Imagine what it would be like if everyone were to undergo such a transformation of consciousness. What if everyone went through the experience of sitting down with others, some of whom were considered to be 'the enemy,' and glimpsed for themselves the *new vision*? What if everyone were to experience the empowerment and hope that comes with the spirit of We the People? What if everyone understood, at a deep level, that that divisiveness in society can be overcome, that We the People can harmonize our needs and concerns?

If everyone were to have this kind of experience, our culture itself would be transformed. Not only would this fill our 'cultural gap' as regards meetings, but also our cultural paradigms about competition and adversarial politics would be neutralized. Although our societal systems would remain unchanged, for a while at least, the culture that supports them would be gone. The elite's divide-and-rule strategy would be fatally undermined. No longer would we feel compelled to choose sides among political parties; no longer would we feel powerless and isolated as citizens. Our culture, beginning in the grassroots, would be transforming into the partnership category.

Harmonization is a transformational force. Spreading the harmonization experience is equivalent to transforming our cultures and our consciousness as individuals. Harmonization is the means by which We the People can wake up, find our identity, and undertake effective collective action.

Cultural transformation at the level of community

Consider the public meeting that followed the Wisdom Council session in Rogue Valley. The session participants were able to communicate their experience to the people who came to that meeting, and the whole meeting was characterized by a spirit of enthusiasm and empowerment. Let us consider how this kind of scenario might be further extended.

Instead of a single harmonization session, suppose that a *series* of sessions were to be organized in a community, each followed by an open public meeting – as envisioned by Jim as part of the Wisdom Council formula. Suppose further that the organizers of this series undertook to publicize the events, and the outcomes of the gatherings, to the wider community. If this were to happen, I suggest that a culture of harmonization would begin to take root and grow within the community.

As the number of 'graduates' (people who have participated in sessions) increases in the community, the time will come when nearly everyone in town knows someone, or is related to someone, who is a graduate. Each graduate, based on the transformation of consciousness that typically occurs, would act as a kind of informal 'evangelist' for the harmonization culture, able to provide first-hand answers to questions, and most likely willing to relate, with some enthusiasm, the session experience to others. In this way familiarity with the harmonization experience would spread on a word-of-mouth basis.

Each harmonization session brings together some microcosm of the community and its concerns. To the extent the various concerns of the community find voice within a session, we can expect the solutions and insights that come out of the session to find resonance in the larger community. As the results of each session are published locally, and people see those results as being relevant to their own concerns, we could expect interest to develop in the community regarding the series of sessions and public meetings.

Presumably the public meetings would grow larger over time, based on the interest generated, with people returning to subsequent meetings, and inviting their neighbors along. We could expect some continuity to develop, with certain issues rising to the fore as recognized community concerns. This might naturally add focus to subsequent harmonization sessions, so that the breakthroughs reached in sessions would become increasingly relevant to recognized community concerns.

A shared *sense of the community* and a sense of *community identity* would begin to emerge. The growing sense of empowerment in the community would be accompanied by a growing understanding of the culture that enables that empowerment: mutual respect and heartfelt dialog. Dialog would carry on informally in the community; the spirit of We the People would become palpable. The sleeping giant would be waking up on the scale of one community. The culture of the community would be transforming, not just for the duration of a single session, but on an ongoing, community-wide basis.

Such a project would not be a formidable undertaking. With a handful of local citizens sharing the work, and some modest fund raising for facilitators and meeting rooms, it would be possible to organize a series of sessions and publicize the results locally. Cultural transformation, on the scale of a single community, appears to be a quite doable project.

> Hope is a dimension of the soul...an orientation of the spirit, an orientation of the heart. It transcends the world that is immediately experienced and is anchored somewhere beyond its horizons. ...It is not the conviction that something will turn out well, but the certainty that something makes sense regardless of how it turns out.
> —Václav Havel, Conversation with Karel Hvízdala, 1986

Community empowerment as a transformational movement

As the sense of the community begins to converge around recognized shared concerns, to continue our scenario, community attention would naturally begin focusing on, "What can we do?" And in a community there are usually many things people can do, when they are acting out of mutual understanding and common purpose. People working together can deal with many problems on a self-help basis: they can give the local school a fresh coat of paint, create a community garden, establish a local currency or credit union, or set up a childcare co-op or a crime-watch network. There is also much that can be accomplished politically. Local officials have a self-interest motivation to listen to the petitions of citizens when those are enthusiastically backed by the general community.

When a whole community has achieved a harmonized sense of itself, as an aware We the People, they can simply choose a slate of candidates from among themselves and elect them, on an essentially unanimous basis, to all the local offices. The official political process, and the administration of the community, can thereby be brought into the space of harmonization. The policy decisions of the community would no longer be made behind closed doors, but would come from the people themselves, by means of harmonization. At the level of community, it is possible for We the People to govern ourselves on the basis of direct, participatory democracy. And we can do this within the current political system. In a local community it is possible for a subculture based on harmonization to be established – a transformed oasis of democratic empowerment embedded within the larger hierarchical society. Consider the following example, which occurred relatively recently in India.

> Four hundred years ago the village of Maliwada, India, was a thriving agricultural center, producing fruits, vegetables, and wines. In 1975, it had little water, no sanitation, few crops. Over 2,000 villagers barely eked out a subsistence living. Muslims and Hindus of many different castes lived with centuries of mutual distrust. The villagers knew about their prosperous past, but it seemed long gone and hopeless to recreate.
>
> The discussions began based on two questions: "What would it take to have prosperity exist again in this village? What can you do to make that happen?" Gradually, as ideas began to pour fourth, perspectives changed. Hindus and Muslims talked together excitedly about how to clean out the ancient well. Brahmins and Untouchables discovered in a joint meeting that all despaired at the lack of medical care for their sick children. They all wanted to create a health clinic in the village. Hope began to creep into their voices and eyes. What had seemed totally impossible suddenly became doable. People organized and tapped resources they had forgotten they had.
>
> They acquired loans from a bank and received government grants. They built a dam, a brick factory, and the clinic. The shared vision of what they wanted for themselves and their community allowed them to go beyond their personal and cultural differences and continued to motivate them. Each success made them stronger, more confident, more self-assured. Today, Maliwada is a prospering village.
>
> When transformation like this takes place, the news travels. Nearby villagers wanted to know how they could do this... (Tuecke, 307).

Based on the enthusiasm generated, the emergence of a few empowered communities might be expected to lead to a chain reaction in the larger society. As in the above example from India, other communities would be impressed by the developments in the transformed communities, and local activists and concerned citizens would be likely to want to try it for themselves. Just as group empowerment can become contagious in a community, so can community empowerment become contagious in the larger society. If this begins to happen, even on a relatively small scale, we would be witnessing the emergence of a *community-empowerment movement* – a movement engaged in spreading a cultural transformation.

This would be a somewhat unusual movement, in that it wouldn't have leaders or central organization. It would be a truly grassroots movement, inspired and guided by local initiative, propagated by grassroots enthusiasm, and focused on democratic empowerment.

In a society suffering under economic decline, an unpopular war, the deterioration of its political system, and many other ills, any ray of hope for democratic empowerment would be likely to generate considerable enthusiasm. The chain reaction could be powerful. Indeed, I strongly suspect that it would be powerful; I could feel the strength of the potential energy when I saw the faces and heard the voices in the Rogue Valley videos.

The movement would be particularly unusual in that it would not be characterized by any particular program or platform. The movement would not be about rallying people behind noble causes, such as world peace or justice, rather it would be about communities discovering their own democratic empowerment. Any particular policy platform would in fact limit the propagation of the movement. Given a platform of policies, there are always some factions, which for one reason or another, do not subscribe to the platform. In that way platforms, no matter how noble, are ultimately divisive, and usually give rise to opposition movements. In the case of our community-empowerment movement, the only 'faction' that could be expected to oppose it would be established elites, who would see it as a potential threat to their own continued power and privilege.

Let us now consider how various kinds of activists would be likely to respond to the emergence of such a movement. There are many activist groups already focusing on community empowerment, working with various constituencies, and pursuing various agendas. There are also many activist groups who would like nothing better than to find more effective directions for activism. If our community-empowerment movement began to gain a bit of momentum, I think it would be noticed by activists, and I imagine many of them would see it as a useful direction for their own energies.

There are many ways that activist energy could accelerate the growth of the movement. Activists could organize sessions in their own communities, and they could get themselves trained as facilitators so that they can support their community and others in the harmonization process. As citizens, they can participate in the dialog process in their own communities, contributing their visions of community empowerment and social reform. As activists, they could use their networks to spread awareness of the movement, and they could help organize networking and conferences among emerging empowered communities.

The focus on community gives the movement a territorial quality, and a self-help quality, both of which characterized the very successful Populist Movement. We can take that as an encouraging and relevant precedent for this phase of the transformational process. Indeed, I think we could expect a harmonization-based, community-empowerment movement to develop in a way similar to the Populists. As the movement spreads, local governments would be brought into the harmonization process, would become agents of democratic agendas, as they rightfully should be in a democracy. The Populists got even to the point where they elected governors of several states. Once a chain reaction gets started, and once that energy begins to synergize with existing activist energy, I suggest we could expect similar results.

What are the prospects for such a movement?

What I have been presenting, in this material, is my own best estimation of what could be expected if we combine the Wisdom Council vision with a focus on community empowerment. I showed you what happened in Michigan, and at the *Maclean's* event, and in Rogue Valley. I cited the community-empowerment experience in India, which is typical of many others throughout the third world, e.g., in Brazil, Argentina, and Venezuela.

What I have suggested, if you look back over this chapter, is that a simple series of harmonization sessions, organized in a few communities, would be likely to start a chain reaction that could end up transforming cultures all over the globe! How could it be possible for so much energy, so much democratic liberation – to be released by so little effort? What could be the driving force behind such a chain reaction?

I believe that we can find the source of that energy by considering the social *separateness* that characterizes modern society. Separateness is multi-faceted: it encompasses the factionalism of our political system, the divisiveness of our ideological and religious beliefs, the psychological sense of isolation that many of us feel as individuals, the absence of a sense of community, and the over-emphasis that our society puts on individualism and competition.

It is not a sign of good health to be well adjusted to a sick society.
—J. Krishnamurti (1895-1986)

The cumulative effect of *separateness*, in all these various manifestations, is extremely disempowering. In a harmonization session the heavy burden of separateness is lifted, and we can understand why this would release liberating energy and a feeling of enthusiasm – as was reflected in the sessions we have looked at. But still, we must ask ourselves why that liberating energy has so much power – why it can be expected to spark a global chain reaction. I believe that we can find the source of that power by taking into account human nature.

Humanity – based on everything we've learned from anthropology, archeology, biology, genetics, ethnology, psychology, sociology – and every other relevant science – is a *social species*. For countless thousands of years we lived in cooperative communities (bands), where we knew we *belonged*, where we shared a common worldview, and where we depended on one another for our survival. We are attuned to body language; our faces are transmitters of emotional energy; we like to hug, and we seek lasting friendships. We like to be part of a group – be it in a church or a social circle – and we care about what people in our group think of us. This is our nature, and we can see it spontaneously expressed whenever children play together.

For such as us, *separateness* is like being in prison. We experience it as stress, and perhaps we blame that on ourselves, increasing our stress further. We seek release from this unnatural isolation by pursuing the perfect relationship, or by making ourselves more attractive (via hair coloring, breast implants, or the right car and after-shave lotion) so that we'll be accepted socially. We use our church, our club, or our place of work, to find a source of community. These things help, at a personal level, but we are still left with the larger divisiveness of our society. Overall, we don't feel that we are part of a supportive culture – and a psychologically supportive culture is the primary characteristic of every social species. We are fish out of water, thrashing about and gasping for life – all due to *separateness*.

From this perspective, we can understand why so much energy is released when separateness is overcome. In a harmonization session participants are able to bond together as We the People: they escape temporarily from their sense of separateness; their spirits are nourished by the support and acceptance of a temporary community; they glimpse a 'new vision' of how people can be in tune with one another; they escape from the cave of separateness and see the sunlight of democratic liberation for the first time; they awaken within themselves a primordial species instinct for cooperation and community, an instinct which dominator societies have long strived to extinguish.

When we were slaves in chains, we were allowed to sing our native songs in the slave camps, maintain our sense of community, and dream of freedom – but all the time our shackles, so to speak, remained fastened. When later we were serfs and royal subjects, our class consciousness was acknowledged, and garrisons were always on the ready to keep us in our place, should a peasant revolt arise – as they often did. Under 'democracy' our shackles are gone and the overt garrisons have disappeared. It is now only *separateness* that keeps us down – and the fact that we have forgotten what freedom feels like.

Imagine that all your life you have dragged around a weight, chained to your ankle. You have never been able to run, jump, swim, or ride a bike. You cannot keep up with your friends or your colleagues. Imagine, then, that one day you are released from your shackles. Imagine how liberated you would feel, how light on your feet, how full of energy and hope for a new and fuller life. That energy has been coiled up during a lifetime of disadvantage and resignation, and it springs forth all at once with great force. Release from separateness, in all its dimensions, is like that. We have carried all of our lives the stressful burden of isolation as powerless individuals, and our ancestors have carried that burden for millennia. It is the burden of domestication, the burden of domination. When we are released from this burden, the pent-up energy of our long-suppressed liberation uncoils all at once, with great force, inspiring us to enthusiastically declare our liberation, as 'We the People.'

This is where the immense energy comes from that can drive a chain reaction, propagate a community-empowerment movement, and thereby bring about a cultural transformation in our societies. It is the energy of a powerful sleeping giant, awakening from long slumber, and eager to claim his rightful heritage.

> What is inconceivable in normal times is possible in revolutionary times; and if at this time the opportunity is missed and what is possible in such great hours is not carried out – a whole world is lost.
> —David Ben-Gurion

Political transformation and regime intervention

Because of the focus on community empowerment, which brings a territorial quality to the movement, we can expect that political transformation will follow in the wake of cultural transformation. As the territory of the movement grows and consolidates, levels of elected government will be gradually integrated into the movement culture, as occurred with the Populists. The political system, the planning process, the policy initiatives, the trade-offs, the budgeting, the implementation strategies – these will all be grounded in an inclusive democratic process within movement territory. The new, democratic society will be creating itself within the shell of the dominator society, like a butterfly developing in a cocoon.

If a movement chain-reaction begins to develop, as I have suggested, then we must expect, sooner or later, a hostile reaction from established elites, backed up by the resources of national government and mass media. Our beautiful butterfly represents a dangerous threat to their power. The more territory that can be captured, and the more momentum that can be generated – prior to evoking some kind of suppressive response – the more likely that the movement will be able to continue growing despite opposition. The struggle will test the power of the waking giant against the suppressive authority of the dominator society. It will test the strength of a people waking up to liberation against the power of the state, a power which depends on obedience from civil servants and military personnel – who themselves are likely to resonate with the emerging spirit of liberation.

Such a scenario is not entirely unfavorable to a robust democratic movement, despite the apparently limitless power of the modern, centralized, state. We need only recall the unexpected fall of the mighty Soviet Union, and the relatively peaceful regime changes in Eastern Europe, to see how powerful a people can be when it feels its own strength as an awakened We the People. Such strength comes not from armed struggle or sabotage, nor does it come from mass demonstrations or confrontations with police. It comes rather from the inner strength of a people united in their determination to achieve their liberation. It is a patient strength, reflecting a deep confidence that We the People will ultimately determine our own destiny.

Those who are at the top of our dominator hierarchies are very savvy people. I'm not referring here to the figure-head political leaders, but rather to those behind the scenes who pull the levers of power, and who employ think tanks and consultants to plan out strategies (e.g., the neocons' PNAC agenda) – and to research all foreseeable scenarios. The management of public opinion, and the orchestrating of media spin and media story lines, are the front-line mechanisms of elite domination. Focus groups are used frequently and regularly in support of this critically important opinion-management process, ensuring that media managers stay in close touch with the various segments of public opinion – the various *propaganda markets*.

Given such a sophisticated early warning system, we can anticipate that any movement with 'dangerous' characteristics would raise alarm bells on elite radar screens sooner rather than later. These alarms, presumably, would be relayed to those consultants that specialize in tracking activist groups, and in finding ways to deal with perceived troublemakers, such as anti-globalization protesters and environmental activists. These consultants are experts in social movements, and they are well aware of the various ways in which movements propagate. By the time our movement begins to achieve any real momentum, these consultants would be blind not to realize that action will be required, to quash this highly contagious democratic virus before it becomes an unstoppable epidemic.

At the same time, however, these are very busy people and they aren't going to jump every time they see a stray blip. They see themselves as masters of the universe, in some sense, given the ongoing success of their propaganda regime. They probably laugh every time they see yet another bold manifesto posted to the Internet, yet another enthusiastic movement send out a hopeful call to action, or yet another book appear about social transformation. And it's been more than a century since a movement as troublesome as the Populists has come along. With considerable justification, they are complacent in their management role. I believe that we can assume our movement will be able to develop a bit of momentum before the opinion-management hierarchy begins to give us any serious attention.

Meanwhile, if the movement is building momentum and generating enthusiasm for democratic empowerment, it will show up on many other people's radar as well. In fact, the alarm bell that would be most likely to arouse Big Brother's attention would be a surge of popular interest in the progress and nature of the movement. Big Brother will pay attention because we are paying attention. We will have a head start. By the time Big Brother smells a virus, the movement will have generated enough momentum to attract the attention of all sorts of activist and community-oriented groups. A de facto race will be underway between the chain-reaction progress of the movement, and the response mechanisms available to Big Brother.

I'm reminded here of a classic science fiction story: Galactic Command Headquarters detects a small invading armada, and sends out a battle cruiser to intercept it. The armada proves stronger than expected, and repels the cruiser. Annoyed, the commanders send out three more cruisers, still a relatively minor force, confident of stopping the armada on the second try. The armada just barely prevails again, and by this time it is too close to Command Headquarters to be stopped – it has broken through the shields! Too little defense, too late, due to the complacency of the powerful: the Galactic Empire is lost to a small armada. This could very well turn out to be the victory scenario of our movement, in a figurative sense.

The problem, in trying to defend against our democratic movement, is that there is no particularly appropriate time to intervene, and no particularly effective means of intervention. With no leadership group, there are no leaders to harass or arrest. As the movement is not associated with any faction or platform, there is no easy target to demonize in the media, no bad guy, no evil race or doctrine. Besides, in the early stages, the movement would be of little perceived consequence: the main activity will be nothing more than community meetings, and these will not be associated with political activism or confrontation. Why would anyone feel threatened? Certainly no one felt threatened by the Rogue Valley Wisdom Council, or any of the other sessions we have examined.

Only after several communities have become involved, after some local governments have been brought into the fold, and after a palpable sense of *movement* is in the air – only then would it make much sense to assign an undercover team to take a closer look. And by then, lots of other people would be taking a look as well. If the movement unfolds in the way I believe it will, it would presumably be seen as a very exciting development by activists and concerned citizens everywhere.

Because of the Internet, with all of its interlinked distribution channels, our chain reaction could go global in a very short time, if it caught people's imaginations in the right way. Fertile ground for community empowerment can be found in every part of the world. And any community anywhere, which embarks on the path of harmonization, becomes an independent center of movement propagation. The pattern of propagation would resemble that of crabgrass, or kudzu, and would be nearly impossible to contain – particularly if seeds have been scattered to the four winds.

Let's consider some of the early counter-measures that the regime might conceivably deploy. Surveillance and infiltration by spies and provocateurs are very common tactics used against movements of all kinds throughout the world. But a harmonization-based movement is relatively immune to such tactics. The movement has nothing to hide as regards its activities, and harmonization sessions are characterized by too much good sense to allow themselves to be sabotaged by a provocateur pushing some counter-productive agenda. More drastic measures, such as arresting organizers or banning meetings among citizens, are unlikely to be undertaken at any early stage. That would be a strategic error on the establishment's part, as it would only bring attention to the movement and generate support for it.

There are other counter-measures that might be deployed, but the one I believe is most likely would be a demonization campaign launched over various media and propaganda channels – a counter-attack within the Matrix. Religious conservatives would be warned, from pulpits and by radio pundits, that harmonization is a *cult movement*, and that it seeks its wisdom not exclusively from the Word of God: good Christians should stay away. To the libertarian-minded would come the warning, from radio chat jocks and online bulletin boards, that harmonization is *communistic* and that it submerges the individual in the collective: stay away and don't risk being brainwashed. Liberals would read in the Op-Ed pages that harmonization is *undemocratic* and that it would lead to one-party tyranny. They would learn that it's hip to dismiss harmonization, in the same way that it's hip to scoff at 'conspiracy theories'.

If the general population adopts a variety of strong negative attitudes toward harmonization, that might stifle or even destroy the early movement. But if the movement can build sufficient momentum in the meantime, and establish sufficient roots, it should be able to hold its ground and respond effectively to such an attack. We can take some comfort from the fact that a demonization campaign would make little sense until after the movement has made noticeable progress; indeed, a premature campaign would contribute unearned notoriety to the movement, and hence would be counter-productive.

The movement would have no incentive to cause any kind of trouble for the regime – until the time came when such initiatives could be effective. Before that time the threat to the regime would exist only in potential, and conflict would be most likely to arise due to preemptive attacks from the establishment, not all of which can be anticipated in advance. We can only trust in our collective wisdom to deal with such challenges as they arise.

Eventually, as we overcome the intermediate obstacles, most of our society will be part of the new culture, and we will have developed a coherent vision of a transformed society. Only then does it make sense to initiate decisive engagement with the regime. One form of engagement could be general strikes; everyone stays home and the system stops operating. Perhaps military units overseas refuse to engage in actions as part of the strike, and police might join in as well. This is similar to how Soviet-era regimes were brought down in Eastern Europe. Eventually elites will realize they no longer have control. They can then either run and hide or they can express a willingness to 'negotiate.' At that point we can invite them to join the rest of us in creative dialog.

Social transformation

Somewhere in this unfolding process, we can be sure that the movement will wake up to the fact that its inherent mission is the total transformation of society. This was not the mission of the Rogue Valley Wisdom Council, nor would I expect it to be the mission of early harmonization events in a fledgling movement. The natural and appropriate focus at the beginning, as in the Rogue Valley, will be on overcoming divisiveness in communities, and seeking solutions to community problems. But as a culture of harmonization spreads, and people become familiar with it on a daily basis, they will become increasing unwilling to accept being controlled by remote dominator institutions, a state of affairs that will increasingly be perceived as being dysfunctional, uncivilized, antiquated, unnecessary – and as being the source of the major problems in our society.

The movement will realize, at some point, that it represents the leading edge of cultural transformation – and that this transformation itself is the movement's most important outcome. As the movement grows larger, and is able to maintain its coherence via networking and inter-community harmonization, people will begin to realize, based on their own experience, that large social projects do not need to be based on centralization and hierarchy. The development of the movement itself will point the way to those organizational forms that are suitable to a democratic society.

Rather than a centralized movement leadership deciding policy for 'the good of the movement,' people will learn in this movement that policies can come from the grassroots, that good ideas and breakthroughs can be rapidly and voluntarily adopted by other communities, and can become part of the movement's 'collective understanding.' Only with the help of harmonization can a movement be both coherent and grassroots based. Without harmonization, a movement must be either disorganized or centrally led.

I imagine that the 'movement structure' would naturally evolve toward a tiered arrangement of temporary councils, where communities send delegates to regional councils, regions send delegates to national councils, and so on up to global councils – with harmonization being used at all levels. Although this may superficially resemble the hierarchical pyramids of our current representative governments, power would flow in the reverse direction, and there would be no permanent decision-making bodies. After a council meets, it disbands and the delegates go back to the communities and their regular activities.

Each delegation to a council would come in with the consensus perspective that has evolved in its own community, and the delegation would not be empowered to reach agreements outside the boundaries of that consensus. If there seem to be conflicts among these incoming perspectives, those conflicts would be addressed as shared problems in the council sessions. Perhaps breakthroughs could be found in the council, overcoming the apparent conflicts, or perhaps delegates would go back home better informed about the concerns of other communities. Each community could then re-examine its thinking in the light of that new understanding. Harmonization would proceed, converging toward overall movement coherence, while power, in terms of movement decision-making, would remain based in the grassroots, in the individual communities.

> It's a wonder I haven't abandoned all my ideals, they seem so absurd and impractical. Yet I cling to them because I still believe, in spite of everything, that people are truly good at heart.
>
> It's utterly impossible for me to build my life on a foundation of chaos, suffering and death. I see the world being slowly transformed into a wilderness, I hear the approaching thunder that, one day, will destroy us too, I feel the suffering of millions. And yet, when I look up at the sky, I somehow feel that everything will change for the better, that this cruelty too shall end, that peace and tranquility will return once more.
>
> —Anne Frank, *Diary*, July 15, 1944

Transformation: the means are the ends

There have been many major revolutionary victories in history, but none has succeeded in escaping from hierarchy and elite rule. There are many reasons for this, which we could analyze from many perspectives. I'd like to offer one particular perspective, because I think it gets down to the root of the problem. I suggest that every 'successful' revolution has been based on this sequential model:

> 1. Achieve victory
>
> 2. Create new political arrangements
>
> 3. Transform culture

This model seems to make a great deal of sense. If we want our new society to be of the *partnership* variety, for example, we certainly need to change our political arrangements first. Right? And before we can do that, we must have the power to do so, which means we need to achieve victory. How could there be any other way? Yet, sensible and inevitable as the model may appear to be, it has consistently failed to deliver the goods.

The flaw in the model, I suggest, arises from we might call 'cultural momentum.' If victory is achieved within the dominator paradigm, and if the new political arrangements are designed by people still embedded in that paradigm, then the old political arrangements are likely to be re-invented – albeit under optimistic new labels (e.g., *democracy* or *peoples' republic*). The dominator culture served to support the old dominator systems, and from that cultural perspective we can expect similar systems to emerge again.

We could also look at the flaw this way: if you've never lived in a democratic society, then you are unlikely to understand the dynamics of such a society, and hence you are unlikely to know what political arrangements might support those dynamics.

Finally, we could look at the flaw in terms of *means and ends*. The old question – *Do the ends justify the means?* – refers to the compromises, the outrages, that have sometimes been committed in the pursuit of a 'glorious revolution.' The choice of reprehensible means arises naturally out of the old, dominator culture. The culture of the revolutionary movement itself becomes a dominator culture. What could we expect from such a movement other than a new dominator society? The truth is that *the means always become the ends.*

Our own transformational movement, based on harmonization and community empowerment, reverses the traditional sequence. It follows this model:

> 1. Transform culture
>
> 2. Create new political arrangements
>
> 3. Achieve victory

Harmonization is the appropriate culture for a partnership society, and the primary activity of the movement is the spreading of the new culture from community to community. Each community retains its autonomy within the movement and operates internally on a harmonized, inclusive, democratic basis. As empowered communities learn to work together, harmonizing their concerns and activities as they network with one another, they are creating the political arrangements that are appropriate to a democratic and equitable society. When victory comes, the new culture and political arrangements are already largely in place. Cultural momentum is on our side; we have already lived in the new culture; the means were the same as the ends from the very beginning.

7

Envisioning a liberated global society

To the size of states there is a limit, as there is to other things, plants, animals, implements; for none of these retain their natural power when they are too large or too small, but they either wholly lose their nature, or are spoiled.

—Aristotle, *Politics*

The basic paradigm: harmonization and community sovereignty

A culture based on harmonization is the primary enabling factor for a transformed global society. Humanity's yearnings for the 'brotherhood of man,' and 'turning swords into ploughshares' are as old as civilization. The new piece in our story is the knowledge that harmonization is *achievable*. We know for sure that harmonization is achievable in face-to-face groups, and by the time you are reading this I hope we are beginning to see it in a larger and ongoing context – in an awakening community. If we succeed in transforming our cultures, building a grassroots movement, and overcoming the elite regime, we have the foundation on which to build a democratic, equitable, and sensible society.

In such a culture, the standard way of resolving disputes and deciding social policy will be by harmonization – why would we use anything else, once we have experienced the benefits? Whatever political arrangements we might set up, the official deliberations and decision-making meetings will use harmonization as their process. The 'good of all' will not be just a hollow slogan, but will be the outcome everyone will seek, because they have learned from experience that they too get the best result that way.

With harmonization as our process, let us move on then to consider what kind of political arrangements would be supportive of a democratic society. I argued in the previous chapter that the empowered community is the appropriate focus for a harmonization-oriented movement. I now suggest that the community is the appropriate unit of primary sovereignty in a democratic society, within a culture of harmonization. The fundamental unit of the movement becomes the fundamental unit of the new society. There are four basic considerations that lead me to this perspective:

Scale and proximity. A community is the right size for democracy to function effectively. In a larger unit the day-to-day interactions, and the sense of face-to-face involvement, are lost. It becomes impossible for everyone to have their say, to feel part of the public conversation; decision-making becomes indirect and remote. At the same time a smaller unit makes little sense because a community has a natural coherence as an entity, otherwise we wouldn't call it a 'community.' As Goldilocks would put it, a community is, 'not too big, not too small, but *just right*.' (In the case of a large city, the equivalent of community would be a neighborhood or borough, based on some kind of agreed boundary lines.)

Commonality of interests. The people in a community tend to have many concerns in common, concerns which are of little interest to people outside the community. Things like parking, traffic, parks, schools, crime, public services – indeed local quality of life generally – concern everyone in the community. This commonality of interests is recognized in most of our societies, where the township or village is typically an official unit of government jurisdiction.

Coherence and efficiency. Feedback loops in a community, if it is operating democratically, are immediate and transparent. If agreed policies are not leading to anticipated results, people can get together, take into account the new information, and develop a new harmonized response. A community is 'just the right size' not only for democracy, but also for the optimization of operations.

Primordial social heritage. We evolved over millions of years in cooperative social groups, where people interacted on a daily basis. We even adapted agriculture and animal husbandry, and established our first civilizations, while still retaining our essential social heritage in *partnership* societies. Only for the past six thousand years have we been subjected to dominator societies. I'm not sure how it is for those at the top, but most of us are being forced to live in a culture that is contrary to our natures. That is why we suffer so much stress, and that is what Freud was talking about in *Civilization and its Discontents*. In a community, with harmonization, it is possible for us to recreate something akin to the social milieu that is 'home' for us as a species. The community, I suggest, is where we can recreate our primordial Garden.

Genuine democracy (inclusive, direct, and participatory) is possible in a community. And it is possible without delegating decision-making power to any centralized mayor or elected council. The people themselves can decide fundamental policy issues; that is what their harmonizing is about. Agencies can be created to manage civic programs, but such agencies have no authority to set or change policy, and they can be disbanded or reorganized if they are not serving the purpose for which they were established. We the People can run our own communities ourselves. With the creative synergy of the whole community awakened, we can expect to handle our affairs wisely, and in the best long-term interest of our communities (i.e., ourselves and our children). Sustainability is simply a matter of common sense.

> I believe that all government is evil, and that trying to improve it is largely
> a waste of time.
> —H.L. Mencken

If the community is to be the unit of sovereignty, we are left then with the question of how larger-scale issues are to be handled. In discussing the movement, recall the suggestion I offered regarding its likely structure:

> I imagine that the 'movement structure' would naturally evolve toward a tiered arrangement of temporary councils, where communities send delegates to regional councils, regions send delegates to national councils, and so on up to global councils – with harmonization being used at all levels. Although this may superficially resemble the hierarchical pyramids of our current representative governments, power would flow in the reverse direction, and there would be no permanent decision-making bodies. After a council meets, it disbands and the delegates go back to the communities and their regular activities.

> Each delegation to a council would come in with the consensus perspective that has evolved in its own community, and the delegation would not be empowered to reach agreements outside the boundaries of that consensus. If there seem to be conflicts among these incoming perspectives, those conflicts would be addressed as shared problems in the council sessions. Perhaps breakthroughs could be found in the council, overcoming the apparent conflicts, or perhaps delegates would go back home better informed about the concerns of other communities. Each community could then re-examine its thinking in the light of that new understanding. Harmonization would proceed, converging toward overall movement coherence, while power, in terms of movement decision-making, would remain based in the grassroots, in the individual communities.

Again, I suggest that the structure of the movement becomes the structure of the new society: the means are the appropriate ends. The community is the unit of political sovereignty, and the larger affairs of society, and the world, are dealt with through dialog among communities, by means of appropriate council sessions, harmonizing the concerns of the communities.

That is the basic paradigm that I envision, as the basis of liberated, democratic society. I believe that this paradigm emerges naturally out of the dynamics of harmonization, and it is from considering those dynamics that I have been led to these ideas. The community has always been a natural unit of society, and empowered by harmonization the community has the ability to run its own affairs sensibly and democratically. Why should it not be allowed to do so? In a culture of harmonization, it seems to me that this is how people would naturally view the situation. And similarly, when larger issues arise in such a culture, the natural thing would be for each affected constituency to send off a delegation to harmonize its concerns with sister delegations.

I believe this paradigm makes sense. It makes sense in terms of 'likely to be achieved' because it arises naturally out of the dynamics of harmonization, in combination with our human habit of living in communities. It makes sense in terms of 'is functional' because it puts political responsibility at the local level, where feedback loops are shortest, where the welfare of the people involved can be under their own control, and where a direct democratic process is practically achievable.

But even if it makes sense, as a basic paradigm, there are still many questions to be addressed. How is peace to be maintained?

How can the global commons be managed? Who controls globally scarce resources? How do we manage large infrastructures, such a transport and communications? How do we prevent the emergence of new hierarchies, which would be taken over eventually by new elites? The rest of this chapter will be looking into these kinds of questions. Our guiding principle will be to keep in mind what it would be like to live in a culture of harmonization, and to imagine how we would naturally deal with the various kinds of challenges that are likely to arise.

Regional affairs

Let's start with the simplest problem, extending organization beyond the community, but not too far. Let's use 'region' to refer to the next level up from 'community.' A region might be the same as a county, province, or bioregion, depending on the local situation. It seems natural to expect that the communities in a region would regularly convene regional council sessions to harmonize regional affairs. Just as in a community, the citizens of a region have many concerns in common that are of lesser interest to people outside the region. A region is basically a community of communities, and by means of regular council sessions, regions will be able to manage their affairs harmoniously and sensibly. We could expect "We the People of our region" to be an element of our personal identities, along with "We the People of our community."

In fact, a region is an important political unit in its own right. The region is the natural unit to develop transport systems, utilities, and other infrastructures, and to manage waterways and other shared resources. In terms of 'optimization of operations,' a region is perhaps more central than a community. We would expect there to be a coherence and continuity to regional affairs, just as there is in today's counties and provinces. Presumably there would be various regional agencies with the responsibility of managing the various regional operations.

What I am describing here is very much the same as how our current societies are organized, and how societies have been organized throughout history: it's basically just towns within counties. The dynamics of this familiar arrangement are transformed, however, in a culture of harmonization. In today's hierarchical societies, centralized agencies are given the power to override local wishes, in the interest of 'efficiency' and the 'larger public interest.' Communities are often destroyed in the process. In a culture of harmonization, decisions will be made in quite a different way.

It seems to me that the natural role of an agency will be one of facilitation. Let me illustrate this with an example. Suppose an agency is charged with the responsibility of establishing a regional rail network. In a culture of harmonization, the first task of the agency would naturally be to meet with each of the communities, to find out their concerns as regards rail transport. Presumably a delegation from the agency would meet with a diverse gathering of local citizens, in an effort to harmonize the objectives of the agency with the concerns of the community. As the delegation visits each community in turn, listening respectfully to local concerns, it is acting as a kind of 'roving facilitator.'

Each harmonization session would not only raise local concerns, but would also give people a chance to offer their ideas about how those concerns might be addressed. Creative breakthroughs could be expected. As the delegation makes its rounds, it will become gradually wiser about how rail can best fit into the region's operations. By the time the delegation gets back to base it will be in a position to draft a regional plan that communities can then review and refine. Not only would such a process be likely to develop creative, appropriate-technology solutions, and fit in with community preferences, but also the planning process would probably go more quickly than it does with the bureaucratic, top-heavy agencies that our societies employ today.

Now let's consider the actual building of the rail network. We all know the hierarchical approach: a crew is assembled, and they march through the region implementing a one-size-fits-all system, according to their own schedule, often disrupting local operations in the process. In a culture of harmonization and empowered communities we can expect more ongoing participation by the communities, acting perhaps through their own local agencies. In some cases it might make sense for each community to take responsibility for its own section of track, so to speak. This would enable construction to go on in parallel, expediting the project. It would also give communities an opportunity to blend their section of the project into the local environment and architectural style. The regional agency would continue to facilitate among the concerns of the communities, and would be responsible for checking that all parts of the project match up to agreed quality standards.

When responsibility begins in the grassroots, a tremendous amount of creative energy becomes available, in contrast to a hierarchical society. Centralized agencies are always bottlenecks. They have a certain budget, and they schedule their projects in some priority order. It seems to take forever from the time a project is conceived until anything really happens. When the tax money that goes to various levels of government is instead retained locally, the community or region has the resources to initiate its own local projects, and manage its part of larger projects, most likely on a more efficient basis. There will be more parallelism in the affairs of society generally, with different creative initiatives rising up in different localities. Democracy liberates popular energy and creativity.

A model for global self-governance

I suggest that the regional scenario provides us with a democratic model that applies to larger-scale affairs as well.

Policy setting is always the province of harmonization sessions, involving councils of delegations from all constituencies that are stakeholders regarding the policies under question. The number of levels of councils depends on the scale involved. If there are many levels, as with global councils, the process may need to iterate, so as to enable harmonization across such a large number of communities. In this way every community participates in the decision-making process regarding society-wide policy, all the way up to global policies.

Once policy is decided, it is necessary to manage the mandated projects and operations, and such activities must be managed on a coherent basis. An agency can be established for that purpose, and it must be able to respond quickly and effectively to unexpected problems, without waiting for a general council to be assembled. The 'agency as facilitator' provides us with a mechanism that can provide that kind of management function without introducing centralized authority.

Because policies that come out of a harmonization process have received the support of all the involved constituencies, cooperation can be expected throughout the affected areas in the implementation of the policy. The agency will begin with this pre-existing consensus on policy, and will then work with the constituencies to maintain harmonization throughout the planning, implementation, and operational phases of a mandated project.

By roving among constituencies, meeting with stakeholder groups, and always using harmonization, the agency can maintain an overall sense of harmony regarding the project and ensure the necessary project coherence. If an unexpected problem arises, that is a shared problem for everyone involved. The role of the agency is then to facilitate a focused dialog among the affected constituencies, so that a harmonious solution can be found to the problem.

In a face-to-face session, the facilitator's role is to ensure that sufficient attention is paid to what participants say. In a large-scale project, the agency's role is to ensure that sufficient attention is paid to the needs of the project. Just as participants in a session may be distracted by their own internal mental chatter, so the constituencies involved in a project have other responsibilities on their minds. Both the facilitator and the agency strive to bring about the necessary focus of attention so as to enable a collective activity to proceed successfully. The facilitator brings no agenda to a session; the agency brings no agenda to a project. In the two cases the role of the facilitator and the agency is to help the participants discover their own collective agenda.

The management of the commons

Issues like fishing on the high seas, global warming, and the exploitation of scarce resources concern everyone, and policies regarding such issues must be the province of global councils. Presumably localities affected most directly, such as those where mineral deposits are located, would be represented directly at such global councils, short-cutting the standard tiered process. The concerns of such localities would be central to the dialog, and the process of harmonization would be expedited by their direct participation. For commons on a smaller scale, such as regional resources, the solution is the same, only with smaller-scale councils.

In dealing with these kinds of issues, the people of the world will be learning how to make strategic decisions together regarding difficult tradeoffs. Petroleum offers a useful example. A policy regarding how much petroleum will be pumped from the ground, and what it will be used for, affects everyone. Such a policy affects global warming and pollution; it affects the operations of societies everywhere, and it has long-term consequences for future generations. Tradeoffs will be required between the desire to reduce burning of fossil fuels, and the need to keep society operating. In order to move toward sustainability, we will need to budget our usage of such finite resources, some for current operations, and some dedicated to the construction of sustainable replacement systems.

In today's world, such global tradeoffs are determined by elites, based on their own self-interest, or else they are left to blind market forces, which amounts to the same thing. Elites have been competent, even astute, in their pursuit of their own self-interest, but wisdom has been absent from their process. No one could be called wise who pursues such destructive agendas. In a democratic society, based on a culture of harmonization, the affairs of the world will for the first time be managed both wisely and coherently. The difficult tradeoffs will not be guided by the simplistic metric of immediate profit, but rather by the harmonized collective wisdom of the world's people, considering not only themselves but their children as well.

We can use harmonizing councils to help us make these kinds of tradeoffs, and we can take the necessary time to enable the harmonization process to converge. It is worth the investment; we will to a large extent be deciding the future of humanity. And when we've settled on our policies, we can establish agencies to facilitate the necessary projects. If we find our policies are flawed, as we try to implement them, we can assemble councils at appropriate levels to address the deficiencies. We can do all of this democratically, and without establishing any centralized authorities, governments, or bureaucracies.

The maintenance of peace

In a culture of harmonization there is little reason to expect hostilities to arise between societies. That would be as unthinkable as Arizona invading California. People have never wanted war; war has always been arranged by elites, as they compete for territories and seek to expand their wealth and power. When people are in charge, in a culture of harmonization, war will be remembered as a regrettable part of humanity's primitive history, like blood feuds among clans.

Nonetheless, one can never predict all eventualities. It is possible that some deranged, charismatic leader, someday in the future, might stir up some society to become aggressive. I doubt it, but I can't deny the possibility. Just as people have antibodies, to protect against potential invasions by disease, societies will need to have defenses, to protect against potential invasions by aggressors. We might recall the case of Switzerland, which has avoided warfare, and which maintains a state of military readiness in case anyone should try to cross the Alps in anger.

Let us consider then some kind of 'peace force,' whose job would be to maintain peace in the face of any kind of aggression that might emerge. We must be very careful in these considerations however, lest the peace force itself become a source of tyranny or aggression. Military coups have been a common occurrence, particularly in our recent history. If a military organization exists, we always have to consider the danger that it might be used against us.

With a peace force, as with all social structures, the path of democracy requires that we avoid hierarchies. It is the existence of a central command structure that enables a coup. If there is no command center to seize, there is no opportunity for a coup. It seems to me that the natural form of a peace force, in a democratic society, is for each community to have its own locally controlled militia.

Suppose then, that every community has such a militia, and there are no other military forces. Presumably a global council would agree on a level of armaments, so that all militias would be comparable in their weaponry. Militia members would be residents of the community, and the community as a whole would need to agree before a militia could be mobilized for action. The purpose of the militias, as set down by the council establishing them, would be strictly to restore order in case aggression occurs.

There would be little danger of a coup scenario to arise with such an arrangement. The local militia is hardly likely to rise up against its own friends and neighbors, and there is no central command that can order a militia into action. Furthermore, a community is unlikely to use its militia to initiate aggression – even if we set aside the culture of harmonization – because all of its neighbors will have comparable militias, and they would surely join forces to resist such aggression.

The aggression scenario we need to guard against would be some larger social unit that goes astray. Perhaps some society begins developing weapons in excess of the agreed limits, or joins its militias together to form an invading force. In the face of such a scenario, the defending militias would need to join forces and coordinate their activities in order to respond effectively.

In a democratic society, I suggest that the appropriate model for defense can be taken from the human body's immune system. Our antibodies normally circulate passively throughout our bloodstreams; when a pathogen invades, the antibodies swarm to surround and neutralize it. When the pathogen is eliminated, the antibodies spread out and resume their normal circulation. Similarly, if an aggressive force arises in the world, local militias – on whatever scale is required – can swarm to surround and neutralize it. When the danger is past, the militias can all go home. No centralized military force need be created, and we can avoid the risk of coups.

Democracy and property rights

The hoopla about a new "Earth Day" or future "Sun Days" or "Wind Days," like the pious rhetoric of fast-talking solar contractors and patent-hungry "ecological" inventors, conceal the all-important fact that solar energy, wind power, organic agriculture, holistic health, and "voluntary simplicity" will alter very little in our grotesque imbalance with nature if they leave the patriarchal family, the multinational corporation, the bureaucratic and centralized political structure, the property system, and the prevailing technocratic rationality untouched.
—Murray Bookchin, *Toward an Ecological Society*

Centralization of power, in any form, is incompatible with democracy. Power can be turned into tyranny, and if power centers exist, someone will always come along and take advantage of that opportunity sooner or later. So far in this chapter, we have seen how harmonization can enable us to avoid power centers in the form of governments, administrative agencies, and military commands. We next need to understand how we can avoid the excessive concentration of economic power and wealth. This core of this problem comes down to finding a proper balance between democracy and property rights.

Different cultures throughout history have had widely varying attitudes regarding property ownership. In hunter-gatherer societies, people owned their own weapons and tools, their clothes and dwelling materials, and little else. The concept of owning land made no more sense to these societies than would the ownership of the atmosphere. Tribes might have their territories, but within a territory nature was to be shared, not owned.

As societies become more complex, with agriculture and fixed dwellings, private ownership naturally comes into existence. Each family owning its dwelling, and being responsible for its maintenance, makes economic sense. And it makes economic sense for a farming family to own its farmland, and to be responsible for managing it. But it also makes sense for a community to own agricultural land jointly, and to farm it communally. Both models of agricultural land ownership have been used throughout history, and are still being used today.

Under modern capitalism, we can see what happens when property rights are placed above all other rights. In the name of 'property rights,' corporations have more power than most governments. This has gotten even worse under neoliberal globalization, with its 'free trade' treaties. Nations are compelled to permit polluting additives in gasoline, because to ban them would violate the 'property rights' of some corporation.

In a democratic society, economic arrangements must be under the control of the democratic process. If a community wants an economic system based heavily on private property, so be it; if it wants a more communal system, so be it. And if a community finds that its chosen arrangements are not working satisfactorily, the community must have the right to modify them. Economic sovereignty is in fact part of political sovereignty. Economics affects every aspect of our lives; if we don't control our economic system democratically, we don't have a democratic society.

If a community is to have political and economic sovereignty, then all property in the community must be owned by the community residents, either individually or collectively. If absentee corporations, landlords, or governments can buy up the land and buildings in a community, then the community would not have the power to control its own affairs and determine its own destiny; its sovereignty would be meaningless.

If ownership of land and structures are localized in this way, then we can avoid the massive concentrations of wealth that we see in today's societies. A giant corporation could not exist; a J.D.

Rockefeller could not accumulate his fortune. We are left then only with the problem of excessive wealth accumulation within a community.

In this regard, permit me to share a story from my youth. One summer at church camp the game of 'coin toss' was all the rage among us boys. A group of us would line up some distance from a wall, and each toss a quarter (25-cent piece) up against the wall. Whoever got his coin closest to the wall won all the quarters that had been tossed. As you might imagine, it wasn't too long before one boy had accumulated all the available quarters. The camp counselor found out about this, made the lucky boy return all the quarters, and told us not to play anymore. As soon as the counselor left, and with our wealth restored, we immediately resumed the game.

Free enterprise is like that. It's a game that some do better at than others. Furthermore, when someone gains an edge, a bit of excess wealth, then it becomes easier for them to gain still more. And yet, most of us like to play the game. We each imagine we too can get lucky, that we too can be rich. One way or another, the game usually leads to the concentration of wealth in a few hands.

Karl Marx suggested that the answer to this problem of accumulation was to ban free enterprise. That would be a very undemocratic solution however, given that most of us like to play the game. In addition, Marx's solution creates problems as regards economic efficiency. When someone owns their farm or business they have a strong incentive to manage it wisely, or at least to the best of their ability. Communal enterprises, unless a culture happens to be highly cooperative to begin with, can be very inefficient. So, as regards private enterprise, we seem to be damned if we do and damned if we don't.

Marx was seeking a solution in terms of economic rules: thou shalt play the game this way, and thou shalt not play it that way. We could seek more flexible rules than Marx did, but we probably wouldn't succeed. People are too good at playing games. No matter what the rules, someone will be clever enough to accumulate wealth anyway. And who can blame them? Most of us would do the same thing, if we were able. Besides, there's nothing wrong with some inequality of wealth; that is the natural outcome of unequal productivity.

A workable solution to excess accumulation, I suggest, lies not in economic rules that attempt to prevent the problem, but rather in the ability to correct problems when they arise. In the ancient Hebrew culture there was something called the *Year of Jubilee*. Once every fifty years wealth would be redistributed, slaves freed, and the game begun again – much like at my summer camp. This was a political solution, a corrective solution, and it could work no matter how the economic game is played in between Jubilees.

In the case of a sovereign, democratic community, we don't need a corrective rule as rigid as the Year of Jubilee. If someone's wealth becomes oppressive to others, the problem can be addressed flexibly by the community's democratic process. Perhaps some kind of direct redistribution would be appropriate, or perhaps some system of local taxation. Whatever solution might be adopted, everyone's interests would be represented, including the one who will need to give up some of his quarters.

The only fixed rule we need is to keep ownership local, and that actually follows automatically if communities are to be sovereign. Within a community, economic problems can be settled democratically when the need arises. The redistribution scenario is a worst case; we need to consider it in order to ensure we aren't creating a system with fatal loopholes. Most likely what would happen is that each community would evolve a way of handling economics that tended to work well for the local culture and residents. Democracy is an ongoing process, and problems would most likely be nipped in the bud before they become serious.

Constitutions

Under a representative form of government, we are rightly concerned about having a constitution and guaranteed rights of various kinds. This is because we know from history that centralized governments tend to be oppressive. And as political conservatives often point out, citizens themselves can be oppressive as well, through a tyranny of the majority. A constitution and its guarantees, in theory at least, are the people's protection from tyranny, both from governments and from majorities. Guarantees regarding private property, for example, are supposed to protect us from arbitrary seizure of our property by either kind of tyranny.

The situation is much different, however, when people have sovereignty over their own communities, and when they use harmonization instead of majority rule. Under such a democratic system, there is no tyranny to protect ourselves against: each of us participates equally in the decision-making process, and our concerns are taken into account along with everyone else's. Any set of pre-determined rules, or constitution, simply becomes a restriction on We the People – something set up in the past by people who couldn't be familiar with current circumstances and problems. The only fixed guarantees needed in a democratic society are guarantees that communities have sovereignty, and that inclusive participatory democracy be used to decide issues within and among communities. And the best guarantee for these things is a culture based on harmonization.

8

The transition process

Beauty is the moment of transition, as if the form were just ready to flow into other forms.

—Ralph Waldo Emerson, "Beauty," from *The Conduct of Life*

The moment of convergence

One can only guess at the precise endgame scenario of our transformational movement, regarding existing elites. Presumably it will be somewhere on the spectrum between, (1) movement slates are elected peaceably and all but unanimously to national power throughout the West (an ideal outcome), and (2) regime troops abandon their tanks and cease suppressing the people (an Eastern-European-like outcome). By one non-violent path or another a moment of convergence will come, and literally everyone will be part of the movement. If we envision the last remaining plutocrats coming out of their towers with their hands up, we see ourselves embracing them, and inviting them to sit down in creative dialog. Don't doubt for a moment that they have unique knowledge and insights to bring to the conversation. They didn't get to the top by being stupid: don't judge them by the cue-card-reading, smiley-faced actors that they pick to sit in places like the White House and #10 Downing Street.

At this moment of convergence humanity will breathe a collective sigh of relief. The global celebrations will be grander than those that followed the ends of our great wars and revolutions, because we will be celebrating not only the end of a bad era, but the birth of a whole new kind of hope, a hope based on the solid personal experience of a *new way of being*, not just on a slogan, such as "The war to end all wars," or "Liberty, Equality, Fraternity."

When we wake up the next morning, and sit down to begin talking business, there will be two obvious agenda items in front of us, one short term and one long term. In the short term we'll need to establish some agreed framework for global order; in the long term our big problem will be to transform our economies and infrastructures to be in synergistic harmony with our natural life-support systems. Sustainability is only a minimal requirement; when we put our collective brains to the subject, we will realize that we are in a symbiotic relationship with the rest of life: the more we nurture the matrix of life, the more we are nurtured. In terms of common-sense economics, being respectful of Mother Nature is simply a good investment in our own health and our own futures. We don't just want to keep her alive; we want her to be healthy and bountiful.

As regards 'global order' I imagine this will be a matter of writing down the obvious. When I suggested that we would 'sit down to begin talking business,' I was presuming that this would happen in the form of large global council, involving delegations from all over the world, comparable demographically to the current UN. These people would already understand what the system of global order in a democracy needs to be: the use of harmonization and the arranging of temporary councils as needed to deal with issues at whatever appropriate level, leading in each case to an eventual consensus that includes all affected communities. This will be obvious to those who have lived through the transformational process (i.e., all of us). It will be how we live and breathe, so to speak.

In the previous chapter I extrapolated in more detail the kind of political and economic arrangements we could expect to develop, when people have come to focus on democracy as being the critical element that needs to be given priority above others. That drives the priority trade-offs as regards property rights, for example. In the rest of this chapter I'd like to explore the problem of converting our societies from exploitive systems to synergistic systems, from the dysfunctional to the functional. The problem is a bit like repairing an aircraft in mid-flight: society cannot be 'closed for renovations.'

Common-sense economics and the management of the commons

The word *economics* comes from a Greek word that means 'management of the household.' As we all know, that kind of management comes down to budgeting. You've got a certain amount of income, fixed expenses, optional items, and the possibility of putting some money into savings or devoting some to upgrading your living environment. There's nothing particularly complicated about it; it's just a matter of facing the reality of your limited income, and making trade-offs according to what's most important to you. The easiest way to get in trouble here is to *not* budget, in which case you might find yourself at the end of the month with no food on the table.

Just as the householder has a certain income, so humanity can access a certain stock of resources: fossil fuels, arable land, fishing stocks, water sources, etc. If we want to move toward more sensible systems, we'll need to budget our resources, particularly the non-renewable ones, in terms of our overall global agenda.

Let's take petroleum as an example. After considering various objectives – reducing global warming and air pollution, keeping our societies running, creating replacement infrastructures – we might decide on a budget something like this:

> Reduce global petroleum production by 20% in the first year.
>
> Allocate petroleum on an equitable basis to different regions, under some scheme of fair exchange between producers and consumers.
>
> Dedicate 20% of petroleum usage to the construction of replacement infrastructures, as appropriate to local circumstances.

For a scarce resource like petroleum, it makes sense to agree at the global level on a basic pace of conversion, and a basic framework for conversion. This enables coherence in our overall use of resources, in the pursuit of agreed common objectives. Note that this is quite a different thing from centralized state planning, as we've seen in some socialist nations. Only the guidelines and general resource budgets are agreed to globally, the implementation and optimization is determined locally and democratically, where the feedback loops are shortest.

When our goal as a society is to make wise use of our resources, and create infrastructures that serve our needs in a sustainable way, the whole basis of economics is transformed.

Let's take rail as an example. The simple fact is that a well-designed and integrated rail system is incredibly more efficient than an automobile-based system in most transport scenarios – not only in terms of energy usage, but in terms of time to destination, pollution, quality of travel, utilization of investment (automobiles spend most of their time parked), and amount of land devoted to transport infrastructure.

Despite these obvious and significant efficiencies, the trend in most parts of the world is toward the automobile. To be sure, a large part of the reason is people's natural desire for the flexibility of personal transport, but the more instrumental factor has been the pursuit of economic growth.

The problem with rail, from the perspective of capitalism, is that it is *too* efficient: it doesn't use up enough resources to generate maximum economic growth. Hence trillions of dollars are invested by governments in ultra-expensive highway systems, artificially subsidizing automobile and truck usage, while rail systems are dismantled and service is intentionally allowed to deteriorate. In this way lots of steel goes into lots of cars, which only last a few years and must be replaced, using an excessive amount of energy, and boosting the GDP figures. What makes no sense in common-sense economic terms makes a lot of sense in capitalist economics – where waste and productivity are essentially synonymous. While the effect of capitalist economics is to maximize the rate at which resources are used up, the effect of common-sense economics is to make the most sensible use of resources.

Just as the economic role of the householder is to manage the household, so the economic role of society is to manage the commons. The commons is partly natural (land, forests, waterways, etc.) and partly artificial (infrastructures: roadways, utilities, communications, etc.). Different parts of the commons would naturally come under the stewardship of different levels of society. The high seas and fossil fuels, for example, need to be managed according to policies set at the global level, with the help of global councils. Transport infrastructures would typically be part of a regional commons, and managed at the regional level. Each community has its own local commons, which includes everything that is not privately owned by residents: land, waterways, forests, roadways, public buildings, water systems, etc.

In this way each part of the commons is managed by the people who benefit from it, and who have a shared interest in seeing that it is managed wisely. Management of the commons is always centered as locally as possible, keeping feedback loops short, and facilitating maximum efficiency of operations.

Common-sense economics could also be called holistic economics, in the sense that it begins where it should begin: with our basic economic relationship to our resource base. This kind of economics is not primarily about money, nor can it be reduced to any such single metric. Decisions about how to use or develop the commons, at any level, involve the consideration of many issues, from productivity to esthetics to local traditions, and there is no mathematical formula that can give a 'right answer.'

Repossessing the commons

The law doth punish man or woman
That steals the goose from off the common,
But lets the greater felon loose,
That steals the common from the goose.
—Anon., 18th cent., on the enclosures

The commons has been stolen from us over the millennia, and the process of theft is still continuing. Sometimes the theft has come in the form of military conquest and imperialism, which is why Western corporations own most of the mineral wealth in the third world. In the 1700's the Enclosure Acts stole a traditional commons from the British people, forcing them off the land and providing cheap labor for the new mills and factories of the Industrial Revolution. Neoliberal privatization steals the infrastructure commons that was paid for and developed by our taxes, enabling corporations to make easy profits. The latest thefts are some of the worst, such as the patenting of traditional seed varieties – claiming private ownership over the very ability to grow food. Seed varieties are rightfully part of the global commons, having been developed and shared freely by individual farmers over thousands of years.

Our first substantive act as a sovereign We the People will most likely be to declare our repossession of the commons. In economic terms, we will simply be taking back what is rightfully ours. But as I pointed out in Chapter 7, the most fundamental principle involved here is political: if we don't own our commons, democracy can only be a sham. If we don't control our resources, we don't really have sovereignty. For political reasons, then, the repossession must be total. We are not talking only about a shift of ownership back to the people; we are talking about a whole new framework of ownership, to be determined by the people.

> Let me issue and control a nation's money and I care not who writes the laws.
> —Amshall Rothschild

One of the commons that we will need to take possession of is our financial and monetary systems. In order for a community to be sovereign, it must control its financial system and currency. Each community doesn't necessarily need to maintain its own currency, but it must have the right to do so at any time it chooses. Most likely we would create local currencies, perhaps at the level of the region, together with some system of global exchange under the stewardship of a democratically controlled clearinghouse.

In our current financial systems, money is created when banks make loans to people, businesses, or governments. Banks don't loan you money they already have, new money is actually created in the form of the loan itself – this is called 'factional reserve' banking. Basically, the bank is betting that you will pay them back. If you do, then you are the one who comes up with the money that makes the loaned money 'real.' If you don't, then the bank must come up with 'real money' to make up the deficit in its books. But most people do pay back, so the system 'works.' Money thus serves as a mechanism to channel wealth to banks, and to those who own the banks.

Currently there is a worldwide movement of people creating local currencies. In parts of the third world, where the IMF has created massive poverty, local currencies are enabling people to create their own productive local economies. Where there is a local currency, people can use it to make exchanges with one another. Without a local currency, the community must transfer wealth away from the community in order to obtain currency to exchange with one another. When the community issues its own currency, it avoids that outward wealth transfer. It turns out that such currencies function very effectively in practice.

Let us next consider the repossession process in the case of corporations. Apart from local businesses that operate within communities, and are likely to remain privately owned, all corporations and all corporate assets become part of the commons. Some corporations are performing useful functions and should continue operating, only under democratic ownership and management. In other cases, the facilities can be recycled and used for other purposes. In some cases, as with weapons factories and nuclear facilities, our challenge will be to dismantle and dispose of them safely.

Presumably the first step would be for each community to take over stewardship of every corporate facility within its territory, each under the temporary management of its workers. In most cases each facility would probably continue doing what it was doing, until a conversion plan can be worked out. Such a plan would be the responsibility of the local community, in dialog with the workers, neighboring communities, other branches of the former corporation, and other interested stakeholders.

Excess corporate facilities would become available for other uses, such as housing, schools, or whatever is needed by the community. In some cases production facilities might be retooled to manufacture more useful kinds of products. But even in cases where a facility continues to operate within the context of the former multi-site corporation, each branch would now be an autonomous entity, collaborating with other branches voluntarily out of self-interest, rather than in response to commands from headquarters. Economies of scale can still be achieved, but on a networking basis rather than a hierarchical basis – and always under democratic control.

Banks, insurance companies, and financial institutions are corporations, and their facilities would be repossessed in the same way. We would have little need of such institutions, freeing up nearly all of their facilities for other uses by their communities, and liberating the former employees for more useful occupations. Similarly, government facilities would no longer be needed for the most part, and could be dedicated to more useful purposes.

In the case of the military, the most sensible thing would probably be to keep the people in uniform for the time being, and give them the task of safely dismantling their weapons systems. But of course they would no longer be under the control of a military command, but would rather be part of the democratic process in the community that has repossessed their particular military installation.

One of the most important commons is agricultural land. Small, independent farmers would presumably continue to own their land and continue operating as usual, apart from the fact that dangerous pesticides and other unhealthy and un-ecological practices would be ended. Very large independent farms would need to be broken up, so as to prevent undue accumulation of wealth, and the threat that brings to democracy. All corporate holdings would be available for re-distribution. These holdings might be taken over by the laborers who currently work the land, or by families and groups that choose to leave urban environments and return to the land.

The global conversion project

Having repossessed our commons, We the People would now be in a position to begin the project of transforming our societies and our economic activities. I would imagine that in many parts of the world there would be a mass exodus from cities to rural areas. Many of the jobs in cities would no longer exist, as they would serve no useful purpose in a democratic society. We could expect a dramatic revitalization of rural areas, and many people would welcome the opportunity to return to the land, creating small businesses, family farms, or co-op farms. Most of these people would have no experience with agriculture, and we would need to develop creative ways for people learn what they need to know, with the help of those who already live in rural areas and have the necessary knowledge.

As with all parts of the conversion project, such transitions would be made incrementally, so as not to interrupt the ongoing operation of society. At the beginning, large agribusiness operations would need to continue, so that food production can continue, but these large operations would now be under the democratic control of the local communities, rather than corporate headquarters. Operations would be gradually converted to a smaller-scale, more labor-intensive basis. Contrary to current mythology, smaller farming operations are actually more productive and efficient. The much-heralded 'efficiency' of modern agribusiness is measured in terms of profits on money invested, not in terms of food productivity per acre or per gallon of irrigation water. Common-sense economics measures things quite differently than does capitalist economics.

As society becomes less urban and more rural, and as economic operations become focused more locally, we would be transforming our requirements for transport systems. Presumably there would be a lot less need for long-distance daily commuting, and less need for transporting goods over long distances, as we move toward a greater emphasis on local production for local consumption. Our replacement transport systems would be much more efficient, but the greatest energy savings comes from using less transport.

Conversion of the shipping industry offers some interesting challenges. With oil being valued as a diminishing resource, rather than as a cheap fuel, and with an agenda of reducing oil usage through budgeting allocations, the whole economics of ocean transport would be redefined. It would no longer make economic sense to transport items thousands of miles across the sea when those same items can be produced closer to the consumer. Besides, much of the motivation for transporting goods over long distances comes from the disparity of incomes in different parts of the world. Under our revised financial arrangements, such disparities would be dramatically reduced.

Large ocean-going vessels would all become part of the commons, as even a single such ship, if owned privately, would represent an undue concentration of wealth. Many of these ships, particularly military vessels, would no longer be needed and could be recycled or rededicated. I'm reminded here of the ocean liner Queen Mary, which now serves as a hotel and tourist attraction in California's Long Beach harbor. Some ships would presumably be part of the global commons, providing a global transport infrastructure, and others might be part of a regional commons, enabling the people of the region to engage in fishing and transport activities.

Of all forms of transport, air travel is by far the most wasteful of energy. It takes more gallons of fuel to carry passengers in a jet airliner from LA to New York, than it would take if all the passengers drove alone the same distance in their various automobiles. Turboprops (gas-turbine-driven propeller craft) are considerably more efficient than either jets or standard propeller planes, and whatever air transport we decide to retain would presumably use turboprop craft. But most air transport would be replaced by either rail or ship transport, both of which are orders of magnitude more energy-efficient than any kind of air transport.

9

Reflections on humanity's future

Someday, after we have mastered the winds, the waves, the tides and gravity, we shall harness for God the energies of love. Then, for the second time in the history of the world, man will have discovered fire.
—Pierre Teilhard de Chardin, *On Love*

Cultural evolution in a democracy

Earlier I suggested that de-specialization was a major step forward for humanity's cultural evolution. With that genetic innovation, Homo sapiens was able to evolve its cultures in drastically shorter time frames than can be accomplished by biological evolution. Our consequent ability to expand into new niches soon outstripped that of our competitor species. And yet, as I also pointed out, the rate of early cultural evolution was strongly limited by the automatic passing down of cultures from generation to generation, with change minimized. This stabilizing aspect of early cultural evolution was suitable to early societies, where changes in basic circumstances occurred relatively rarely. Early societies were strongly conservative, and rightly so.

With the advent of civilization, the rate of our cultural evolution has been limited by elite-sponsored mythologies. These mythologies have been relatively rigid, changing only when elites needed to adjust their system of control – as when Henry VIII abandoned Catholicism, or capitalists adopted neoliberalism and the mythology of 'free trade.'

In a democratic society, we need not be so conservative as our earliest societies, nor need we any longer be held back by elite-sponsored mythologies. A democratic community can transform its culture simply by dialoging and adopting changes. De-specialization moved our scale of cultural evolution from the realm of genetic changes into the realm of behavioral adaptation.

Democracy accelerates the scale of cultural evolution further into the realm of conscious cognition. To door will be opened onto a global cultural renaissance.

Early societies needed rigid mythologies as an effective means of passing on successful cultural adaptations. Hierarchical societies need relatively rigid mythologies in order to subjugate the people. *A democratic society has no need of mythology.* People can believe in myths if they want to, that's their sovereign right – but the maintenance of a democratic society does not depend on everyone subscribing to one particular mythology. This lack of *enabling mythology* is in fact the most revolutionary aspect of this particular cultural transformation. Not only are we going back to before hierarchy began, but we are abandoning something that humans have always had: a relatively rigid, inherited culture.

This is not to say that people in a democratic and sustainable society would not tend to adopt shared beliefs and a shared *worldview*. By operating in a culture of harmonization, and a society based on sustainability, people could be expected to adopt such beliefs as these: *people have the right to govern themselves; we must respect nature; violence is never necessary; people can always work out their differences amicably; everyone's opinion is equally important.* The reason such beliefs are not an *enabling mythology* is that youth can be encouraged to question them – and adults can be encouraged to reconsider them – in each generation. These kinds of beliefs, or worldview, need not be *programmed into the youth* – such beliefs are likely to become widespread and survive only because of their *inherent utility and ongoing demonstrated validity.*

For the first time ever, humanity will be free to define its own destiny, unencumbered by systematically conditioned beliefs and superstitions. *Defining our own destiny rationally* was part of the original Enlightenment vision, but it was in that case betrayed. To the elites who ran the new 'democracies,' keeping the people under control was the most important priority. Desirable cultural evolution under elites has been systematically minimized, being forced only by effective grassroots activism, or occurring fortuitously as a result of elite agendas. Meanwhile undesirable cultural evolution, as we've seen under neoliberalism, has been initiated whenever such has been required to further enrich elites.

As we launch into transforming our societies, free at last from elites and conditioned myths, we will most likely experience an initial, explosive *speciation* of new cultures. This does not mean, however, that our democratic cultures will be plastic affairs, changing with every season and fashion. What it does mean is that our cultures will be free to co-evolve from the grassroots, along with the economic, infrastructure, life-style, and other decisions we make as we transform our societies. In fact, we can expect our cultures to tend to stabilize over time due to the constraints of sustainability.

Sustainability and stability go hand in hand. Sustainable agriculture, for example, tends to involve rotating through those crops that are most suitable for the local soil and climate. Hence one might expect regular cycles of agricultural activity to develop. Sustainable businesses would want to have markets and suppliers whose demands and productivity are relatively stable over time. Hence we might see a stabilization of business enterprises, perhaps somewhat akin to the medieval guild system, but guided by democratic principles.

We also have reason to expect that our cultures will become more *holistic*, as were early human cultures. When our cultures are free to evolve, instead of being constrained by relatively rigid myths, the various aspects of our cultures are likely to converge toward some kind of mutual coherence. As we universally adopt sustainable practices, for example, we are likely to regain respect for nature at a spiritual level, as was characteristic of early human cultures. And as we become accustomed to using harmonization in our political affairs, we are likely to develop a more cooperative and loving ethic toward our fellow humans generally.

As regards respect for nature in early cultures, it is true that exceptions can be found when tribes migrated to new territories. They often opportunistically exterminated vulnerable food species. But eventually equilibrium would be reached and respect for nature would become part of the culture. We can view industrialization as such a *new territory*, leading to the opportunistic decimation of nature. When we leave exploitive practices behind us, as did early societies when the vulnerable species disappeared, we too can expect our worldview to come into alignment with our new economic practices.

Education outside the Matrix

> [T]he old Lakota was wise. He knew that man's heart away from Nature becomes hard; he knew that lack of respect for growing, living things soon led to lack of respect for humans too. So he kept his children close to its softening influence.
> —Chief Luther Standing Bear, Oglala Lakota

> If you must hold yourself up to your children as an object lesson... hold yourself up as a warning and not as an example.
> —George Bernard Shaw, "Treatise on Parents and Children"

> A father lectured his son on the real values of life. The father said, "We were put on Earth to help others." The boy said, "What are the others here for?"
> —Milton Berle

In our current societies, the primary role of 'education' is to fill the youth with disempowering myths and condition them to the practical requirements of a regimented society. Indeed, general public 'education' was not established until industrialism came along, requiring a literate work force that could understand and obey complex instructions. Before that, illiteracy had served as one more mechanism to subjugate the masses. In a democratic society, we can restore education to the original meaning of the word. The word comes from *educe*, which means to *bring out or develop something latent or potential*. Instead of force-feeding children myths and 'useful facts,' we can seek to *bring out* their innate wisdom and allow their learning to be guided by their innate curiosity. There have been educational pioneers who have applied such educational methods in today's societies, and the results have been remarkable.

When children are programmed with myths, then as adults they are constrained by those myths. To the extent children are liberated from myths, they as adults will be that much closer to personal and psychological liberation. The full flowering of our new democratic societies will be realized by future generations, who have been freed in this way during their formative years of learning. We will envy them and we can only dimly imagine the personal and cultural renaissance that is likely to occur.

At the same time, we must respect the right of families to raise their children according to their own family values, even if some of us consider those values to be based on deceptive myths. For us to instill in children a belief in 'atheistic humanism' or the 'Mother Goddess,' for example, would be manipulative programming – just as much as if we instill in them the mythology of hierarchical religions. My own bias against religion has been clear from this material, but I would not impose that bias on others. I have faith that in a liberated, democratic society, a harmonious balance will be reached between those with religious beliefs and those who lack or even scorn them. This too was part of the original Enlightenment vision, and this too was betrayed by elites who found that in secular 'democracies' religion could be exploited as a tool to divide and subjugate the masses. We can take hope from the experience of the Michigan gathering where, by the process of harmonization, religious conservatives and outspoken leftists were able to find common ground and declare their solidarity as *We the People*.

Democracy and personal liberation

> The most remarkable aspect of the transition we are living through is not so much the passage from want to affluence as the passage from labor to leisure... Leisure contains the future, it is the new horizon... The prospect then is one of unremitting labor to bequeath to future generations a chance of founding a society of leisure that will overcome the demands and compulsions of productive labor so that time may be devoted to creative activities or simply to pleasure and happiness.
> —Henri Lefebvre, *Everyday Life in the Modern World*

While representative democracy promises personal liberty, it is under genuine democracy that we will experience personal liberty for the first time in millennia. Actually participating in the decisions that affect our lives will be not only politically liberating, but psychologically liberating as well. We have been in a dark prison for millennia, and emerging into the daylight of freedom will liberate our spirits in more ways than we can imagine. Like the lion in *Born Free*, we will be able to re-discover our true natures as free beings.

One of the things we will discover, in a society that is governed for the benefit of the people, is that we have been *working entirely too hard*. It is not our needs that force us to work ten hours a day or more, but rather the needs of capitalism. The scarcity that we experience in our lives is an artificial scarcity, required so that elites can extract profits from our labor. Indeed, a major problem for capitalism has been the excess production enabled by industrial methods. If applied sensibly, modern technology can produce whatever artifacts we need with a small fraction of the effort currently devoted to *work*. In a democratic society based on local sovereignty and ownership, we will find that we have lots of free time on our hands.

Free time plus a liberated spirit is a formula for unleashing creativity. Not only will we experience a renaissance of creativity at the level of our societies, but art, poetry, music, science and all manner of personal creativity will be enabled as well. In our societies today, it is very difficult to be an artist. You must have a special talent and dedication in order to make a living by art in a society that does not assign much economic value to art. And if you want to pursue scientific inquiry, you are restricted to what will be funded by establishment institutions.

> I believe the world is beautiful,
> that poetry is like bread, for everyone.
> —Roque Dalton, "Like You"

When we don't need to spend most of our waking hours working to support a dysfunctional system, then we will find there are artists and poets all around us. Indeed, some indigenous societies today do not have a special word for *artist* or *musician*. These societies understand that everyone has such talents. And when scientific inquiry can be pursued free of elite agendas, who knows what breakthroughs might be possible? Instead of being constrained by the needs of corporate profit making, our only scientific constraints will be those imposed by our democratic will. Rather than most of our research going toward developing weaponry and frivolous consumer products, our research can be guided by the needs of society and the pursuit of understanding.

Many social visionaries today believe that personal transformation on a massive scale is necessary *before* social transformation can be attempted. I suggest that this is a disempowering myth, a means of subjugation just like our other myths. It inhibits us from pursuing social transformation and it blames us, the victims, for a society that has in fact been fashioned by elites for their own benefit.

This *necessity of personal transformation* myth can be seen as a vestige of the religious myth of *original sin*. The myth fails to recognize that the deficiencies in our current level of personal consciousness are due not to our inherent natures, but are largely the result of systematic conditioning. If the conditioning is removed, the path to personal transformation will be a far easier one.

The conditioning can be removed by appropriate social transformation. If we insist that personal transformation occur first, we are prevented from moving forward. The teachings of Buddha and Christ have been known for thousands of years, and yet massive personal transformation – of the kind they themselves personified – has never occurred. How can we expect that it will suddenly happen in our own time, unless we try a different approach?

In fact, we can expect personal and social transformation to proceed together, in a mutually reinforcing way. We have seen the empirical evidence: participants in harmonization sessions *do* frequently experience personal transformations of one kind or another. Humans have always been highly social animals. Our identities and beliefs have always been closely linked to the societies we live in and the people we choose to associate with. It should not be surprising that our personal transformation can most readily be brought about in the context of social transformation.

I see friends shakin' hands, sayin' "How do you do?"
They're really saying "I love you"

I hear babies cryin', I watch them grow
They'll learn much more than I'll ever know

And I think to myself, what a wonderful world

—George Weiss & Bob Thiele, *What a Wonderful World*

Afterword

With knowledge comes responsibility

If the fundamental systems of our societies need to be transformed, and if only We the People working together can bring about the needed changes, then we must – each of us – take responsibility for getting on with the project. And if our dysfunctional systems are taking us rapidly toward the precipice, we cannot afford to put this responsibility off until later.

In accepting this responsibility, we are in fact beginning the process of our own personal transformation. Werner Erhard, in his *est*-training days, talked about being *at cause*, rather than *at effect*. By *at cause* he meant something deeper than simply *exercising initiative*. He was talking about a fundamental change in your perception of yourself. To be *at effect* is to see yourself as one who *responds* to circumstances; to be *at cause* is to see yourself as one who *creates* circumstances. In both cases your efforts may be limited by your talents and skills, but by being *at cause*, you vastly expand the scope of your personal potential.

In the context of est, learning to be *at cause* is a central part of a program of personal transformation and empowerment. In the context of transforming society, learning to be *at cause* is precisely what happens to us when we accept our share of the responsibility for our own – and humanity's – salvation. By taking this first step toward social transformation – the acceptance of responsibility – we are also taking a big step toward personal transformation and empowerment.

Just as the est term *at cause* has a deeper meaning than the mere words imply, so does *accepting responsibility*, in our context, have a deeper meaning than the mere words imply. Permit me to articulate this deeper meaning in the form of a credo. As I see it, *taking responsibility* – in the context of social transformation by We the People – is equivalent to subscribing to a personal credo more or less like this one:

> Neither governments, nor politicians, nor organizations, nor special leaders are going to create the changes that the world desperately needs. It is up to me, my neighbors, my co-workers – and all the other ordinary people all over the world – to learn how to work together and begin to build the kinds of cultures and societies that can enable us all to live fruitful lives in harmony with one another.

In this formulation, I'm trying to capture the essential elements of our discussion in a way that may help inform our attempts to 'get on with the project.' The credo reminds us that *whomever we are with* is a potential – and eventually necessary – *partner* (in Riane Eisler's sense) in changing the world, not just those who agree with our beliefs and agendas. It reminds us that *wherever we are* is the right place to begin creating a culture of harmonization, and *our every interaction* is the right time to practice respectful listening. It helps us see the reciprocity that is inherent in democratic empowerment: just as we seek to be *at cause*, so do we encourage, and expect, others to be *at cause*; even those we don't agree with. It reminds us that our mission is not to sell some agenda or idea, but rather to learn how to hear and respect the concerns of those around us, and to learn how to speak from our hearts when we express our own concerns.

In the last half of this book I've outlined what I believe to be a viable scenario for a transformational movement. I've convinced myself, if not anyone else, that the basic features of that scenario are a necessary and inevitable part of the path that we will follow in our creation of transformation. But I could be wrong.

When paradigm shifts happen, those who anticipated the shift tend nonetheless to be surprised by the actual outcomes. Thomas Edison was a primary visionary behind the shift to electrical power, but his concept of generator plants in every community failed to anticipate new technologies, i.e. alternating current and efficient long-distance transmission of power. The credo, above, is an open invitation for creative initiatives. Personally, I still recommend community empowerment as a focus, but I'm not asking anyone to be *at effect* with that suggestion. As one who subscribes to the credo, I offer my scenario as a heartfelt contribution to our collective dialog, and what I most hope for in response are the *at cause* initiatives of those who are ready to *accept responsibility*.

I invite you to join me in accepting responsibility for creating our future world, and I hope to see you there some sunny day.

References

Arends, Brett, "Economic 'Armageddon' predicted," *Boston Herald,* November 23, 2004, p. 35.

Atlee, Tom, "Empowered Dialogue Can Bring Wisdom to Democracy," http://www.co-intelligence.org/CIPol_EmpoweredDialogue.html.

Blum, William, *Killing Hope: U.S. Military and CIA Interventions Since World War II,* Common Courage Press, Monroe, Me., 1995. OR Updated Edition, Common Courage Press, Monroe, Me., 2004.

Briars, The, "To Clarify a Vision," 1991, http://www.co-intelligence.org/MacleansStatement.pdf

Chossudovsky, Michel, "The Anglo-American Military Axis," March 10, 2003.
http://globalresearch.ca/articles/CHO303B.html

Crozier, Michel, Samuel P. Huntington, and Joji Watanuki, *The Crisis of Democracy: Report on the Governability of Democracies to the Trilateral Commission* (Trilateral Commission. Task Force Report. TFR-08), New York University Press, New York, 1975.

Dawkins, Richard, *The Selfish Gene,* Oxford University Press, New York, 1976.

Engdahl, William, *A Century of War: Anglo-American Oil Politics and the New World Order,* Revised Edition, Pluto Press, London, 2004.

Higham, Charles, *Trading with the Enemy,* Dell Publishing Co., New York, 1984.

Kreis, Steven, "1968: The Year of the Barricades," from *The History Guide: Lectures on Twentieth Century Europe,* Lecture 15.
http://www.historyguide.org/europe/lecture15.html

Lappé, Frances Moore and Joseph Collins, *World Hunger: Twelve Myths,* Grove Press, New York, 1986.

Madsen, Wayne, "Suffering and Despair: Humanitarian Crisis in the Congo," Prepared Testimony and Statement before the House Subcommittee on International Operations and Human Rights, Washington, D. C., May 17, 2001.
http://www.totse.com/en/politics/central_intelligence_agency/162600.html

McCoy, Alfred W., author of *The Politics of Heroin: CIA Complicity in the Global Drug Trade,* from an interview by David Barsamian conducted at the University of Wisconsin-Madison, February 17,1990.
http://www.lycaeum.org/drugwar/DARKALLIANCE/ciah4.html

Montague, Peter, "The WTO Turns Back the Clock," *Rachel's Environment & Health News,* Nov. 4, 1999.
http://www.rachel.org/bulletin/index.cfm?issue_ID=1634

Mullins, Eustace, *Secrets of the Federal Reserve,* unpublished, available online: http://www.apfn.org/apfn/reserve.htm

NEF (National Energy Foundation), "Fuel Consumption Stats," 2002.
http://www.nef1.org/ea/eastats.html

NSSM (National Security Study Memorandum, NSSM 200), "The Kissinger Report," December 10, 1974.

Perloff, James, "Pearl Harbor: The Facts Behind the Fiction," *The New American*, June 4, 2001.

PNAC (Project for the New American Century), *Rebuilding America's Defenses: Strategies, Forces and Resources for a New Century*, PNAC, Washington, D. C., September, 2000.
http://newamericancentury.org/RebuildingAmericasDefenses.pdf

Shoup, Laurence, and William Minter, "Shaping a New World Order," in *Trilateralism: The Trilateral Commission and Elite Planning for World Management*, pp. 135-166, edited by Holly Sklar, South End Press, Boston, 1980.

Tuecke, Patricia R, "Rural International Development," in *Discovering Common Ground*, by Marvin R. Weisbord, et. al., Berrett-Koehler, San Francisco, 1992.

UN, High-level Plenary Meeting of the General Assembly, "Draft Outcome Document," Printer friendly version, September 14, 2005.
http://www.un.org/ga/president/59/draft_outcome.htm

USIP (United States Institute of Peace), *American Interest and UN Reform, Report of the Task Force on the United Nations*, June, 2005.
http://www.usip.org/un/report/usip_un_report.pdf

Wolfe, Alan, "Capitalism Shows Its Face: Giving Up on Democracy," in *Trilateralism: The Trilateral Commission and Elite Planning for World Management*, edited by Holly Sklar, South End Press, Boston, 1980, 295-307.

Zinn, Howard, *A People's History of the United States: 1492–Present*, HarperPerennial, New York, 1995.

Bibliography and online resources

This material is maintained and updated online at
http://EscapingTheMatrix.org/resources/

Most highly recommended

The Breakdown of Nations, by Leopold Kohr. Totnes, Devon, UK:
Green Books in association with New European Publications;
White River Junction, VT: Distributed in the USA by Chelsea
Green Publishing Company, 2001, c1957.

> "So let us solve the great problem of our time, the disease of excessive size
> and uncontrollable proportions, by going back to the alternative to both right
> and left—that is, to a small-scale social environment with all its potential for
> global pluralistic cooperation and largely unaffiliated self-sufficiency, by ex-
> tending not centralised control but by decontrolling locally centred and nour-
> ished communities, each with its own institutional nucleus and a limited but
> strong and independent gravitational field."
> —Leopold Kohr

*A Century of War: Anglo-American Oil Politics and the New World
Order*, by William Engdahl. Revised Edition. London: Pluto
Press, 2004.

> People often ask me, "If there are 'ruling elites,' then who, exactly, are they?
> Who is it that runs the world?" In *A Century of War*, Engdahl meticulously
> documents the rise to preeminent power of one particular elite group: the top
> banking interests in London and New York. Control over global finance is
> their lever of power, and control over oil sources is the underpinning of that
> lever. By working with their covert contacts in the Intelligence services and
> oil industry in Britain and America, this group has dictated the course of his-
> tory over the past century, arranged the two World Wars, and generally done
> what has been necessary to maintain and increase their hold on global
> power.

The Chalice & The Blade: Our History, Our Future, by Riane Tennenhaus Eisler. Special Edition, with a new epilogue by the author. San Francisco, Calif.: HarperSanFrancisco, 1994.

"The phenomenal bestseller, with more than 500,000 copies sold worldwide, now with a new epilogue from the author–The Chalice and the Blade has inspired a generation of women and men to envision a truly egalitarian society by exploring the legacy of the peaceful, goddess-worshipping cultures from our prehistoric past."
    —The publisher

The New Pearl Harbor: Disturbing Questions About the Bush Administration and 9/11, by David Ray Griffin. Updated Edition. Northampton, Mass.: Olive Branch Press, 2004.

"The disturbing questions emerge from every part of the story, from every angle, until it is impossible not to seriously doubt the official story, and suspect its architects of enormous deception. Long a teacher of ethics and systematic theology, Griffin writes with compelling and passionate logic, urging readers to draw their own conclusions from the evidence outlined. The New Pearl Harbor rings with the conviction that it is possible, even today, to search for the truth; it is a stirring call that we demand a real investigation into what happened on 9/11."
    —Interlink Publishing website

See also his *The 9/11 Commission Report: Omissions and Distortions*, also from Olive Branch Press, 2005.

The Story of B, by Daniel Quinn. New York: Bantam Books, 1996.

Besides being a good read, this novel profoundly changed my understanding of human history and the development of civilization. Quinn shows how the agricultural revolution brought a shift in world view, toward what he calls the "taker mythology" which is much the same thing that Eisler refers to as a "dominator" culture.

Toward an American Revolution: Exposing the Constitution & Other Illusions, by Jerry Fresia. Boston: South End Press, 1988.

If you're an American – whether on the left or the right – then you haven't been fully awakened until you read Toward an American Revolution. In 200 fully referenced and readable pages, Fresia cuts through the matrix of American political history – revealing a continuous pattern of elite manipulation that began even before the Constitution was written.

"Venezuela's Democracy is an example for the world to follow," Katherine Lahey.
http://www.vheadline.com/readnews.asp?id=22431

"The stitching of the fabric of the revolution is unmatched in its strength and breadth of anything I have ever seen. Throughout the country, not just in the urban barrios, social programs called 'misiones' – a social development strategy borrowed from the Cuban revolution – are being implemented by the people with the support of government resources."
    —From the article

Media and propaganda

History as Mystery, by Michael Parenti. San Francisco: City Lights Books, 1999.

"Those who keep secret the past, and lie about it, condemn us to repeat it. Michael Parenti unveils the history of falsified history, from the early Christian church to the present; a fascinating, darkly revelatory tale."
—Daniel Ellsberg, author of *The Pentagon Papers*

Inventing Reality: The Politics of News Media, by Michael Parenti. Second Edition. New York: St. Martin's Press, 1993.

"In this passionate, provocative critique of the news media, Michael Parenti examines the subtle but profound ways in which the media influence and manipulate the public's perception of reality. It attacks the widely held belief that the news media are controlled by liberals and liberal opinion – and clearly depicts the news media as a controlling institution of the American capitalist system, an institution that serves the interests of the rich and powerful while appearing to serve the many."
—Robin Good, MasterNewMedia.org

Make-Believe Media: The Politics of Entertainment, by Michael Parenti, New York: St. Martin's Press, 1992.

"In Make-believe Media, Parenti turns his eye to entertainment for an absorbing, challenging look at the way America's "free and independent" television and film industries actually promote the ideas of the economic and political forces that control them. Even viewers who claim to be immune to the obvious messages of film and television will find Parenti's analysis provocative and compelling as he urges us to become more critical about what we choose to watch."
—The author's website

Manufacturing Consent: The Political Economy of the Mass Media, by Edward S. Herman and Noam Chomsky. New York: Pantheon Books, 1998; Updated Edition, 2002.

"In this pathbreaking work, now with a new introduction, Edward S. Herman and Noam Chomsky show that, contrary to the usual image of the news media as cantankerous, obstinate, and ubiquitous in their search for truth and defense of justice, in their actual practice they defend the economic, social, and political agendas of the privileged groups that dominate domestic society, the state, and the global order."
—The publisher

See also: *Media Control: The Spectacular Achievements of Propaganda,* by Noam Chomsky. (An Open Media Book) Second Edition. New York: Seven Stories Press, 2002.

Orwell Rolls In His Grave (Film). Written, directed, filmed and
edited by Robert Kane Pappas; produced by Miriam Foley.
Sag Harbor-Basement Pictures, a Sky Island Films release in
association with Magic Lamp, 2003.

> Director Robert Kane Pappas' Orwell Rolls in His Grave is the consummate
> critical examination of the Fourth Estate, once the bastion of American de-
> mocracy. Asking whether America has entered an Orwellian world of dou-
> blespeak where outright lies can pass for the truth, Pappas explores what the
> media doesn't talk about: itself.
>   —The producer

Unreliable Sources: A Guide to Detecting Bias in News Media, by
Martin A. Lee and Norman Solomon. (A Lyle Stuart Book)
New York: Carol Publishing Group, 1990.

> "This is one of the single most thought provoking books I've ever read. It
> provides the reader with a real behind the curtain look at the media and poli-
> tics. This is a must read for every American!"
>   —Review by a reader

Online news and information

Centre for Research on Globalization – http://globalresearch.ca

> "The Centre for Research on Globalization (CRG) is an independent research
> and media group of progressive writers, scholars and activists committed to
> curbing the tide of "globalisation" and "disarming" the New World Order.
> The CRG webpage publishes news articles, commentary, background re-
> search and analysis on a broad range of issues, focusing on the interrelation-
> ship between social, economic, strategic, geopolitical and environmental
> processes."
> http://globalresearcch.ca/about

Environmental Research Foundation – http://www.rachel.org

> "Environmental Research Foundation (ERF) was founded in 1980 to provide
> understandable scientific information about the influence of toxic substances
> on human health and the environment."
> http://www.rachel.org/about_eng.htm

Independent Media Center (IndyMedia) – http://www.indymedia.org

> "The Independent Media Center is a network of collectively run media out-
> lets for the creation of radical, accurate, and passionate tellings of the truth.
> We work out of a love and inspiration for people who continue to work for a
> better world, despite corporate media's distortions and unwillingness to
> cover the efforts to free humanity."
> http://www.indymedia.org/en/static/about.shtml

Online Journal & Progressive Press – http://www.onlinejournal.com

> "Dedicated to providing readers with the news, views and analysis missing
> from today's major print and broadcast media."
>   —Google.com

Truthout – http://www.truthout.org

> "Covers latest international news, current political issues and various topics. Also includes forum, editorials and contact details."
> http://www.joeant.com/DIR/info/get/14067/74220

Venezuelanalysis.com – http://www.venezuelanalysis.com

> ...an editorially independent website produced by individuals who are dedicated to disseminating news and analysis about the current political situation in Venezuela... Our goal is to become the primary resource for information and analysis on Venezuela in the English language.
> http://www.venezuelanalysis.com/about.php

ZNet – http://www.zmag.org/weluser.htm

> "Very extensive online progressive magazine and community of alternative news, opinions, discussion forums, and resources from Z Magazine."
> —Open Directory Project

The current regime and how it got that way

The Clash of Civilizations and the Remaking of World Order, by Samuel P. Huntington. A Touchstone Book. London: Simon and Schuster, 1997.

> A classic by one of the foremost spinners of matrix illusion. In the guise of historical analysis, Huntington fabricates a worldview designed to justify Western domination under globalization. According to The Economist, Huntington's civilization-clash paradigm has already become the "sea" in which Washington policy makers swim. The book reveals the backbone structure of modern matrix reality, putting day-to-day official rhetoric into an understandable framework. And it clearly reveals the real intentions of elite planners regarding the tactics of global management through selective interventionism.

Colossus: How the Corporation Changed America. Edited by Jack Beatty. New York: Broadway Books, 2001.

> The corporate way of doing business needed both a revolution and the Constitution of the U.S. to succeed. While some fought against it, the authors of the Constitution were wealthy men whose interests lay in England, and who were involved with the East Indies Company, and saw the opportunity that existed in America.

Confessions of an Economic Hit Man, by John Perkins. San Francisco: Berrett-Koehler Publishers, 2004.

"In his controversial book, John Perkins tells the gripping tale of the years he spent working for an international consulting firm where his job was to convince underdeveloped countries to accept enormous loans, much bigger than they really needed, for infrastructure development – and to make sure that the development projects were contracted to U.S. multinationals. Once these countries were saddled with huge debts, the American government and the international aid agencies allied with it were able, by dictating repayment terms, to essentially control their economies. It was not unlike the way a loan shark operates – and Perkins and his colleagues didn't shun this kind of unsavory association. They referred to themselves as 'economic hit men.'"
    —The publisher

CovertAction Quarterly magazine, published quarterly by Covert Action Publications, Inc., Washington D.C.

Keeps you up-to-date on covert activities, cover-ups, military affairs, and current trouble spots. Contributors include many ex-intelligence officers who came to see the error of their ways.

See also their website: http://www.covertactionquarterly.org

Dark Alliance: The CIA, the Contras, and the Crack Cocaine Explosion, by Gary Webb. New York: Seven Stories Press, 1998.

"Gary Webb was a cherished friend of ours, and one of the best investigative reporters we've ever known. He attacked stories with a unique blend of zeal and skepticism. Gary had no axe to grind, and typically Gary himself didn't fully believe in his own stories until he'd finished them. If he could overcome his own skepticism then he'd done his job. Anything less than that would have been unworthy of him, and he was incapable of lowering his standards, although he must have been tempted sometimes."
    —Daniel Simon, Publisher.

The Fed: the Inside Story of How the World's Most Powerful Financial Institution Drives the Market, by Martin Mayer. New York: Free Press, 2001.

Foreign Affairs, a journal published quarterly by the Council on Foreign Relations, New York.

The best source I've found to track the latest shifts in the matrix and to glean an understanding of current elite thinking. As the publisher accurately puts it on its webage: "Since 1922, the Council has published Foreign Affairs, America's most influential publication on international affairs and foreign policy. It is more than a magazine—it is the international forum of choice for the most important new ideas, analysis, and debate on the most significant issues in the world. Inevitably, articles published in Foreign Affairs shape the political dialogue for months and years to come."

See also: See also the Council's website: http://www.foreignaffairs.org

Friendly Fascism: The New Face of Power in America, by Bertram Gross. New York: South End Press, 1980.

Illuminates the increasing collusion between Big Government and Big Business to "manage" our society in the interests of the elite.
    —The publisher

The Globalization of Poverty: Impacts of IMF and World Bank Reforms, by Michel Chossudovsky. Second Edition. Shanty Bay, Ont.: Global Outlook, 2003.

This detailed study by an economics insider shows the consequences of "reforms" in various parts of the world, revealing a clear pattern of callous neo-colonialism and genocide.

The Global Trap: Globalization and the Assault on Democracy and Prosperity, by Hans-Peter Martin and Harald Schumann. Translated from the German by Patrick Camiller. London, New York: Zed Books; New York: Distributed in the USA exclusively by St. Martin's Press, 1997.

"This remarkable book explores the spread of globalization and the likely consequences for jobs and democracy. Written by experienced journalists on Der Spiegel, it is informed, up-to-date, thought-provoking and compelling reading."
    —From book jacket

The Grand Chessboard: American Primacy and Its Geostrategic Imperatives, by Zbigniew Brzezinski. New York: Basic Books, 1998.

Brzezinski expresses his apparent worldview when he quotes (p. 31) Samuel P. Huntington: "The sustained international primacy of the United States is central to the welfare and security of Americans and to the future of freedom, democracy, open economies, and international order in the world." Anything less than world domination, evidently, would be a disservice to humanity! Brzezinski traces the history of the world's notable empires, characterizes the U.S. as being the first truly global empire, and sets out to establish a framework for U.S. global hegemony, based on the premise that Eurasia is the Grand Chessboard of world affairs. This book can be seen as the academic version of the PNAC's "Rebuilding America's Defenses."

The Growth Illusion: How Economic Growth Has Enriched the Few, Impoverished the Many and Endangered the Planet, by Richard Douthwaite. Revised Edition. Dublin: Lilliput Press, 2000.

"Douthwaite's captivating book makes the arguments used to support economic growth look unconvincing and indefensible."
    —David Hickie, An Taisce, the National Trust for Ireland

Guns, Germs, and Steel: The Fates of Human Societies, by Jared Diamond. With a New Afterword. New York: W. W. Norton & Company, 1996, 2005.

> The author traces the development of civilization, seeking to establish the preeminence of geography as a determining factor. He perhaps carries his thesis a bit too far, but in the process he presents a broad and colorful account of the development of civilization in different parts of the world.

> See also his latest book: *Collapse: How Societies Choose to Fail or Succeed*, Viking Books, New York, 2005.

Hegemony or Survival: America's Quest for Global Dominance, by Noam Chomsky. (The American Empire Project) New York: Metropolitan Books, an imprint of Henry Holt and Company, 2003. Paperback: Owl Books, 2004.

> If you have to pick just one book on the American Empire, pick this one. It's Chomsky at his best…"
>   —Arundhati Roy, from the cover

Money and Power: The History of Business, by Howard Means. New York: Wiley, 2001.

> "This sweeping business history shows the dramatic movement of power from east to west, providing an expansive global view of choice moguls across various industries, including finance, transportation, communication, and more. It's an engaging narrative about greed, money, and the moguls and dynasties that have defined business."
>   —The publisher

On the Rampage: Corporate Power and the Destruction of Democracy, by Robert Weissman and Russell Mokhiber. Monroe, Maine: Common Courage Press, 2005.

> "Mokhiber and Weissman again strike at the heart of corporate power and malfeasance in this excellent book, On The Rampage. These journalists uphold the time-honored and now all-too-rare tradition of dogged muckraking, exposing corporate criminals and their bought politicians in the spirit of Ida Tarbell, Lincoln Steffens, and I.F. Stone."
>   —Amy Goodman, Democracy Now!

A People's History of the United States, by Howard Zinn. New Edition. New York: HarperCollins, 2003.

> "Known for its lively, clear prose as well as its scholarly research, A People's History of the United States is the only volume to tell America's story from the point of view of – and in the words of – America's women, factory workers, African-Americans, Native Americans, working poor, and immigrant laborers."
>   —The publisher

The Politics of Heroin: CIA Complicity in the Global Drug Trade: Afghanistan, Southeast Asia, Central America, Colombia, by Alfred W. McCoy. Second Revised Edition. Chicago: Lawrence Hill Books; Distributed by Independent Publishers Group, 2003.

"The Politics of Heroin includes meticulous documentation of dishonesty and dirty dealings at the highest levels from the Cold War until today. ...this groundbreaking study details the mechanics of drug trafficking in Asia, Europe, the Middle East, and South and Central America. New chapters detail U.S. involvement in the narcotics trade in Afghanistan and Pakistan before and after the fall of the Taliban, and how U.S. drug policy in Central America and Colombia has increased the global supply of illicit drugs. ...Alfred W. McCoy is a professor of history at the University of Wisconsin-Madison. He holds a doctorate in southeast Asian history from Yale University and is the recipient of the 2001 Goodman Prize from the Association for Asian Studies."
  —The publisher

Rogue State: A Guide to the World's Only Superpower, by William Blum. Updated Edition. Monroe, Maine: Common Courage Press, 2001.

"In Rogue State, learn about decades of ubiquitous U.S. cruelty, kept – remarkably – from penetrating world consciousness or shocking world conscience. Though President Clinton called America 'the world's greatest force for peace,' William Blum shows that our Rogue State is really a marauding Western brute."
  —The publisher

See also Blum's earlier book, *Killing Hope: U.S. Military and CIA Interventions Since World War II,* also from Common Courage Press, 1986; Second Updated Edition, 2004.

Trilateralism: The Trilateral Commission and Elite Planning for World Management. Edited by Holly Sklar. Boston: South End Press, 1980.

This well-researched anthology explains the role in global planning played by such elite organizations as the Trilateral Commission, the Council on Foreign Relations, and the Bilderbergers. Examples from various parts of the world are used to show what kinds of considerations go into the formation of on-the-ground policies.

When Corporations Rule the World, by David C. Korten. Second Edition. San Francisco: Berrett-Koehler Publishers; West Hartford, Conn.: Kumarian Press, 2001.

"This is 'must read' book – a searing indictment of an unjust international economic order, not by a wild-eyed idealistic left-winger, but by a sober scion of the establishment with impeccable credentials. It left me devastated but also very hopeful. Something can be done to create a more just economic order."
  —Archbishop Desmond M. Tutu, Nobel Peace Laureate.

Who Will Tell the People: The Betrayal of American Democracy, by William Greider. A Touchstone Book. New York: Simon & Schuster, 1993.

This best seller shows in detail how the American democratic process is sub-verted at every stage by corporate interests. Greider was a highly respected journalist for many years at the Washington Post and his high-level contacts permit him to present an insider's view of how the influence-peddling sys-tem actually operates.

World Hunger: 12 Myths, by Frances Moore Lappé, Joseph Collins and Peter Rosset; with Luis Esparza. Second Edition, Fully Revised and Updated. New York: Grove Press, 1998.

Debunks Malthusian thinking, among other things. Here's a sample: "During the past twenty-five years food production has outstripped population growth by 16 Percent. India – which for many of us symbolizes over-population and poverty – is one of the top third-world food exporters. If a mere 5.6 percent of India's food production were re-allocated, hunger would be wiped out in India" (Lappé, 11).

Toward a sensible society

The Battle of Venezuela, by Michael McCaughan. (An Open Media Book) First North American Edition. New York: Seven Stories Press, 2005.

"McCaughan gives a vivid eyewitness report of the extraordinary events of the coming to power of Hugo Chavez... His book will be welcomed by all those interested in the complexities of the most original political experiment in Latin America since the Cuban Revolution."
    —Richard Gott, author of *In the Shadow of the Liberator*

"Brazil's New Experiment: Participative democracy in Porto Alegre," by Bernard Cassen. *Le Monde diplomatique,* October 1998.

"The town has set up a parallel organisation operating alongside the munici-pal council, enabling local inhabitants to take real decisions for their city. And it works. Especially for the least well-off for whom it offers a way to stake a claim on public funds normally spent on the more prosperous areas of the city."
    —From the article

The Case Against the Global Economy, and For a Turn Toward The Local. Edited by Jerry Mander and Edward Goldsmith. San Francisco: Sierra Club Books, 2001.

This fine collection of forty-three chapters by knowledgeable contributors analyzes the broad structure of globalization and its institutions, and ex-plores locally based and sustainable economic alternatives.

Collaborative Spunk: The Feisty Guide for Reviving People and Our Planet, by A. Gayle Hudgens, PhD. Helena, MT: SOS Press, 2002. See: http://www.collaborativespunk.org

"For us to thrive, even survive, Hudgens contends that we all need to take rapid, meaningful, and effective action. Her groundbreaking strategy synthesizes two well-established systems to help that happen: the brilliance of The Natural Step Framework, an award-winning, scientifically rigorous initiative pioneered in Sweden that has already fostered health and prosperity for thousands of communities, organizations, businesses, and individuals worldwide; and, Life Coaching, the hugely popular goal-oriented, human development technology that enables extraordinary personal success that began sweeping the U.S. and abroad in the '90s."
      —The publisher

See also the author's website: http://www.coach5.net

Crazy Horse: The Strange Man of the Oglalas, by Mari Sandoz. With an introduction by Vine Deloria Jr. New Edition. Lincoln: University of Nebraska Press, 2004.

An account taken from the recollections of a Sioux who lived in the time of Crazy Horse – provides an insider's view of Sioux society and its decision making process.

Envisioning a Sustainable Society: Learning Our Way Out, by Lester W. Milbrath. SUNY Series in Environmental Public Policy. Albany, NY: State University of New York Press, 1989.

"The evidence is increasingly persuasive. We are changing the way our planet's physical systems work – irrevocably. These changes are global and interconnected and unavoidable. They are upon us already, making it virtually impossible for any modern society to continue its present trajectory of growth. This book provides a penetrating analysis of how we have come to this point, of why science and technology will fail to solve these problems, and of how we as a society must change in order to avoid ecological catastrophe. The scope is broad, the urgency of the message is impossible to ignore."
      —Back cover

Gaian Democracies: Redefining Globalisation and People-Power, by Roy Madron and John Jopling. Totnes, Devon: Published by Green Books for the Schumacher Society, 2003.

"Gaian Democracies would tackle the task of co-creating a global network of just and sustainable societies that could co-exist symbiotically with Gaia's systems. ...Throughout the Briefing, the authors stress the systems framework on which they have based their proposals. They draw on examples such as the Mondragon Cooperatives of Basque Spain, Visa International, the Semco Corporation, the Athenian city state and the hundreds of Participative Budgets initiated by Brazilian Workers' Party to show how many of the principles of Gaian democracies have been successfully applied in the real world."
      —The publisher

Governing the Commons: The Evolution of Institutions for Collective Action, by Elinor Ostrom. Cambridge (Eng.), New York: Cambridge University Press, 1996, c1990.

"In contrast to the proposition of the tragedy of the commons argument, common pool problems sometimes are solved by voluntary organizations rather than by a coercive state. Among the cases considered are communal tenure in meadows and forests, irrigation communities and other water rights, and fisheries."
    —The publisher

The International Journal of Inclusive Democracy

"Inclusive Democracy aims to become the international forum for the new conception of inclusive democracy. That is, direct political democracy, economic democracy (beyond the confines of the market economy and state planning), as well as democracy in the social realm and ecological democracy. In short, inclusive democracy is a form of social organisation which re-integrates society with economy, polity and nature."
    —The journal

Mondragon Cooperative Corporation – http://www.mcc.es

"Mondragón Corporación Cooperativa is the fruit of the sound vision of a young priest, Don José María Arizmendiarrieta, as well as the solidarity and efforts of all our worker-members. Together we have been able to transform a humble factory, which in 1956 manufactured oil stoves and paraffin heaters, into the leading industrial group in the Basque Country and 7th in the ranking in Spain, with sales of 10.400 million euros in its Industrial and Distribution activities, 10.000 million euros of administered assets in its Financial activity and a total workforce of 71.500 at the end of 2004."
    —Their website

"The Mondragon Co-operative Federation: A Model for our Time?" by Mike Long. Reprinted from *Freedom*, Winter 1996.

"The Mondragon Co-operative Federation (MCF) is a community of economivcally highly successful worker-owned, worker-controlled production and consumption co-operatives centred around Mondragon, a town in the Basque region of northern Spain, and now spreading throughout the Basque provinces and beyond. The MCF is an experiment in participatory economic democracy rooted in a powerful grassroots movement for Basque cultural revival and autonomy, but inclusive of non-Basques."
    —From the article

"Mondragón: The Remarkable Achievement," by Robert Gilman. In: Economics In An Intellegent Universe, *In Context* #2, Spring 1983, page 44.

"The village and the corporation – they seem like opposite poles, yet the previous article suggests that at least some corporations are rediscovering the importance of community and of the village scale. The following article is about a group of industrious people who have carried this process considerably further and developed a form of business organization that could well be the basis for a significantly new economic system."
    —*In Context* website

The Natural Step – http://www.naturalstep.org

Since 1988, The Natural Step has worked to accelerate global sustainability by guiding companies, communities and governments onto an ecologically, socially and economically sustainable path. More than 70 people in twelve countries work with an international network of sustainability experts, scientists, universities, and businesses to create solutions, innovative models and tools that will lead the transition to a sustainable future.
—Their website

A New Way to Govern: Organisations and Society after Enron, by Shann Turnbull. (NEF Pocketbook No. 6) London: New Economics Foundation, 2002.

"Networks of network organisations achieve economies of scale and scope, provided that no higher level network undertakes activities that are better carried out by a lower level self-governing unit. This principle of subsidiary function is illustrated by the nested networks that make up the stakeholder control enterprises around the town of Mondragon in Northern Spain that operate more efficiently than investor owned firms. Like a mutual enterprise the Mondragon firms do not require equity investors."
—From the abstract

No Space, No Choice, No Jobs, No Logo: Taking Aim at the Brand Bullies, by Naomi Klein. New York: Picador USA, 2000.

"With a new Afterword to the 2002 edition. No Logo employs journalistic savvy and personal testament to detail the insidious practices and far-reaching effects of corporate marketing—and the powerful potential of a growing activist sect that will surely alter the course of the 21st century. First published before the World Trade Organization protests in Seattle, this is an infuriating, inspiring, and altogether pioneering work of cultural criticism that investigates money, marketing, and the anti-corporate movement."
—The publisher

Participatory Democracy: Prospects for Democratizing Democracy. Edited by Dimitrios Roussopoulos and C. George Benello. New Edition. Montréal, New York: Black Rose Books, 2005.

"This wide-ranging collection probes the historical roots of participatory democracy in our political culture, analyzes its application to the problems of modern society, and explores the possible forms it might take on every level of society from the work place, to the community, to the nation at large. Part II, 'The Politics of Participatory Democracy,' covers Porto Alegre, Montreal, the new Urban ecology, and direct democracy."
—The publisher

The Post-Corporate World: Life After Capitalism, by David C.
   Korten. San Francisco, Calif.: Berrett-Koehler Publishers;
   West Hartford, Conn.: Kumarian Press, 1999.

> "David Korten, amongst a few prescient others, predicted the collapse that
> was set in motion in Asia and is now spreading worldwide. [Korten] once
> again looks ahead, envisioning the rudiments and principles of an economy
> that is guided by life rather than currency. It is an articulate and hopeful ex-
> pression by one of the leading architects for a positive future."
>   —Paul Hawken, author, *The Ecology of Commerce* and Chairman of The
>   Natural Step U.S.A.

See also The People-Centered Development Forum, David C. Korten, foun-
der & president, at: http://www.pcdf.org

The Simultaneous Policy – http://www.simpol.org

> "The Simultaneous Policy is a peaceful political strategy to democratically
> drive all the world's nations to apply global solutions to global problems, in-
> cluding combating global warming and environmental destruction, regulat-
> ing economic globalization for the good of all, and delivering social justice,
> peace and security, and sustainable prosperity."
>   —Their website

*Society's Breakthrough!: Releasing Essential Wisdom and Virtue in
   All the People*, by Jim Rough. Bloomington, Ind.,
   AuthorHouse, 2001.

> "Society's Breakthrough! presents two social innovations and suggests that in
> a particular context, they could be used to transform the global paradigm so
> that all-of-us-together would act responsibly, respectfully and intelligently.
> The two innovations are: 1) Dynamic Facilitation – a proven approach to
> helping small groups of people address "impossible" issues creatively and
> collaboratively and reach unanimous conclusions; and 2) the Wisdom Coun-
> cil – a way to dynamically facilitate a whole system of people (a city, corpora-
> tion, county, high school, etc.) to do the same thing and to create a voice of
> "We the People." Used together at a national or international level, these
> tools offer the prospect of facilitating a transformation in thinking, and a shift
> to actions that are collectively intelligent."
>   —The book's webpage: http://www.societysbreakthrough.com/

See also: *Dynamic Facilitation Skills* (Jim Rough & Associates, Inc.) –
http://www.tobe.net

*The Tao of Democracy: Using Co-Intelligence to Create a World that
    Works for All,* by Tom Atlee, with Rosa Zubizarreta. Cranston,
    R.I.: Writers' Collective, 2003.

"Demonstrating that groups, communities and whole societies can be more
intelligent and wise collectively than most brilliant individuals, Tom Atlee
shows how 'collective intelligence' could revolutionize politics and governance, bringing wise common sense to every issue – from city budgets to terrorism to global warming. ...Readers will find descriptions and links to over a
hundred proven approaches to this new form of democracy – organizations,
participatory practices, innovations, books and more. The most powerful innovations – citizen deliberative councils – have been used hundreds of times
around the world – from Denmark to India, from Brazil to the U.S."
    —The publisher

See also: The Co-Intelligence Institute – http://www.co-intelligence.org

Dialog and community empowerment

*■Appropriate technology" –
    http://en.wikipedia.org/wiki/Appropriate_technology

This entry, from Wikipedia, the free encyclopedia, begins with a definition:
"Appropriate technology is a term which refers to using the simplest and
most benign level of technology which can effectively achieve the intended
purpose." Contains cross-references ("See also") to related Wikipedia articles
and URLs to appropriate technology websites.

*Building Sustainable Communities: Tools and Concepts for Self-
    Reliant Economic Change,* by C. George Benello, Robert S.
    Swann, Shann Turnbull, and others. Edited by Ward More-
    house. (A Toes Book) New York: Bootstrap Press, 1989. Sec-
    ond Edition, Revised, 1997.

"This book presents the underlying ideas and essential institutions for building sustainable communities. Three major sections deal with community land
trusts, worker managed enterprises and community currency and banking."
    —The Sustainable Communities Network website:
        http://www.sustainable.org/economy/commecon.html

Citizens Jury Process
    http://www.jefferson-center.org/index.asp
        ?Type=B_BASIC&SEC={2BD10C3C-90AF-438C-B04F-88682B6393BE}

"A Citizens Jury provides the opportunity for citizens to learn about an issue,
deliberate together, and develop well-informed, common ground solutions to
difficult public issues. The Citizens Jury process also allows decision-makers
and the public to discover what people really think once they have heard
witnesses and taken a close look at a topic."
    —Their website

Co-Intelligence Institute – http://www.co-intelligence.org

"Healthy communities, institutions and societies – perhaps even our collective survival – depend on our ability to organize our collective affairs more wisely, in tune with each other and nature. This ability to wisely organize our lives together – all of us being wiser together than any of us could be alone – we call co-intelligence. Co-intelligence is emerging through new developments in democracy, organizational development, collaborative processes, the Internet and systems sciences like ecology and complexity. Today millions of people are involved in co-creating co-intelligence. Our diverse efforts grow more effective as we discover we are part of a larger transformational enterprise, and as we learn together and from each other."
—Their website

Community Crossroads – http://communityx-roads.org

"The purpose of the Community Crossroads site is to provide a clearinghouse for information regarding the activities of community-building groups and individuals around the world – announcements, information on upcoming events, 'reports from the field' – and also to provide a source of related information that may be of interest to those engaged in the Community Building effort."
—Their website

See also facilitator listings by country and state:
http://communityx-roads.org/facilitator

Conversation Cafés – http://www.conversationcafe.org

"The Conversation Café project addresses the need to increase social intelligence, to build social capital and generate the social engagement so we can actually HAVE a wise democracy. I am doing this by building a network of Cafés where people can have weekly drop-in dialogues about the key inner and outer issues of our times.

"I envision a culture of conversation — a culture where people talk freely — without fear or taboos — with friends and strangers alike. I once asked a Dane how Denmark had resisted the pressures of globalization. He said two words: study circles. Most Danes throughout their adult lives have the habit of conversation about things that matter in small groups."
—Vicki Robin, President of the New Road Map Foundation

Culture Change – http://www.culturechange.org

"Through independent thinking and cooperative action it is possible to attain bioregionally based economic security that would greatly heal the Earth's and our own wounds. We are not only "concerned" about global climate change; we present a realistic analysis of the so-called techno-fix. We demonstrate alternatives to sprawl and petroleum dependence while fighting unwise development such as new road construction."
—Their website

Dynamic Facilitation for Group Transformation, by Tree Bressen. Eugene, Oregon: The Co-Intelligence Institute, August 25, 2000.
http://www.co-intelligence.org/dynamicfacilitationGT.html

"This great article about Jim Rough's remarkable group process was written by a student of Jim's who is majorly involved with consensus process and the intentional communities movement. It is the best material currently available in writing on the process behind the Wisdom Council."
    —Tom Atlee, Co-Intelligence Institute.

See also Atlee's brief write-up on dynamic facilitation at:
    http://www.co-intelligence.org/P-wisdomcouncil.html#facilitation

The E. F. Schumacher Society – http://www.smallisbeautiful.org

"Building on a rich tradition often known as decentralism, the Society initiates practical measures that lead to community revitalization and further the transition toward an economically and ecologically sustainable society."
    —Their website

TheFacilitator.com – http://thefacilitator.com

"*The Facilitator* is a quarterly publication written for facilitators by facilitators since 1993."
    —Its website

See also: Facilitation User Groups Contact:
http://www.thefacilitator.com/htdocs/tf_usrgrp.html

Fellowship for Intentional Community – http://fic.ic.org

"The Fellowship for Intentional Community nurtures connections and cooperation among communitarians and their friends. We provide publications, referrals, support services, and sharing opportunities for a wide range of intentional communities, cohousing groups, ecovillages, community networks, support organizations, and people seeking a home in community."

FIC Process Consultant Clearinghouse – http://fic.ic.org/process.html

Are you dissatisfied with the quality of your meetings? Is your group confused about process agreements? Do you need help dealing with a "hot" issue? The people listed here may be able to help.
    —Their website

Global Village – The Institute for Appropriate Technology
http://www.i4at.org

"Global Village is a non-profit organization created in 1974 and chartered as a tax-exempt charity in 1980 for the purpose of researching promising new technologies that can benefit humanity in environmentally friendly ways. The philosophy of the Institute is that emerging technologies that link the world together are not ethically neutral, but often have long-term implications for viability of natural systems, human rights and our common future."
    —Their website

Going Local: Creating Self Reliant Communities in a Global Age, by Michael Shuman. New York: Free Press, 1998; paperback: New York: Routledge, 2000.

> Ask your family, friends, and neighbors what matters most to them, and you're likely to hear words like love, security, spirituality, beauty, good health, even. This book cuts through all of the conventional public discussions on the economy and society to make a clear, convincing case for reviving local communities.
> —amazon.com

Horizons of Change – http://www.horizonsofchange.com

> "HORIZONS is a group of experienced organization development consultants and community organizers, specializing in "whole system" approaches to organization and community development and change."
> —Their website

International Association of Facilitators (IAF) – http://www.iaf-world.org

> "The IAF encourages and supports the formation of local groups of facilitators to network and provide professional development opportunities for their members. Regional groups from around the world are invited to become affiliated with the IAF to help promote the profession of facilitation as a critical set of skills in the global society of the 21st century."
> —Their website

See also: Certified Professional Facilitators
http://www.iaf-world.org/i4a/pages/index.cfm?pageid=3329

The National Coalition for Dialogue and Deliberation (NCDD)
http://thataway.org

> "The National Coalition for Dialogue & Deliberation is a network of nearly 300 organizations and individuals who regularly engage millions of Americans in dialogue around today's critical issues. Often led by trained facilitators and oriented toward community problem-solving, these groups offer one of the few hopeful signs of growth in American democracy today."
> —Their website

National Issues Forums – http://www.nifi.org

> "National Issues Forums (NIF) is a nonpartisan, nationwide network of locally sponsored public forums for the consideration of public policy issues. It is rooted in the simple notion that people need to come together to reason and talk – to deliberate about common problems. Indeed, democracy requires an ongoing deliberative public dialogue."
> —Their website

Recreating the World: A Practical Guide to Building Sustainable Communities, by Michael Bopp and Judie Bopp. Calgary, Alberta: Four Worlds Press, 2001.

"Recreating the World is a comprehensive field guide to sustainable community development. Rooted in more than 20 years of hands-on development work in North America and around the world, it is written to be used by people who are working to bring about change in their own communities, and by professionals working with communities to solve critical human problems."
—amazon.com

Study Circles Resource Center – http://www.studycircles.org

"The Study Circles Resource Center is dedicated to finding ways for all kinds of people to engage in dialogue and problem solving on critical social and political issues. SCRC helps communities by giving them the tools to organize productive dialogue, recruit diverse participants, find solutions, and work for action and change... In addition, many colleges and high schools are organizing study circles to engage young people in dialogue and problem solving."
—Their website

Tools for Change Institute – http://www.instituteforchange.org

"Tools for Change Institute is dedicated to inspiring a cultural transformation in which history, heart, spirit, values, and vision are all at the center of public life. ...We work with communities and organizations, assisting them to create sustainable and democratic structures in which people can reclaim their wholeness and contribute their best. ...We envision a time in which decisions are made by those most affected by them while honoring the natural world upon which all life depends – a time in which trust, care and creativity are the currency of culture. We strive to model just relations and inspire reaffirming leadership for building a movement to bring this about."
—Their website

Tree Bressen's Group Facilitation Site – http://www.treegroup.info

"Tree Bressen is an experienced facilitator working with nonprofits, cohousing groups, activists, schools, and a wide variety of other organizations. Her base is in intentional communities, groups of people who live together and have to deal with each other every day! Her work arises from a desire for people to learn the communication skills that will enable all of us to build a better world together. Tree gives workshops on consensus decision-making, meeting facilitation, conflict resolution, and related subjects."
—Her website

The World Café – http://www.theworldcafe.com

"The World Café is a flexible, easy-to-use process for fostering collaborative dialogue, sharing collective knowledge, and discovering new opportunities for action. Based on living systems thinking, this is a proven approach for fostering authentic dialogue and creating dynamic networks of conversation around your organization or community's real work and critical questions, improving both personal relationships and people's capacity to shape the future together."
—Their website